ALEXANDER MONTGOMERIE

POEMS

Alexander Montgomerie

Poems

Volume I: Text

Edited by

David J. Parkinson

The Scottish Text Society
27 George Square
Edinburgh

2000

©

THE SCOTTISH TEXT SOCIETY 2000

ISBN 1 897976 15 1

Printed by Cromwell Press,
Trowbridge, Wiltshire, England

Distributed by Scottish Book Source
137 Dundee Street, Edinburgh EH11 1BG
Tel: 0131 229 6800

Table of Contents

Contents

Contents

Contents

Contents

Contents

Contents

ABOUT THIS EDITION

The first volume of this edition offers texts of all poems ascribable on the authority of early manuscript witnesses to Alexander Montgomerie, sixteenth-century Scottish poet. The Appendix to this volume contains musical settings to seven of these poems. The second volume includes the following: an introduction to Principal Witnesses and the Author; select Bibliography; Notes (including marginal glosses at the first occurrence of each difficult word); and a Word List in which every occurrence of each word in the poems is cited according to its spelling(s), without separation of homographs, and with proper nouns capitalised.

I. Poems

In manuscript and print, the early sources for Montgomerie's poems seem legion. At first sight, the many seventeenth-century printed editions of *The Cherrie and the Slae* predominate, followed by those of the so-called *Flyting of Montgomerie and Polwart*. A closer look reveals a host of occurrences of individual lyrics (often unascribed) in manuscripts of various kinds: literary miscellanies and music books especially. The present edition draws on the earliest and fullest of these diverse sources, as listed in *Sigla* (xv-xvi, below).

The order, titling, and text of the poems in this edition reveal the precedence given herein to manuscript evidence, especially where that evidence includes clear indication of authorship. Priority goes to the principal source, the Ker Manuscript; the first ninety-eight poems follow the order in which they appear there. Poem 99 is *Invectives* ('The Flyting of Montgomerie and Polwart'), based on the Tullibardine Manuscript text. Following this appears a parallel-text edition of *The Cherrie and the Slae* (100, based on the second Waldegrave print of 1597, and 101, based on the Wreittoun print, 1636). A small group of poems ascribed to Montgomerie in the Maitland Quarto and Bannatyne Manuscript completes the text proper.

Where supported by textual evidence, poems are treated as parts of one item. In such cases (sonnet sequences, *Invectives*), each part has a roman numeral subordinate to the arabic numeral for the whole item.

Accidentals
In spelling, punctuation, and lineation, the text of this edition reflects the evidence of the witnesses, with a few exceptions, listed here.

1. In place of the swash (ſ) appears *s* without comment. In place of the z (which indicates the phonemes /y/ and /ċ/ as well as /ʒ/) appears ʒ. Digraphs (*æ*, *œ*) and thorn (*þ*) follow the witnesses.

2. Capitalisation follows the witnesses, with the following exceptions: lines begin with capitals; new sentences that begin in the middle of a line begin with a capital; quotations begin with capitals.

3. Punctuation reflects rhetorical practices of the witnesses. For grammar, punctuation is added to line endings. Mid-line, the comma appears as in copy-text (where it signals divergence between syntax and metre) or as demanded by clause structure. Parentheses indicate interjection. Question marks, exclamation points, and apostrophes follow the witnesses, as do colons, though in the *Cherrie* these appear more sparingly than in the prints. Additional quotation marks indicate direct discourse.

4. Abbreviations and suspensions in the witnesses (for instance, & for *and*, $\overline{m}$ for *mm*, w^t for *with*) are silently expanded.

5. Lineation and indentation follow copy-text.

6. Folio numbers from the principal manuscript witnesses appear outside the line numbers.

Emendation

For each of the three major sets of texts in this edition, copy-text has been subject to emendation on the following principles.

1. Where the copy-text has been damaged, missing words are supplied after comparison of available witnesses, or from extant paleographical evidence. The ellipsis appears where a loss or omission of text can not be conjectured within limited possibilities.

2. Where a reading in the the copy-text is demonstrably in error and alternate witnesses are available with variant readings, such readings are compared and one is substituted. Where no alternate witnesses are available, substitution is only rarely attempted. Emendation occurs case by case, justification and support for each case being evaluated in the Notes. The harder reading is adopted only when it draws on ample testimony (from other witnesses; in the case of clear errors, from previous editors) to resolve a metrical or semantic uncertainty.

3. Substantive variations between witnesses are recorded in footnote form, the lemma being followed by a closing square bracket and the variants separated by semi-colons. Usually, spelling variations are not listed; nor are common variations between Scots and English (*quhilk/which*, *luik/look*, *sik/such*), or variation in case, punctuation or lineation. In the notation of a variant, the spelling is that of the first witness listed.

4. In the textual notes, suspensions and abbreviations of variant readings are silently expanded, and capitalization is standardized; where an ellipsis appears in textual notes, it indicates that scribal omission has been filled editorially.

5. Omissions of lines or words are indicated as either *cropped* (due to damage to the witness) or *om.*[itted] (due to scribal error); reversals of lines or stanzas are indicated *rev.*[ersed]; scribal deletions appear *del.*

6. In the textual notes to *Invectives*, "F" refers to readings common to F1-4 and Ru.; in the textual notes to *The Cherrie and the Slae*, "C3" indicates a reading common to C3, C4 and C5 unless otherwise specified.

II. Songs

The volume ends with a group of song settings of Montgomerie poems. These four-part settings derive from seventeenth-century songbooks; with one important exception (the last poem in the Ker Manuscript, 'Come my children dere'), only those songs for which all four vocal lines are attested by early witnesses have been included.

Music

The music in the Appendix to this edition is presented in modern notation, the four parts appearing on two staves, with clefs (treble and bass) and note values (generally half those of the witnesses) following modern practice. Harmonically and melodically justifiable accidentals in one part in the witnesses are extended without comment to the other parts affected. Substantive variants are recorded thus: bar number (arabic), part number (roman), and sequence number of note or rest (arabic) are followed by a colon, after which variant time-values and pitches appear. Since variants occur within an octave of the reading given, note names are simply given as *A* through *G*, with dotted values indicated by a period, and accidentals provided (e.g., ♭, ♮). Time values are given as *s* (semibreve), *m* (minim), *c* (crotchet), *q* (quaver), and *sq* (semiquaver).

Text

For comparison with the text provided earlier in this volume, the lyric for each song has been selected from one of the principal musical witnesses.

III. Illustrations

Each of the sections of this volume begins with transcriptions of relevant title pages. For the first three sections, these title pages present features of layout, type and image derived from those in the principal witnesses: the Ker Manuscript, the Tullibardine Manuscript, and the Waldegrave and Wreittoun prints of *The Cherrie and the Slae*. Elsewhere in the volume, illustrations derived from seventeenth-century Scottish books indicate the beginnings and endings of sections.

SIGLA

I. Manuscripts

Ba Bannatyne MS. NLS Adv. 1.1.6

Ed Robert Edwards's Commonplace Book. NLS Add. 9450

Fc Alexander Forbes's Cantus Partbook. Fitzwilliam Museum Music 687

He Archibald Hegate's Protocol Book. Glasgow City Archives B10.1.7

K Ker MS. EUL Drummond De.3.70

La Laing MS. EUL Laing III.447

Mb David Melvill's Bassus Partbook. BL Add. 36484

Mi2 Inscription in *The Mindes Melodie* (Edinburgh: Robert Charteris, 1606). Glasgow UL, STC 18051.3

Mq Maitland Quarto MS. Magdalene College Cambridge Pepysian Library 1408

Mx John Maxwell's Commonplace Book. EUL Laing III. 467

Po Timothy Pont's 'Description of Cunningham'. NLS Adv. 33.2.27

Rc William Mure of Rowallan's Cantus Partbook. EUL Laing III.488

Ro Margaret Robertson's MS (19c copy). NLS 59137

Ru John Rutherford's MS. BL Harleian 7578

Sc William Stirling's Cantus Partbook. NLS Adv. 5.2.14

Ta Robert Taitt's MS. University of California at Los Angeles. William Andrews Clark Memorial Library T135Z B724

Ti William Murray of Tibbermure's MS. Cambridge UL K.k.5.30

Tu Tullibardine MS. Henry E. Huntington Library 105

Wa Thomas Wode's Psalter: Altus Partbook. BL Add. 33933

Wb, Wc, Wt Thomas Wode's Psalter: Bassus, Cantus and Tenor Partbooks. EUL La.III.483

We Lady Margaret Wemyss's Songbook. NLS, Dep. 314, no. 23

Wq Thomas Wode's Psalter: Quintus Partbook. Trinity College Dublin F.5.13

II. Prints

C1 Alexander Montgomerie. *The Cherrie and the Slae*. Edinburgh: Robert Waldegrave, 1597. STC 18049

C2 ---. Edinburgh: Robert Waldegrave, 1597. STC 18049.5

C3 ---. Edinburgh: John Wreittoun, 1636. STC 18050 [see this edition, 1.xiii]

C4 ---. Aberdeen: Edward Raban, 1645. Wing M2498

C5 ---. ?London: For I.D., 1646. Wing M2498A

F [see this edition, 1.xiii]

F1 Alexander Montgomerie and Patrick Hume. *The Flyting betwixt Montgomerie and Polwart*. Edinburgh: Andrew Hart, 1621. STC 13954.3

F2 ---. Edinburgh: Heirs of Andrew Hart, 1629. STC 13954.7

F3 ---. Edinburgh: Heirs of Thomas Finlason for J. Wood, 1629. STC 13955

F4 ---. Edinburgh: John Wreittoun, 1632. STC 13955.5

Fo John Forbes. *Songs and Fancies*: Cantus Partbook. Aberdeen: John Forbes, 1662. Wing 379

Ja James VI. *Essayes of a Prentise in the Divine Arte of Poesie*. Edinburgh: Vautrollier, 1584. STC 14373

Me James Melville. *Ane Frvitfvl and Comfortable Exhortatioun anent Death*. Edinburgh: Robert Waldegrave, 1597. STC 17815.5

Mi1 *The Mindes Melodie*. Edinburgh: Robert Charteris, 1605. STC 18051

The fear of the Lorde is

the beginning of wisdom

W

All ȝe that feir this holy Name adore

This sacred one with offring hie

That may cut of at his vintage

The breath of Princis in his rage

To Eirthly Kings

To earth

Captain Allexander Montgommeries Poëm[s]

Will is þe man

In my defence god me defend

And bring my saull to ane gud

Margarat Ker

1 The First Psalme to the tone of the Solsequium 2

Weill is the man,
ȝea blissed than,
Be grace that can
Esheu ill Counsell and the godles gait,
That stands not in 5
The way of sin
Nor does begin
To sitt with mockers in the scornefull sait
Bot in Jehovahis lau   Delyts aricht
And studies it to knau   Both day and nicht 10
For he sall be
Lyk to the trie
Quhilk plantit by the running river grouis
Quhilk frute does beir
In tym of ȝeir 15
Quhais leaf sall never fade nor rute sall louis.

His Actionis all
Ay prosper sall
Quhilk sall not fall
To godles men bot as the chaffe or sand 20
Quhilk day by day
Winds dryvis away.
Thairfor I say
The wicked in the judgment sall not stand 2ᵛ
Nor sinners ryse na mair   Vhom god disdanes 25
In the Assembly vhair   The just remanes.
For why? the Lord
Doth beir record

1 Weill] Blist Miı 2 blissed] happie Miı 4] Eschew þe wicked and þe godlesse
gates Miₐ ill] evill Ba gait] gaitis Ba Miı 5 That stands] Quha walkis Ba; And
walkes Miı; That walkes Miₐ 8 the] thair Ba sait] saitis Ba Miı 11 For he]
That man Miı 12 the] ane Ba 13 Quhilk] (Quhilk, *del.*) (that; *LH margin*) Ba;
Fast Miı 14 Quhilk] That Miı 16] Miₐ ends here leaf] leivis Ba sall louis]
vnlowis Ba Miı 19 Quhilk] So Ba 20 To] The Miı godles] wicket Ba or] and
Ba 21 Quhilk] That Miı 22 Winds dryvis] Wind driuth Miı 25 ryse] cum Ba
28 Doth beir] Quha beiris Ba; Who bearth Miı

He knauis the Richteous Conversatioun ay,
30 And godles gaits
Quhilk he so haitis
Sall doutles perish and decay aluay.

2 The 2 Psalm to the Tone of In throu the
windoes of myn ees

Quhy doth the Heathin rage and rampe
And peple murmur all in vane?
The Kings on earth ar bandit plane
And princes ar conjonit in Campe
5 Aganst the Lord and Chryst ilk ane.
'Come let our hands
Brek all thair bands'
Say they, 'and cast from vs thair yoks'.
Bot he sall evin
10 That duells in hevin
Laugh thame to scorne lyk mocking stoks.

In wraith then sall he speik thame till
And vex thame in his anger sore
And say, 'I set my king with glore
3 15 On Sion Mount my holy hill'.
I will declair his will thairfoir,
That is that he
Hes said to me,
'Thou art my sone beloved ay
20 From vhome my Love
Sall not remove.
I haif begotten thee this day.

1.29 He knauis] Doth know Mɪ Conuersatioun] conuersations Mɪ 31 haitis]
hait is K 32] Shall quite die, perish, and doubtlesse decay Mɪ doutles] quickly
Ba decay aluay] but dowt decay Ba
2.title the windoes of myn ees] the &[c] K 12 In] ... K 13 And] ...nd K 14 And]
...nd K

'Ask thou of me and thou sall haive
The Heathin to enherit haill
And all the Earth thou sall not faill   25
For thy Possessioun to resaive.
Thy Princely scepter sall prevaill
       For they sall feill
       It made of steill
To render thame thair just reuaird   30
       Quhairvith thou sall
       Evin bruis thame all
In peces lyk a potters shaird'.

Be wyse thairfor ȝe Kingis and heir.
Ȝe Judges of the earth, I say   35
Be leirnd and instructit ay.
Rejoyce and serve the Lord in feir
And kisse the SONE and him obey
       Leist vhen his yre   3ᵛ
       Sall burne as fyre   40
Ȝe perish in the way and fall
       And sik as trust
       In god most just
Sall happy be and blissed all.

3   The Poets Dreme

God give me grace for to begin
My spousing garment for to spin
And to be one till enter in
       With the brydgrome in blisse
And sleep na mair in sleuth and sin   5
Bot rather ryse and richtly rin
That hevinly wedfie for to win
       Vhilk he prepairs for his.

The way is strait, the nomber small,
Therfor we may not entir all   10
Ȝit he hes said that sik men sall
       Vhais faith brings furth gude frute.

2.41 ȝe] ȝea K

5

My saull then fash not for a fall,
Contineu knocking, clim and call.
15 Thair is no winning ouer the wall
      Fra ains the dur be shute.

4   Tak tym in tyme or tym be tint
    To stryve with sin and nevir stint
    And vhar thou may not, mak a mint
20   Sa that thy faith be fast.
    As raynie dropis do peirce the flint
    Throu falling oft and not throu dint,
    Of hope if thou hold fast the hint
         Thou sall prevaill at last.

25 Presume not nor dispair to speid.
    To lyf that leddir sall the leid
    Quhilk stude at godly Jacobs heid
         Quhen he to dream wes drevin,
    Quhairby the Angels come and 3eid
30 From Hevin to earth as thou may reid.
    That is the only way indeid
         To help the vp to hevin.

    Assure thy self it is the sam
    Vharby the godly fathers clam
35 Vha war the heires of Abraham
         Beloved of the Lord.
    If thou beleive into that Lamb
    Vha said, 'I am evin that I am'
    The De'ill dou nevir the condam.
40   Thy warand is the word.

4ᵛ When he wes rent vpon the rude
    He boght belevers with his blude,
    I mene the godly men and gude
         Quha keepit his Commands
45 And by Instinction vnderstude
    Thair saulls resau'd his flesh for fude.
    Then clim by Chryst for I conclude
         Thy help lyes in his hands.

13 saull] (faith; *del.*) K; ...ll *LH margin* K

6

4   A godly Prayer

Peccavi Pater, miserere mei.
I am not worthy to be cald thy chylde
Vho stubburnely haif look't so long astray,
Not lyk thy sone bot lyk the prodigue wyld.
My sillie saull with sin is so defyld   5
That Satan seeks to catch it as his pray.
God grant me grace that he may be begyld.
Peccavi Pater, miserere mei.

I am abash'd hou I dar be sa bald
Befor thy godly presence to appeir   10
Or hazard anes the hevins to behald
Vha am vnworthy that the earth suld beir,
3it damne me noght vhom thou hes boght so deir
Sed salvum me fac dulcis fili Dei
For out of Luk this leson nou I leir.   15
Peccavi Pater, miserere mei.

If thou o Lord with Rigour woldst revenge   5
Vhat flesh befor the faultles suld be fund?
Or vho is he vhois Conscience can him clenge?
Bot by his birth to Satan he is bund,   20
3it of thy grace thou took auay that grund
And sent thy Sone our Penalty to pay
To saiv us from that hiddious hellish hund.
Peccavi Pater, miserere mei.

title] C.A.M. His Lamentation C3 1] I have sinned, O Father, bee mercyfull to
mee C3 3 Vho] That C3 haif look't so long] hes went so lang La Ba; so long
have gone C3 4 lyk thy] lyke the La; as thy C3 lyk the] as the Ba C3 prodigue]
prodigal La C3 5 sin] synnis La Ba 6 seeks] thinks C3 his] a Ba C3; (ane; *del.*)
a La 7 God] Lord C3 9 abash'd] abaysed La; abaisd Ba; abasde C3 I dar] dare I
C3 11 to] for to La Ba C3 12 vnworthy] not worthy Ba C3; nocht wourdie La 15
leson] leasing La nou I] we doe C3 18 suld] shal Ba C3 19 vhois] his C3 can]
cowld Ba clenge] cleanse C3 20] Bot by his brother he is to Sathan bound La;
To sin and Sathan from his birth's not bound La 21 thy] meer C3 took]
took'st C3 that] the C3 23 that] the La hellish] hels C3

25   I hope for mercy thoght my sinnis be huge,
      I grant my gylt and grones to thee for grace.
      Thoght I suld flie vhair sall I find refuge?
      In hevin o Lord? thair is thy duelling place,
      The erth thy futstule, 3ea in hel is (alace)
30   Doun with the dead, bot all must the obey.
      Thairfor I cry vhill I haif tyme and space
      Peccavi Pater, miserere mei.

      O gratious God my gyltines forgive
      In sinners death since thou does not delyte
35   Bot rather that they suld convert and live
      As witnessis thy sacred holy wryte.
      I pray the then thy promise to perfyte
      In me, and I sall with the Psalmist say
      To pen thy prais and wondrous works indyte.
40   Peccavi Pater, miserere mei.

      Suppose I slyde, let me not sleep in sleuth,
5ᵛ   In stinking sty with Satans sinfull swyn
      Bot mak my Tongue the Trompet of thy treuth
      And lend my Verse sik wings as ar divyne.
45   Sen thou hes grantit me so good Ingyn
      To Loif the, Lord, in gallant style and gay
      Let me no moir so trim a talent tyne.
      Peccavi Pater, miserere mei.

25 thoght] although C3 26 grones] grone C3 27 suld] wald La; would C3 sall] suld La; shuld C3 28 In] Till Ba; To C3 29 3ea in hel is] 3ea in hels La; 3e in hell Ba; and to the hels C3 30 Doun] Dam Ba with] goes C3 bot] for C3 34 does not] hast no C3 35 rather] rader Ba that] would C3 36 witnessis thy sacred] witnes for thy sacret La; doe witnes the Prophets in C3 37 then] Lord C3 38 In] With La and I sall] that I may C3 Psalmist] psalmes La 39 To pen] I will C3 40] Therefore deare Father be mercifull to mee C3 41 Suppose] Though I doe C3 slyde] sled La 42] Mee to revive from sin let grace begin C3 43 Bot make] Make Lord C3 44 lend] send Ba 46 To Loif the, Lord, in] To praise thy Name with C3

Thy Spirit my Spirit to speik with speed inspyre.
Help holy Ghost, and be Montgomeries muse. 50
Flie doun on me in forked tongues of fyre
As thou did on thy oune Apostills vse
And with thy fyre me fervently infuse
To laud the, Lord, and longer not delay.
My former folish fictiouns I refuse. 55
Peccavi Pater, miserere mei.

Stoup stubborne stomock that hes bene so stout,
Stoup filthie flesh and carioun of clay,
Stoup hardnit hairt befor the Lord and lout,
Stoup, stoup in tyme, defer not day by day. 60
Thou knouis not weill vhen thou man pass away.
The Tempter als is bissie to betrey.
Confes thy sinnis and shame not for to say
Peccavi Pater, miserere mei.

To grit Jehovah let all glore be gevin 65
Vha shupe my saull to his similitude
And to his sone vhom he sent doun from hevin
Vhen I wes lost to buy me with his blude 6
And to the holy Ghost my gyder gude
Vho must confirme my faith to tak no fray. 70
In me cor mundum crea, I conclude.
Peccavi Pater, miserere mei.

49] My sprit to speak let thy sptit, Lord inspire C3 50 Montgomeries] mine
heavenly C3 51 in] with C3 52] As on th'Apostles, with thy feare mee infuse C3
53–55] All vice expel, teach me sin to refuse, / And all my filthy affections, I
thee pray, / Thy fervent love on mee powre night and day C3 54 laud] luif La;
love Ba 55] *om*. Ba 57 so] ay C3 58 carioun of] carion made of C3 61 knouis not
weill vhen] watt not quhen La; wait not weill quhen Ba; wots not when that C3
man] may C3; must C5 62] *om*. La; The tempter to is reddy to betray Ba; To
the great glore where thou must be for ay C3 63 sinnis] syn Ba shame not for]
thinke no shame C3 say] stay C5 65 To] O C3 let] salt La; to thee C3 66, 67
his] thy C3 67 he sent] thou sentst C3 68 to buy] He boght C3 70 to tak no
fray] in the right way C3 72] O Heavenly Father be merciful to mee C3

5   A walkning from sin

Think on the end and thou sall seindle sin.
Since vnadwysment wraks or thou be war
To call for grace betyms at god begin
Befor thou folou on the flesh too far.
5   Throu vnadvertance (oh) hou mony ar
Involvit so, vhill out they can not win.
Wald thou be clene, touch nather pick nor tar.
Think on the end and thou sall seindle sin.

As Trees hes leafis then florishis, syn fruit
10   So thou hes thoghts, syn words and actions last
Thus grie by grie sin taks in the sik rute
Infecting saull and body baith so fast
To stay Repentance till the tyme be past.
Then turne in tym and not so rekles rin
15   Or thou thy self in Condemnation cast.
Think on the end and thou sall seindle sin.

Or thou be sommound by vncerten Death
Count with thy Conscience, knau if it be clene,
Defer not to the latter blast of breath
6ᵛ 20   Sen lait Repentance seindle sure is sene,
Then thrau the wand in tyme vhill it is grene.
Sen tym is precious, tak it or 3e tuin,
Sen thou began, look bak vhat thou hes bene.
Think on the end and thou sall seindle sin.

25   Sen Death is debt, prepair thee for to pay.
Thou knauis not vhen thy Creditour will crave.
Remember Death and on that dreidfull day
Quhen as thy Saull hir sentence sall resave
Of endles pain or endles joy to haive
30   (The goatis ar many thoght the Lambis be thin),
Seek thy salvation, be not Satans slaive.
Think on the end and thou sall seindle sin.

18 clene] cle... K

Seik, knok and ask in Faith with Hope and Love
And thou sall find and enter and obtene.
Obey his blissed bidding from above   35
So thou sall purchess proffeit to betuene.
Inclyne thyn eiris, and open wp thy ene
To heir and sie and comfort all thy kin.
Do good, repent, in tym to come abstene.
Think on the end and thou sall seindle sin.   40

Thoght Natur force thee to commit offence
Ʒit it is Divelish daylie to delyte
Or perseveir inonder this pretence
That Chryst sall be compeld to mak the quyte.
As some will say, sen flesh is Imperfyte   45
God mon forgive or think his Court bot thin.   7
These words ar vain but warrand of the wryt.
Think on the end and thou sall seindle sin.

6   A lesone hou to leirne to die

Be war, be war, leist it be war.
The dreidfull day drauis to the duris.
Exame ʒour selfis, sie vhat ʒe ar
And spy hou death comis at the spurris
      Whais sharpe seveirest summond sayis   5
      Without Contineuing of Dayis.

He keepis no dyet, day nor Table
Bot vhen he calis thou mon compeir
Euen vhen thou art vnmetest able.
Then fruitles faith is fraught with feir,   10
      That message so thy mynd dismayis
      Without Contineuing of Dayis.

Quhen all thy sensis the forsaikis
And thou persaivis no dome bot dead
Then Courage lyk a Couart quaikis,   15
Vane hope dar not hold vp his head,
      Thy sinfull saull astonisht stayis
      Bot no contineuing of dayis.

Fra Conscience brings furth his Books
20 Into thy stomok is a stryfe.
7ᵛ   It is no laughter vhen thou looks
Vpon the Legend of thy lyfe
    Vharin ar writtin all thy wayis
    Without contineuing of dayis.

25 That Register may mak thee rad
Reveiling both thy good and evill.
Thy saull sall sie to mak hir sad
Hir vgly enemie the Divill
    Quhilk all that Lybel to hir layis
30   Without contineuing of Dayis.

Fra sho haif gaȝed in that glasse
Sho hes a gesse vhair sho suld gang.
Be sho provydit or sho passe
It's weill, if not, all will be wrang.
35   To lait for pardon then sho prayis
    Quhen no contineuing of dayis.

A bitter battell sall sho byde
Betuixt quick hope and dead dispair
Quhen sho sall trimble to be tryde
40 Remembring on long Euermair
    Quhair peirles pain or plesur ay-is
    Without contineuing of Dayis.

Thoght, word and Deid all sall be weyde
Befor thy lingring lyf disluge.
8 45 Vhat ferly, freind, thoght thou be fleyd
To go befor so grit a Judge
    Vhais feirfull face the wicked frayis
    Without contineuing of dayis?

Thy Beutie, Riches, Wit and Strenth
50 Quhilk God thee to his glory gaive
Sall caus the cry alace at lenth

43 Deid all] Deid (and; *del.*) all K

Quhen he thy Checker Compt sall craive
    Vho will allou the no delayis
    Nor yit contineuing of dayis.

Thair thou that in this warld wes wont   55
To griev thy God without regaird
Sall be compeld to give account
And, as thou thoght, resave rewaird
    Of him vho presently repayis
    Without contineuing of Dayis.   60

Then Prayers, Almesdeids and tearis
Vhilks yit to skorne yee skantly skar
Sall mair availl than Jaks and spearis
For to debait thee at that bar
    Quhair nane rebelis bot all obeyis   65
    Without contineuing of Dayis.

Quhen Justice halds the Ballance evin
Sho mettis no inshis with the ell.
The hevy saulis ar had to hevin   8ᵛ
The light alace ar hoyde to hell   70
    Quhair Belȝebub in burning brayis
    In wter darknes vhair no day is.

Quhat wald thou give if god wold grant
Thee longer licience for to leive?
Wald thou not sueir to be a Sant,   75
And all thy goods for gods saik give?
    Ȝea and instruct all sik as strayis
    Without contineuing of Dayis.

Quhy art thou miserable o Man?
Quhy pretermits thou tyme and place?   80
Quhy art thou ydler nou nor than?
Quhy speids thou not vhill thou hes space?
    Quhy tyins thou tyme that the betrayis?
    Quhy dreeds thou not these duilfull dayis?

72 day is] dayis K 82 Quhy speids] Quhy (hyds t; *del.*) speids K

13

85 3it hear vhill Chryst knokis at thy hairt
   And open it to let him in
   Or thou sall abill efteruard
   Crave entrie vhair thou sall not win
       As the fyve folish Virgins playis.
90   Then with the wyse redeme thy dayis.

7   A Description of Tyme

    Tak tyme in tym or tym will not be tane.
9   Thairfor tak tent hou thou this Tyme suld tak.
    Sho hes no hold to hold hir by bot ane,
    A toppe befor bot beld behind hir bak.
5   Let thou hir slippe or slipperly grou slak
    Thou gettis no grippe agane fra sho be gane.
    If thou wald speid remember vhat I spak.
    Tak tyme in tyme or tym will not be tane.

    For I haif hard in Adagies of auld
10 That tyme dois waist and weir all things auay
    Then trou the taill that treu men oft hes tauld,
    A turne in tyme is ay worth other tuay
    Siklyk I haif hard ofttymis suith men say
    That Negligence 3it nevir furtherit nane
15 Als, seindle tymis luck foloues long delay.
    Tak tym in tyme or tyme will not be tane.

8   The Oppositione of the Court to Conscience

   (9) The Court and Conscience wallis not weill. (a)
   (8) These tua can nevir weill accord. (b)
   (9) Quha leivis in Court and halds him leill (a)
   (3) Lang or that lyf mak him a Lord (b)
5   (8) And Conscience sten3ies if he steill (a)
     (9) So Court and Conscience walis not weill. (b)

7.15 delay] delayis K

(9) The Court some qualities requyrs
(8) Quhilk Conscience can not bot accuse
(9) And specially sik as aspyris
(8) Mon honest Adulation wse.   10
   (9) I dar not say and doubly deill   9ᵛ
   (8) Bot Court and Conscience wals not weill.

First thou mon preis thy Prince to pleis
(Thoght contrare Conscience he commands)
With Mercuris mouth and Argo's eis   15
And with Briarius hundreth hands
    And seme vhatsoevir he sayis to seill
    So Court and Conscience wallis not weill.

Syn evirie minioun thou man mak
To gar thame think that thou art thairs   20
Houbeit thou be behind thair bak
No furtherer of thair effairs
    Bot mett thame moonshyn ay for Meill.
    So Court and Conscience wallis not weill.

To pleis men vhen thou art imployde,   25
Give glorifluikims in thair face
Quhilks wald be cunningly convoyde
To gar thame haif the griter grace
    To mak thame fonde that hes no feill.
    So Court and Conscience walis not weill.   30

9   An invectione against Fortun contening ane Admonitione to his freinds at Court

Not Clio nor Calliope I chuse,
Megera thou must be my mirthles Muse
For to inspyre my spreit with thy despyte
And with thy fervent furie me infuse   10
Quhat Epithets or Arguments till vse   5
With fals and fein3ed fortun for to flyte.
Both wey my words and waill my verse to wryte
That curst, inconstant Cative till accuse
Quhais variance of all my wois I wyt.

9.7 wryte] wry... K

10 Sho is mair mobile mekle nor the Mone.
It keeps a Course and changis not so sone
Bot in ane ordour waxis ay and wanis.
Sing sho tua notis, the one is out of tone
As B acre lau and B moll far abone.
15 In mesur not a moment sho remanes.
Sho givis by gesse, sho weyis no gold by granes.
Hir doings all ar vndiscreitly done
Without respect of persons or of pains.

For men of merit sho no mater maks
20 Bot vhen a toy intill hir heid sho taks
But ryme or reson or respect to richt
The worthiest and valiantest sho wraks
And honours out waills for wnworthie acts
As of a kitchin knaive to mak a knicht.
25 That witch, that warlok, that vnworthie wicht
Turnis ay the best men tittest on thair bakis
Syn settis vp sik as somtym war bot slycht.

Quhen with a quhisk sho quhirlis about hir quheill
Rude is that rattill running with a reill
10ᵛ 30 Quhill top ouer tail goes honest men atains
Then spurgald sporters they begin to speill,
The Cadger clims neu cleikit from the Creill
And ladds vploips to lordships all thair lains.
Doun goes the bravest, brecking al their banis.
35 Sho works hir will, god wot if it be weill.
Sho stottis at strais, syn stumbillis not at stanis.

How sho suld hurt or help sho neuer huiks.
Luk as it lyks sho laughis and never luiks
Bot wavers lyk the widdircok in wind.
40 Sho counts not Kings nor Caȝards mair nor Cuiks.
Reid bot hou scho hes bleckit Bocas buiks,
Thairin the fall of Princes sall ȝe find.
That bloodie Bitch, that buskit belly blind
Dings dounuards ay the duchtiest lyk Duiks.
45 Quha hopped highest ofttyms comes behind.

25 wicht] wic... K 26 bakis] baki... K

I neid not nou to nominat thair Names
Quhom sho hes shent and dayly shifts and shames.
That longsome labour wold be ou'r prolixt.
3our selfis may sie I think a thousand thames
Quhilks (Poets as hir Pursevants) proclames.   50
Hir fickle freindship is not firmely fixt.
Quhair ane is now, his nichtbour may be nixt.
Sho causles cul3ies, and but falt defames.
Hir mirrines with missheif ay is mixt.

Thairfor my freinds vha nevir feirs to fall,   55   II
Resaiv my eirnest admonition all.
Quhillis 3e ar weill I wish 3ou to be war.
Remember (shirs) that somtym 3e war small
And may be 3it, I will not say 3e sall
For (I confes) that war a fut too far.   60
Houbeit 3e think my harrand something har
Quhen 3e leist wein 3our baks may to the wall.
Things byds not ay in ordour as they ar.

Tak tyme in tyme and to my Taill tak tent.
Let 3e it pas (perhaps) 3e may repent   65
And wish it war vhen 3e may want 3our will.
Had Cæsar sene the Cedul that wes sent
3e wat he had not with the wicked went
Quha war concludit causles him to kill
Bot in his bosome he put vp that bill   70
The vhilk at last (thoght lait) maid him repent.
His vnadvertence only did him ill.

Judge of 3our self by Julius my Joyes
Quhais fen3eid freinds wer worse then open foes
If that 3e stand not in a stagring stait.   75
Think 3e that sho will thole 3ou more nor those
Quha war 3our auin Compan3ons, I suppose,
Quhom sho gart slyde or 3e sat on thair seat?
Some got a blind vho thoght they war not bleat.
Chuse or refuse my Counsel, tak 3our chose.   80
Fairweill my freinds, I bot with Fortun fleat.

11ᵛ   10   The Poets Complaint of his Nativitie

Since that the Hevins ar hinderers of my hap
And all the starris so strange against me stand
Quhy kild not Jove me with his thunderclap?
Hou soon the Midwyfe held me in hir hand
5   Quhy wald not Mercure with his wrethin wand
Depryve me baith of senses, wit and shape?
Since that the Hevins ar hinderers of my hap

Quhy thoild my Mothers bouels me to breath?
Quhy wes hir belly not my bureall bed?
10 Quhy wes not hir delyverie my death?
Quhy suelt I not so soon as we wer shed?
Quhy come the Muses and my Cradle cled?
Quhat movit these Vestall Virgins me to wrap?
Since that the Hevins ar hinderers of my hap

15 Quhy wes my Mother blyth vhen I wes borne?
Quhy heght the Weirds my weilfair to advance?
Quhy wes my birth on Eister day at morne?
Quhy did Apollo then appeir to dance?
Quhy gaiv he me good morou with a glance?
20 Quhy leugh he in his golden chair and lap?
Since that the hevins ar hinderers of my hap

Quhy had he me to Helicon to heive?
Quhy wes I novece to the Nobles nyne?
Quhy did the Gods for godbarne gift me geive
25 Ambrosian bread and hevinly Nectar wyn?
12 To quintessence a goldin grave Ingyne
Both for Invention and for vttrance apt
Since that the Hevins ar hinderers of my hap

Quhy wes I nurisht with the Noble Nymphs?
30 Quhy wes I fostred for to flie with fame?
For drinking of these Ladyis hallouit lymphs
Extold Among Ye Rare Men wes my name.

17 day at] day (and; *del.*) at K

18

Quhy did Apollo Poet me proclame?
To cleith my heid with his grene laurell Cap
Since that the Hevins ar hinderers of my hap.   35

Quhat helpeth me thoght Maja or Minerve
With hevinly fury haif my spreit infusde?
Quhat do these sacred Ceremonies serve?
Quhilks they haif on thair auin adoptit wsde
Quhat profits me vhom fortun hes refusde?   40
Thoght with my King in credit once I crap
Since that the Hevins ar hinderers of my hap

Quhy wes my will to Vertue mair then Vyce?
Quhy wes I faithfull and refusde to fane?
Quhy soght I aye warme water vnder yce?   45
Quhair wylis availls and Veritie is vane
Forgive me this, and if I do-it agane
Then tak me with the foxis taill a flap
Since that the Hevins are hinderers of my hap.

11   The Poets Complante aganst the wnkyndnes of his 12ᵛ
      Companions vhen he wes in prisone

No wonder thoght I waill and weip
     That womplit am in woes.
I sigh, I sobbe vhen I suld sleep.
     My spreit can not repose.
My persone is in prisone pynit   5
And my Companionis so vnkynd
(Melancholie mischeivis my mynd)
     That I can not rejose.

So long I lookit for relief
     Vhill treulie nou I tyre.   10
My guttis ar grippit so with grief
     It eitis me vp in yre.
The fremmitnes that I haif felt

10.48 tak] tak(e; *del.*) K

19

For syte and sorou garris me suelt
15   And maks my hairt within me melt
    Lyk waxe befor the fyre.

Quhen men or wemen visitis me
    My dolour I disguyse
By outuard sight that nane may sie
20   Quhair inward langour lyis.
Als patient as my pairt appeirs
With hevy hairt vhen no man heirs
For baill then burst I out in teirs
    Alane with cairfull cryis.

13 25 All day I wot not vhat to do
    I loth to sie the licht
At evin then I am trublit to,
    So noysum is the nicht.
Quhen Natur most requyrs to rest
30   With pansing so I am opprest
(So mony things my mynd molest)
    My sleiping is bot slicht

Remembring me vhair I haif bene
    Both lykit and belov't
35   And nou sensyne vhat I haif sene
    My mynd may be commov't.
If ony of my dolour dout
Let ilkane sey thair tym about.
Perhaps vhois stomok is most stout
40   His Patience may be prov't.

I sie and namely nou a dayis
    All is not gold that gleitis
Nor to be seald that ilkane sayis
    Nor water all that weitis.
45   Sen fristed goods ar not forgivin,
Quhen Cuppe is full then hold it evin
For man may meit at vnset stevin
    Thoght Montanis nevir meits.

47 vnset stevin] vnsetstevin K

Then do as yee wald be done to,
    Belouit brethren all   50
For (out of dout) vhat so ȝe do   13ᵛ
    Resaiv the lyk ȝe sall
And with quhat mesur ȝe do mett
Prepair again the lyk to gett.
ȝour feet ar not so sicker sett   55
    Bot fortun ȝe may fall.

12   A late regrate of Leirning to Love

Quhat mightie motione so my mynd mischeivis?
Quhat vncouth cairs throu all my corps do creep?
Quhat restles rage my Resone so bereivis?
Quhat maks me loth of meit, of drink, of sleep?
I knou not nou vhat Countenance to keep   5
For to expell a poysone that I prove.
Alace, alace that evir I leirnd to Love.

A frentick fevir thrugh my flesh I feill,
I feill a passione can not be exprest,
I feill a byll within my bosum beill,   10
No Cataplasme can weill impesh that pest,
I feill my self with seiknes so possest.
A madnes maks my mirth from me remove.
Alace, alace that evir I learnd to love.

12.title] *om.* Ed We Wq Ro 1 Quhat] Of Ed motione] motive Wq my mynd] my (many; *del.*) my Ro 2 Quhat] That Ed cairs] cair Ed We Wq Ro all my corps] all crops Ro do] doth Ed We 3] Quhat restless raige so my mynd bereavs Wq Quhat] Þat Ed Ro so bereivis] soverein is Ed 4] that maks mei lath bath meatt both drink and sleep We Quhat] Quhich Ed of drink, of sleep] and drink and sleep Ro; of drink and sleep Wq 5 nou] then We vhat] þat Ed Countenance] continence Ed Ro 6 a poysone] the poyson Ed Wq; that pasion We; the treassons Ro that] quhilk Ed; that We 8 A frentick] And (ane; *del.*) fanting Ro thrugh] in We flesh] self Ro 10 beill] veill Ro 11 impesh that] infest that We; remeid this Ro 12] my siknes sore with sorow so posestt We possest] oppresst Ro 13] that madnes doth from mei my mirth remeu We A madnes maks my mirth] All mirrines makes Ro; that madnesse maks all mirth Wq

15 My hopeles hairt, vnhappiest of hairts
    Is hoild and hurt with Cupids huikit heeds
    And thirlit throu with deidly poysond dairts
    That inwardly within my breist it bleids
14 3it fantasie my fond affection feeds
20 To run that race but ather rest or rove.
    Alace, alace that evir I leirnd to love.

    Nou sie I that I nevir sau afore.
    Nou knou I that (vhill nou) I nevir kneu.
    Nou sie I weill that servitude is sore
25 Bot vhat remeid? It is no tym to reu.
    Quhair Love is Lord, all Libertie adeu.
    My baill is bred by destinies above.
    Alace, alace that evir I leirnd to Love.

    All gladnes nocht bot aggravats my grief.
30 All mirrines my murning bot augments.
    Lamenting toons best lyks me for relief,
    My sicknes soir to sorou so consents
    For cair the cairfull comounly contents.
    Sik harmony is best for thair behove.
35 Alace, alace that evir I leirnd to love.

    I felt fra anis I entred in that airt
    A grit delyte that leson for to leir
    Quhill I become a prentise ou'r expert
    For but a book I cund it soon perqueir.
40 My doctours wage and deuty will be deir
    I grant, except I get hir jelous glove.
    Alace, alace that evir I leirnd to Love.

15–35] *om.* We 15 hopeles] haplesse Wq of hairts] of all hearts Ro 16 hoild] healed
Ro; held Wq huikit] huckes Ro 17 deidly poysond] many dead Ro; poysound deadly
Wq 18 breist it bleids] bossome bleids Ro Wq 19] My fantacies and full effectione
leads Ro 3it] but Wq 20] And makes me say þis ay but rest or roue Ro; and maks
me runn that race but rest or ruve Wq 21] *end of Ro text* 22 sie ... sau] feel ... felt Wq
25 no] not Wq 27 by destinies] my despaires Wq 36 anis] once Wq 38 Quhill] till
We 39 For] how We I cund it soon perquier] canditt shun perquier We 39–42] that
I then could have proved a master ther / yett never could win in within hir sphear /
nor never will except she pitie move / that then wee both may end our livs in lov Wq
40 and] ane We 41 hir jelous glove] your gles glou lou We

13   A Counsell aganst Dispair in Love   14ᵛ

Drie furth the inch as thou hes done the span,
My gentle hairt, and die not in dispair.
I sheu the first vhen thou to Love began
It wes no moues to mell with Loves lair.
Thou wald not ceis till thou wes in that snair.   5
Think of it nou as thou thoght of it than.
With patience thou mayst thy self prepair
To drie the inch as thou hes done the span.

Quhat meins thou nou fra thou be in hir waird?
Thy Libertie alace, it is to lait.   10
Except hir grace thou hes no other gaird.
Thair is no chose for nou thou art chekmait.
Thair is no draught that dou mak the debait.
Thou art inclosde for all the craft thou can.
With patience persaiv thy auin estait.   15
Drie furth the Inch as thou hes done the span.

The mair thou grudgis the griter is thy grief.
The mair thou sighis the mair thou art ou'rsett.
The mair thou loipis the les is thy relief.
The mair thou flings the faster is the net.   20
The mair thou feghts the mair thou art defett,
The mair behind the faster that thou ran.
Tak Patience sen dolour peyis no dett.
Drie furth the inch as thou hes done the span.

ʒit werie not thoght of thy will thou want   25
I am assuird that shortly thou sall sie   15
Thy Love and Lady grace vnto the grant
Sa far as may stand with hir honestie.
Hir gentlenes and hir humanitie
War Advocats till thou thy proces wan   30
Provyding aluayis thou suld stedfastly
Drie furth the inch as thou hes done the span.

Then mak thy self als mirrie as thou may.
The tyme may come thou longis for so fast.
35 Rome wes not biggit all vpon ane day
And ȝit it wes compleitit at the last.
Of all thy pains account the perrils past.
For vhy? Sho is not come of Cresseids clan.
Be glade thairfor and be no more agast.
40 Drie furth the inch as thou hes done the span.

O noblest Nymph of Naturs nurishing
O most excellent only A per se
O fairest flour in firmnes florishing
O treuest Turtle, root of Constancie
45 O worthie wicht both wyse and womanlie
O Myn but mo shau mercy to thy man
To plesur him vho dois so patiently
Drie furth the inch as he hes done the span.

15ᵛ   **14 ECHO**

To the Echo and thou to me agane
In the deserts among the wods and wells
Quhair Destinie hes bund the to remane
But Company within the firths and fells
5 Let vs complene with wofull ȝouts and ȝells
On shaft and shooter that our hairts hes slane.
To the Echo and thou to me agane.

Thy pairt to mine may justlie be compaird
In mony poynts vhilk both we may repent.
10 Thou hes no hope and I am clene dispaird.
Thou tholis but caus, I suffer innocent.
Thou does bewaill and I do still lament.
Thou murns for nocht, I shed my teirs in vane.
To the Echo and thou to me agane.

14.2 among] amangs Ja 3 the] the Ja; him K 6 On shaft and shooter] A shaft, a
shooter Ja 7] *end of Ja text*

Thou pleins Narcissus, I my love also.   15
He did the hurt, bot I am kild by myne.
He fled from the, myne is my mortall fo
Without offence, and crueller nor thyne.
The weirds vs baith predestinat to pyne
Continually to others to complane.   20
To the Echo and thou to me agane.

Thou hyds thy self, I list not to be sene.
Thou banisht art and I am in exyle
By Juno thou and I by Venus Quene.
Thy Love wes fals and myn did me begyle.   25   16
Thou hoped once, so wes I glaid a vhyle
3it lost our tyme in love, I will not lane.
To the Echo and thou to me agane.

Thy elrish skirlis do penetrat the Roks,
The roches rings and rendirs me my cryis.   30
Our saikles plaints to pitie thame provoks
Quhill they compell our sounds to pierce the skyis.
All thing bot Love to plesur vs applyis
Quhais end, alace I say, is bot disdane.
To thee Echo and thou to me agane.   35

Somthing Echo thou hes for to rejose.
Suppose Narcissus sometyme the forsook,
First he is dead, syne changed in a Rose
Quhom thou nor nane hes pouer for to brook.
Bot be the contrair evirie day I look   40
To sie my Love attraptit in a trane
From me Echo and nevir come agane.

Nou welcome, Echo. Patience perforce!
Anes eviry day with murning Let vs meet.
Thy Love nor myne in mynds haif no remorse.   45
We taist the sour that nevir felt the sueet.
As I demand then ansueir and repeit
(Let teirs aboundant ou'r our visage rane)
To thee Echo and thou to me agane,

19 weirds vs] weirds (is; *del.*) vs K

16ᵛ 50   Quhat Lovers, Echo, maks sik querimony?   Mony
      Quhat kynd of fyre doth kindle thair Curage?   Rage
      Quhat Medicine (o Echo, knouis thou ony?)   Ony
      Is best to stay this Love of his Passage?   Age
      Quhat merit thay that culd our sighs assuage?   Wage
55   Quhat wer we first in this our Love profane?   fane
      Quhair is our Joy (o Echo tell agane)?   gane.

15

    Blind Love if euer thou made bitter sueet
    Or turnd the sugar to the taist of gall
    Or ȝit dissolvit a frostie hairt with heet,
    If on thyn altar sacrifice I sall
5   As to the Lord of Love vho may do all,
    Vhois pouer maks the stoutest stomoks yeeld
    And waikest somtyme for to win the feeld,

    If thou can brek ane allabaster breist
    Or if no sheeld be shotfrie vhare thou shoots,
10 Let not thy Lau be lichtliet at the leist
    Bot tak revenge vhen Rebels thee reboots.
    If thou be he of vhom so mony moots
    Quha maks the hardiest flintie harts to melt
    And beirs thame ay about the lyk a belt,

15 Or if thou be that Archer so renound
    That vhair thou mints thou missis not the mark
    Bot lyk a king is for thy Conqueis cround
17 To vhom all stoupis thoght they war neuer so stark,
    If of thy fyr be resting ȝit a spark,
20 I pray thee nou thy cunning for to kyth
    And burne hir breist that of my baill is blyth.

15.10 Let not] Let (t; *del.*) not K 18 stark] s... K

16   A descriptione of vane Lovers

Nane lovis bot fools vnlov'd agane,
Quha tyns thair tyme and comis no speid.
Mak this a Maxime to remane
That Love beirs nane bot fools at feid
(And they get ay a good goosheid   5
In recompense of all thair pane)
So of necessitie mon succeid.
Nane lovis bot fools vnlov'd agane.

3e wot a wyse man will be war
And will not ventur but advyse.   10
Greit fuills for me I think they ar
That seeks warme water vnder yce.
3it some mair wilfull ar nor wyse
That for thair Lovis saik wold be slane.
Buy on Repentance of that pryce.   15
Nane lovis bot fools vnlov'd agane.

Thoght some we sie in evry age
Lyk glaikit fools gang gooked gaits
Quhair Reson gets no place for rage,
They Love best them vhilk thame bot haits   20
Syne of thair folies wyts the faits
As Destinie did thame disdane,   17ᵛ
Quhilks are bot cappit vane conceats.
Nane lovis bot fools vnlov'd agane.

title] *om.* La 2 tyns] spendis La 3 remane] remeid La 4 That Love] That (f; *del.*)
Love K; luifis La 5 goosheid] geis heid La 7 mon] man La 9 3e wot] 3itt will La
12 warme] hett La 14 be slane] be scene La 15 Buy on] Bayand La of] on La 18
glaikit] gukitt La gang] gangis La 19 rage] age La 20] Thay luf þame best þat
þame bott cancentis La 21 Syne] Same La 22 Destinie] desteneis La 23] *line
om.* La 24] *end of La text*

25 Some by ane Proverbe fane wald prove
(Quha skantly nevir sau the scuills)
That Love with resone is no Love
Nor constance vhare Occasion cools.
Thair they confes lyk frantick fools
30 That wilfully thay will be vane.
But Reson what ar men bot mulis?
Nane loves bot fools vnlov'd agane.

They speik not leirnd lyk at the leist
That rage in steid of Reson ruisis.
35 Vhat better ar they nor a beist?
Fra tym that Reson thame refuisis
Some beistlily thamselfis abusis
As Constancie did them constrane,
Quhilks ar bot Ignorant excusis.
40 Nane lovis bot fools vnlov'd agane.

For ding a Dog and he will byte,
And fan on him vha givis him fude,
And can (as caus requyrs) acquyt
As ill with ill and good with good.
45 Than love nane bot vhare thou art lude
And vhar thou finds tham fayn'd, refrane.
Tak this my Counsell, I conclude.
Nane Lovis bot fools vnlov'd agane.

18   17   ## The well of Love

Among the Gods that sittis above
    And ruleth in the skyis,
That blindit boy the god of Love
    All Creatur espyis.
5 Vha may withstand his stroke, I say,
    Quhen he list for to shute?
For to reveill I minted ay
    Bot yet it was no bute.
Fra tym that winged God did sie

16.45 Than love] Than (nane; *del.*) love K   art lude] art (v; *del.*) lude K

28

That I did Love disdane,   10
He took a shaft and shot at me
    And peirsit evirie vane.
The head so deeply in me sank
    That al my body brist.
Then of the well of Love I drank   15
    To quench my burning thrist.
So soon as I thairof did taist
    My breist began to burne
Then to the Gods of Love in haist
    My visage did I turne,   20
With trimbling teirs, vpon my knees
    My pains for to deploir,
Then they did open vp my ees
    Quhilk long wer shut before.
Quhen that my dimmit sight greu cleir   25
    Incontinent I sau
A palice stand before me neir   18ᵛ
    And thidder did I drau
For to refresh my werynes
    Quhilk I susteind before   30
Bot then my pains they did incres
    And vexd me more and more.
Into that place I sau repair
    Of Nymphs mony one.
Lyk burning gold thair glistering hair   35
    Thair shulders hang vpon.
Amongst thame one I sau appeir
    Quhilk did excell thame all,
Lyk Venus with hir smyling cheir
    That wan the goldin ball,   40
Hir deasie colour rid and vhyte
    Lyk Lilies on the laik,
Hir glistring hair of grit delyte
    Behind hir nek did shaik,
Of Diamonds hir ees were maid   45
    That in hir heid did stand,
With armis long and shulders braid
    And middle small as wand.
Fra I beheld hir beuty bright

50   I had no strenth to steir.
        I wes so woundit with that sight
            That I micht not reteir.
19   The Gods of Love reliev my pain
            And caus hir for to reu
55   For nou the fyre of Love agane
            Is in me kindlit neu.
        O happie war that man indeid
            Quha micht hir love obtene!
        For hir my thirlit hairt does bleid,
60   Sair vexit is my splene
        Sen I haif lost my Libertie
            In bondage for to duell
        God give her grace to reu on me
            And meit me at the well.

18   Of the same Well

        To the o Cupid king of Love
            We pray vhair thou does duell
        That but respect thou wold remove
            All rebells from thy well,
5   And if to drink they haif desyre
            This water then thou turne
        Into the Element of fyre
            With baill thair breist to burne,
        And let thame with Apollo prove
10   The fury of thy fyre
        And let them haif no luk in Love
            Bot droun thame with desyre,
        Bot vnto vs that subjects ar
            To Love and to his lauis
19ᵛ 15 Mair mercifull I wald thou war
            Nor ȝit thy self thou shauis.
        As we do serve thy Celsitude
            In hope to haif reuaird,
        Let thame vhom we haif so long lude
20   Our service once regaird.

19   The Commendatione of Love

I rather far be fast nor frie
Albeit I micht my mynd remove.
My Maistres hes a man of me
That lothis of euery thing bot Love.
        Quhat can a man desyre,   5
        Quhat can a man requyre,
        Bot tym sall caus him tyre
            And let it be,
        Except that fervent fyre
        Of burning Love impyre?   10
        Hope heghts me sik a hyre.
I rather far be fast nor frie.

But Love vhat wer bot sturt or stryfe?
But Love vhat kyndnes culd indure?
But Love hou lothsum war our lyfe?   15
But Love vhairof suld we be sure?
        But Love vhair wer delyt?
        But Love vhat bot despyt?
        But Love vhat wer perfyt?
            Sure suld we sie.   20
        But Love vhat wer to wryt?
        But Love vha culd indyt?
        No, nothing worth a myte.   20
I rather far be fast nor frie.

Love maks men galȝard in thair geir.   25
Love maks a man a Martial mynd,
Love maks a man no fortun feir,
Love changes Natur contrare kynd,
        Love maks a Couard kene,
        Love maks the clubbit clene,   30
        Love maks the niggard bene,
            That vho bot he?
        Love maks a man, I mene,
        Mair semely to be sene.
        Love keeps ay Curage grene.   35
I rather far be fast nor frie.

2 micht my] micht (my; *del.*) my K

Love can not be bot from above
Quhilk halds the hairt so quik in heit.
Fy on that freik that can not Love
40   He hes not worth a sponk of spreit.
Remember ony man
In Chronikle ʒe can
That ever worship wan
But Love, let sie,
45   And once that rink he ran.
Sen this is treu, vhy than,
I end as I began.
20ᵛ   I rather far be fast nor frie.

20 AGANE of Love

I rather far be frie nor fast.
I hope I may remove my mynd.
Love is so licht it can not last.
It is smal plesur to be pynd.
5   Sen I haif ees tuo
Vhat neid I blindlings go
Ay fundring to and fro
Quhill clods me cast?
I am not one of tho
10   To work my wilfull wo.
I shaip not to do so.
I rather far be frie nor fast.

But libertie vhat micht me meis?
But libertie all things me grieve.
15   But libertie vhat might me pleis?
But libertie I loth to leive.
But libertie, alace,
Hou cairfull wer my case.
But libertie, my grace
20   And joy wer past.
Suppose I for a space

19.40 of spreit] of (heet; *del.*) spreit K
20.title] A... f L... K 13 me meis] me (s; *del.*) meis K

    War Captive in a place?
    I reu that rekles race.
I rather far be frie nor fast.

Of prisone fredome brings me furth.   25
My fredome maks contentment kyth.
But fredome all things war no worth.
My fredome maks me glade and blyth.
    My fredome maks me fain   21
    In mirth vhair I remain   30
    I pas the tym but pain
        And vnagast,
    Quharas I purpose plain
    From folies to refrain
    Sen Love hes syndrie slain.   35
I rather far be frie nor fast.

Love can not be bot very ill
That folk with fury so infects,
Abusing manheid, wit and skill.
No ryme nor resone it respects   40
    Bot ramping in a rage
    Not sparing ony age
    Of Caȝard, king nor page
        Bot byds thair blast.
    Sen sik as suld be sage   45
    Ar korpit in that Cage,
    I work not for sik wage.
I rather far be frie nor fast.

21

    Lyk as the dum
    Solsequium
    With cair ou'rcum
And sorou vhen the sun goes out of sight

21.1 dum] doul Ro   4 And] does Wq Ba; Doth Ed Fo C3; Deed Ro

5   Hings doun his head
21ᵛ   And droups as dead
And will not spread
Bot louks his leavis throu langour of the nicht
Till folish Phaeton ryse   With vhip in hand
10   To cleir the cristall skyis   And light the Land,
Birds in thair bour
Luiks for that hour
And to thair Prince ane glaid good-morou givis.
Fra thyn that flour
15   List not to lour
Bot laughis on Phœbus, lousing out his leivis.

Sa fairis with me
Except I be
Vhair I may se
20   My lamp of licht, my Lady and my Love.
Fra sho depairts
Ten thousand dairts
In syndrie airts
Thirlis throu my hevy hart but rest or rove.
25   My Countenance declairs   My inward grief.
Good hope almaist dispairs   To find relief.

5 his] her Wq Ro Fo C3 6 droups] drops Fo as] lyk Ti 6–7] And will not spred / but droups as dead Wq 7 And] Nor Ba spread] come Ro 8 louks his] luirks his Ti; lurk her Ro; lurks her C3 of] all Ti Ba Ro C3 8] lurking in leavs the langnesse of the nicht Wq; but lurkes her leaves through longer of the night Fo; but lurks her leaves throgh langour al the night C3 9 ryse] arise C3 10 cleir] purge Ba 12 Luiks for] Waits on Ti Ba Ro; Waites for Fo; waite on C3 13 Prince] king Wq Ba Ro Fo C3 glaid] great Ti Ro 14 thyn] thence Wq Fo C3; hence Ti Ro 15 List] likes Wq Ro Fo C3 to] till Ba 15] Lists nocht ane boure Ti 16 laughis] lachis Ti lousing out] lousing furþ Ti; opning out Ro Fo C3 his] her Wq Ro Fo C3 17 fairis] it stands Ti Ba Wq Ro; stands't C3 Fo 18 I be] I (se; *del.*) be Ba 21 Fra] When C3 Wq Ro Fo 22 Ten] ane Ba 23 airts] artes Fo 24 Thirlis] Thirle C3 my] my (hart; *del.*) Ba hevy] heavnlye (heavy) Ro rove] ruth Wq; raiffe Ti 26 Good] My Wq; And C3 Ba Ro Fo

I die, I duyn,
Play does me pyn,
I loth on euiry thing I look, alace
    Till Titan myne   30
    Vpon me shyne
That I revive throu favour of hir face.

    Fra she appeir
    Into hir spheir
    Begins to cleir   35   22
The dauing of my long desyrit day,
    Then Curage cryis
    On hope to ryse
    Fra he espyis
My noysome nicht of Absence worne auay.   40
    No wo vhen I aualk   May me impesh
    Bot on my staitly stalk   I florish fresh.
    I spring, I sprout,
    My leivis ly out,
My color changes in ane hartsum heu.   45
    No more I lout
    Bot stands vp stout
As glade of hir for vhom I only greu.

28 Play] lov Wq 29 on] of Wq Ti look] lov Wq 30 Till] While Ro Fo C3 32 hir face] hir (face; *del.*) long desyred face Ti; her grace Ro Fo C3 33 appeir] appeirs Ti 34 Into] Wq Fo C3; And in Ti; in to Ba; Int... K; hir speir] Ti; h... s...hi... K 35 Begins] she ginns Wq 36 dauing] drawing C5 37 cryis] cryes (tryes) Ro 39 Fra] quhen Ba he] she Wq Ti Ro Fo C3 40 My] The Wq Ti Ba Ro C3 noysome] langsum Wq Ti worne] went Ti Ba Fo C3 41] No vois mey me awaill Ti; No noyis fra I awalk Ba; No woe can me awake C3 Wq Ro Fo 41] nor yett redresse Wq May me] Nor yet C3 Ti Ro Fo; Can me Ba impesh] impash Ti in posch Ro 42 my] thy C5 44 ly] break Fo C3; Lyis Ti Ba Ro; stairtes Wq 45 changes] hanges Ro in ane hartsum heu] in evrie helthsum heu Ti 48] Throu sight of her on quhom I only grew Wq As] Alse Ro for] on C3; of Fo

O happie day
50   Go not auay.
         Apollo stay
Thy Chair from going doun into the West.
         Of me thou mak
         Thy 3odiak
55   That I may tak
My plesur to behold vhom I love best.
         Thy presence me restores   To lyf from death
         Thy Absence also shores   To cut my breath.
         I wish in vane
60   Thee to remane
Sen Primum mobile sayis aluayis nay.
         At leist thy wane
         Turn soon agane.
Fareweill with patience perforce till day.

22   A regrate of Hard luck in Love

O vhat a martyrd man am I.
I freat, I fry,   I wreist, I wry,
I wrassill with the wind
(Of duill and dolour so I dry)
5   And wot not vhy   This grit invy
Of Fortun nou I find.
Bot at   This tyme hir spyt I spy.
O vhat   A martyrd man am I.

21.52 Chair] Cart Ro Fo C3 into] wnto Ba West] vaist Ti 53 mak] makes Ro
57 Thy] Her Wq Ro C3; Quhois Ti 57 To lyf from death] (from de; *del.*) To
lyf from d... K; frome deth to lyfe Ti C5; from life to death Wq C3 58 Thy]
Her Ro Fo C3 also] lykvayis Ti Ba shores] schoures Ro 58 breath] brea... K;
breath Ti Ba Ro Fo C3 60 Thee] Ye Ro 61 sayis aluayis] Sayis me alwayis Ba;
doth say me Wq Ro Fo C3 62 At leist] yett haist Wq thy wane] I veene Ti; thy
vayne Wq Ro; my Wane Fo 63 Turn soon] Turn shoone Ti; bring sone Ba;
Hast soone Ro Fo C3; right soone Wq 64] Ba Ro Fo C3; ... K; that I may joy
into my lightsome day Wq till] to Ti 72, *infra*: Finis quod thomsone with my
hand Ti
22.8 martryd man] martyrd (e; *del.*) man K

Quhat pen or paper can expres
The grit Distres   and hevynes   10
Quhilk I haif at my hairt.
My Comfort ay grouis les and les,
My cairs incres   With sik excess,
I sigh, I sobbe, I smarte
So that   I am compeld to cry,   15
'O vhat   a martyrd man am I'.

With weping ees my Verse I wryt
Of comfort quyt,   Adeu delyt,
My hairt is lyk the lead.
Of all my sorou and my syte   20
The weirds I wyt   That span with spyt
My thrauart fatall threid.
God wat   That Barrat deir I buy.
O vhat   A martyrd man am I.

Of ill befor I vnderstude   25
It had bene gude,   Into my cude
Bereiving me my breath   23
Nou to haif bene of noy denude
Quhilk boyllis my blude.
Come ʒit, conclude   30
My dolour, gentle Death
And lat   me not in langour ly.
O vhat   a martyrd man am I.

23

Quhen first Apollo Python sleu
Sa glorious that God he greu
Till he presumit to perseu
    The blindit Archer boy
Quhais Turkie bou and quaver bleu   5
Quharin appeirit noks aneu
He bad him ʒeild to him as deu
    Quha best culd thame imploy.
Quod Cupid, 'Shortly sall thou reu
That euer thou sik Cunning kneu'.   10

Syne to Parnassus fast he fleu
    His shaft for to convoy.
Thair he ane deidly dairt outdreu.
At proud Apollo he it threu,
15   Syn him a sight of Daphne sheu
        Quhose beutie wroght him noy.

Ʒit crabit Cupid not content
Apollois anger to augment
Did nok agane Incontinent
20   And amit aneu a flane
23ᵛ   With fethers rugh and all too rent.
At Daphne slaulie doun he sent
Quhais frostie head vhair so it went
        Bedeaʒit evry vane.
25   That winged Archer insolent
Did wound thame baith bot different,
Apollois harte to Love he bent,
        Bot Daphnes to disdane.
To lait Apollo did repent
30   That he with Cupid wes acquent
Quha wilfullie did ay invent
        Hou to augment his pane.

His hurt wes with the goldin heid
Quhilk inward in his hairt did bleid.
35   No medicin micht him remeid
        From Cupids angrie yre.
Hirs with the blunted bolt of leid,
Ane hevy mettall, cauld and deid,
Repelling Love as yee may reid,
40   And quencher of desyre.
His pain wes lyk the Pyralide,
A beist in birning that does breid
And in the fyry flammis dois feid
        And fosters of the fyre.
45   Cupido bare him so at feid
That in his love he come no speid.
Both his persute and Daphne's dreid
        To tell my tongue suld tyre.

20 A...d ... fl... K

About PENNEUS did repair
This noble Nymph of beuty rare   50   24
Quhais comely clothing to declare
    My Author does indyt.
Most from the belt vp scho wes bair.
Behind hir hang hir hevinly hair
Vnkamed, hovring in the air,   55
    Shed from hir visage vhyt,
With blinks dulce and debonair
Lyk Beuties freshest florish fair
Exem'd clene from Loves lair
    To work Apollo spyt.   60
Hir Countenance did move him mair
Quhen throu hir garments heir and thair
Appeirit hir lustie lims square
    As sho ran by him quyt.

Quhen as he sau that Virgin flie   65
He folloude in a frenesie
And cryde, 'O daphne, deir to me,
    Quhy does thou tak the chace?
Go slau and sie vha folouis thee,
Thy lover and no enemie.
Nixt michtie Jove into degrie   70
    I bruik the cheifest place,
And I sall stay my course', quod he,
'Leist thou resave some hurt from me.
Thou sees thair is no remedie   75
    But thou must lose the race'.
Sho prayd the Gods hir helpers be
To saif hir pure Virginitie,
Quha shupe hir in a laurell trie   24ᵛ
    As he did hir embrace.   80

Nou lovesome Lady let vs leir
Example of these Ladyis heir.
Sen Daphne boght hir love so deir
    Hir fortun suld effray ʒou.
Bot I haif no sik caus to feir   85
82 Ladyis] Lady is K

39

That obstinat ȝe perseveir.
On Lovis book my self I sueir
    Ȝour bundman til obey ȝou.
Then lyk Penelope appeir
90 Quha wes so constant tuenty ȝeir
Quhen ȝour Vlysses is not neir.
    Tentation may assay ȝou,
Ȝit vary not I ȝou requeir,
And I sall stoppe Vlysses eir.
95 Fairweill my Love and Lady cleir,
    Be permanent I pray ȝou.

24

As Natur passis nuriture
(Of Natur all things hes a strynd)
So evrie leving Creature
Ay covets comounly thair kynd,
5 As Buk the Dae, the Harte the Hynd.
Lyk drauis to lyk, we sie this sure
So I am aluayis of that mynd
That Natur passis Nuriture.

Thoght Nuriture be of that strenth
10 To war the Natur vhylis a wie,
25 Ȝit Natur ay prevailis at lenth
As by Experience we sie,
Except throu Destinie it be
In some vhilk does not long indure.
15 Vhat fortun will may no man flie,
Bot Natur passis nuriture.

To prove this Proverbe to be true
Difficultie I think is nane
By ald Examplis past aneu
20 Quharof I micht haif tuentie tane.
Nou I will vse bot only ane
Quhilk lang within my breist I bure
And let the lave nou all alane
Hou Natur passis Nuriture.

23.96, *infra*: Finis. K

40

Thair wes a gentle girking gay   25
Of plesand plume and fair of flicht
Quha wes so proud vhen he wald pray
That he outsprang all halks for hight
He wes so lordly for to light
He wald not look vpon a lure   30
Bot fleu (ay soaring) out of sight
As Natur passis Nuriture.

The falconis folouit vhair he fleu.
To fang his freindship they war fane,
Quharof so glorious he greu   35
That he thair offers did disdane
Quhilks vhen they sau they wroght in vane
The formels fair auay they fure.   25ᵛ
Ingratitude gets sik agane,
As Natur passis Nuriture.   40

This girking pearkit in a place
Quharin ouer long he did delyt
Quhill at the last throu Love alace
He come acquantit with a kyt
And quat his auld acquentance quyt.   45
Of his oun kynd he took no cure.
Wo worth the weirds that had the wyt
That Natur ʒeildt to Nuriture.

Fra once hir Company he vsit
He greu so goked with that gled,   50
Blind Love his reson so abvsit,
He suore that they suld neuer shed.
Fra sho with fedrit flesh wes fed
(Quhilk prayd befor on poddoks pure)
With tym sho tystit him to tred.   55
Thair Natur ʒeild't to Nuriture.

39 agane] a gane K

Hir meit of Modeuarts and myce
He chang'd in Partridge and in pout.
Ʒit Natur nottheles is nyce.
60 Thair brald a Bissat neir about
Quhilk vs'd hir vhen the Halk fleu out,
Suppose they held it long obscure.
Do vhat ʒe dou, thair is no dout
Bot Natur passis nuriture.

26 65 Thair Companie wes not so quyet
Bot or they wist they wer beuryde
And that throu pearking of a Pyet
Besyde thame vhilk thair palks espyde.
To tell the halk in haist sho hy'de.
70 The kyt wes palʒard and perjure.
The Tersel troude not vhill he tryde
That Natur passis Nuriture.

25

Quhill as with vhyt and nimble hand
My Maistres gathring flours doth stand
    Amidst the florisht meid
Of Lilies vhyt and violets,
5 A garland properly sho plets
    To set vpon hir heid.
O Sun that shynis so bright above,
If euer thou the fyre of Love
    Hes felt (as Poets fayne)
10 If it be sik as sik it semes,
Of Courtessie withdrau thy bemes
    Leist thou hir colour stayne.
She if thou not hir Beutie burne
Sall quyt thee with a better turne,
15   To close hir cristall ees
(A brightnes far surmounting thyne)
Leist thou thairby asham'd suld tyne
    Thy Credit in the skyis.

26

Evin dead, behold I breath.
My breath procures my pane,
Els dolour eftir death
Suld slaik vhen I war slane.
Bot Destinies disdane   5
So span my fatall threid
But mercy to remane
A martyr quik and deid.
O cruell deidly feid,
O Rigour but remorse!   10
Since thair is no remeid
Come Patience perforce.

The faits, the thrauard faitis,
The wicked weirds, hes wroght
My state of all estates   15   27
Vnhappiest to be thoght.
Had I offendit oght
Or wroght aganst thair will,
But mercy than they moght
Conclude my Corps to kill,   20
Bot as they haif no skill
Of gude nor ȝit regard,
The Innocent with ill
Ressaves the lyk reuard.

---

1 dead] death Ro Fo Sc 2 procures] procured Ro 3] Els D (*space*) eftir death Ro
4 slaik] sleip Ro; slack Fo 6 So] Who Sc Ro fatall] froward Fo 9 O cruell] Mb
Tc Rc Ed Fo; O fatall K; A crewell Ro deidly feid] Lie seid Sc 13–36] Mb Tc
Rc Ed Fo Ro; *stanzas rev.* K 13] The faith the froward faitis Ro the thrauard]
the froward Sc; my froward Fo 14] My vikid threids has vroghte Ed The]
With Ro Fo 17 Had] Have Fo 18 thair] ȝour Sc Ro 19 they] yee Sc; the Ro
moght] might Fo 21 they haif] there is Sc Ro 22] Of reasoune nor regard Sc
Ed Ro Fo 23 with] and Sc Ed Fo Ro 24 Ressaves the] receaves a Sc Ed; Re-
ceive a Fo

26ᵛ 25   My hairt but rest or rove,
         Reuth, reson or respect,
         With fortun, Death, and Love
         Is keipit vnder check
         That nou thair is no nek
30   Nor draught to mak debate
         Bot let it brist or brek,
         For Love must haif it mait.
         Relief, alace, is lait,
         Quhen I am bund, to flie.
35   I stand in strange estate.
         I duyn and dou not die.

27   3it tyme sall try my Treuth
         And panefull patient pairt
         Thoght Love suld rage but reuth
40   And Death with deidly dairt
         Suld sey to caus me smart,
         Nor fortuns fickill vheill—
         All suld not change my hairt,
         Quhilk is als true as steill.
45   I am not lyk ane eill
         To slippe nor 3et to slyde.
         Love, Fortun, Death fairueill
         For I am bound to byd.

25 rove] rueth Sc; ruff Ro; rauffe Ed 26 Reuth] butt Sc 27 With] Twixt Mb
Sc Ed Fc; Cairis Ro fortun] Fortunes Fo and Love] or lyfe Sc 30 draught]
strenkthe Ed 31 let it] neids must Sc Ro Fo; meues most Ed or] and Sc Ro Fo
32 must] will Sc Ro it] its Sc; his Fo 33 Relief] releise Sc; Retrite? Ro 34
bund] forcit Sc Ro Fo 36] I loue I duyne I die Ro; I live I duyne I die Sc; I love,
I dwyne, I die Fo; Recaue allyk rewaird Ro 36, *infra*: Finis amen so be it Ro
26.37–48] *om.* Ro 39 Love] lyfe Sc suld] would Fo 41] Should stay to cure my
smart Sc Fo S 42 Nor] And Sc; On Fo 43 suld] sall Sc Fo 46 nor 3et to] away
and Mb Fc Sc St Fo; away or Ed 48 For] Wher Fc St Sc Ed Mb Fo to] I Mb
Fc St Sc Ed; I'le Fo

27

Love, if thou list I pray the let me leiv,
Devoir me not, withdrau thy deidly dairt.
Quhat right or resone hes thou to bereiv
Me (wofull wretch) of my vnhappie hairt?
Thy fyre
Through yre } My bailfull bosome burnis   5   27ᵛ
Quhat gloir
The moir } Vnto thy Trophee turnis   10
      To prove on me thy pith,
      Ane innocent but ill
      That ȝoldin am in will?
      If thou thy Captive kill
      I dou not do thairwith.   15

O Reson thou regards not to be reft.
Weill I persaiv thy pairt is to reprove.
Quhy hes thou me alone in langour left
Delyvring me vnto this lokman Love,
Vhose strenth
At lenth } Sall shuff the by the skaith   20
That I
Deir buy } And thou be banisht baith   25
      Quhilk sore we may repent.
      Fra thou be in exyle
      That boy will me beguyll.
      O waryit be the vhyle
      That euer we wer acquent.   30

Quhen I wes lous, at Libertie I lap.
I leugh vhen Ladyis spak to me of Love.
To hald me sa, alace, I had no hap
Bot purposly I wald gang pastym prove.
I thoght
I moght } But perrell pas the tym   35
Fra hand
I fand } My fethers in the lyme   40   28

5–7 *See Notes*

45

Quhair I took leist regaird
And lothest wes to look
Bot seimd that I forsook,
Sho had me on hir hook.
45   O welcome, just reuard!

My pane is bot hir pastyme and hir play.
As fyr I burne, lyk yce sho is als cauld.
I sie the man vha will not vhen he may,
The tym sall come he sall not vhen he wald.
50   I sie
        In me   { This Proverbe to be true
55   Quha wald
        Not hald   { Me frie, vhilk I may reu,

Bot proudly wald presume
And haȝard to come speid.
Quhen gone is all remeid,
Dispair will be my deid.
60   I sie nane other dome.

28

In throu the windoes of myn ees
(A perillous and open pairt)
Hes Cupid hurt my hevy hairt,
Quhilk daylie duyns bot nevir dees
5   Throu poyson of his deidly dairt.
    I bad him bot
    To sey ane shot.   { I smyld to se that suckling shute.
28ᵛ   'Boy, with thy bou
  10 Do vhat thou dou' { Quod I, 'I cair the not a cute'.

27.49 come he] come (s; *del.*) he K
28.2] Ane oppen and a peralous pairt Mb Fc 3 Hes] And Ro 4 daylie duyns
bot] daylie dwynes and Fc; never dewynes and Ro 4–5] *rev.* Fc 5 Throu]
Though Ro 6–8 *See Notes,* 27.5-7 7 To sey] sey Ro 11 I] he Fc

'Fell peart', quod Cupid, 'thou appeirs'.
Syn to his bou he maid a braid
And shot me soon be I had said
Quhill all my laughter turnd to teirs. 15
'Now gesse', quod he, 'if thou be glaid.
Nou laugh at Love.
That Pastym prove. {Am I ane Archer nou or nocht?'
His skorne and skayth{
I baid thame baith {And got it sikker that I socht. 20

Fra hand I frei3'd in flamis of fyre
I brint agane als soon in yce.
My dolour wes my auin devyce. 25
Displesur wes my auin desyre.
All thir by Natur nou ar nyce.
Bot Natur nou
(I wot not hou) {Sho meins to metamorphose me 30
In sik a shappe
As hes no happe {To further weill nor 3it to flie.

Quhen I wes frie I micht haif fled.
I culd not let this Love allane. 35
Nou out of tym vhen I am tane
I seik some shift that we may shed,
Becaus it byts me to the bane
Bot pruif is plane {It war bot mouis thairat to mint.
I work in vane. { 40
Fra I be fast, {My Tym and travell war baith tint.
That pairt is past.{

12 Fell peart quod] 3e are full pert Ro 13 Syn] Then Fc his] þis Ro 14 And
shot me soon be] Syne schot him thorough befor Ro soon] syne Fc 15 turnd
to] burnt in Fc 19 nou] guid Fc 23 frei3'd] fry Fc 24 brint] freis Fc 25–6] *rev.*
Fc 27 All thir by] As ar my Ro nou ar nyce] wald surmeice Fc 28 Natur] Cupid
Fc 28–9 nou / I wot not hou] quhen I went not hew Ro 30 Sho meins] Thow
shaipis Fc; Sho seames Ro 34–55] *om.* Fc 37 we may] weman lie (be?) Ro 39–
40 plane / I] prime but Ro 41 war] was Ro mint] meane Ro

29 45   Micht I my Ariadne move
       To lend hir Theseus a threed
       Hir leilest lover for to leed
       Out of the Laberinth of Love
       Then wer I out of dout of deed,

   50   Bot sho, alace   { Hou can I then the better be
       Knauis not my cace.

       Quhill I stand au   { The Minotaur does murdre me.
  55   My self to shau?

       Go once my longsome looks, reveill
       My secrete to my Lady sueet.
       Go sighs and teirs, for me intreet
       That sho by sympathie may feill
   60   Pairt of the Passionis of my spreet,

       Than if hir grace   { Ineugh, or covets sho to kill
       Givis Pitie place

       Let death dispetch   { I wold not live aganst hir will.
  65   My lyf. Puir wretch,

29

       If faithfulnes suld friendship find,
       If Patience suld purches Pitie place,
       If Resone love with bands micht bind,
       If service gude suld guerdond be with grace,
    5   If loving all for ane,
          If loving hir allane
            Suld Recompence resave
         Sen tym hes tryde my treuth
         If rigour reiv not reuth
  10   Some hope of helth I have.

28.45 move] now move Ro 46 lend hir] land to hir Ro 47 to] the Ro 49 out] dure
Ro of deed] bot duers Ro 53–4] Quhilk I sould have my self to save Ro 55 murdre
me] Mb Fc; murdr... K; murdred me Ro 56 once my] 3e my Fc; out by Ro reveill]
releife Ro 57 secrete] serveice Fc; secreats Ro 58 Go] With Ro teirs] sobis Fc Ro
59 feill] seik Ro 60] The passioues of my trubillit spirit Fc 61 Than if hir] I
wald 3our Fc; Ther give her Ro 63 covets sho] compt 3e Fc; bellies she Ro kill]
Mb Fc Ro; ... K 66 live] luve Fc hir will] Mb Ro; hi... K; 3our will Fc
29.10 ...] Some h... of h...l...h I h...e K

Quhat neids thou, Cupid all thir dairts   29ᵛ
Me to ou'rthrou that els am cum thy thrall?
Thoght I had had ane hundreth hairts,
Long syne my Lady had bereft thame all.
 Since that a hairtles man   15
 Mak na resistance can,
  Quhat worship can ȝe win
 To slay me ouer agane
 That am alredy slane?
  That war baith shame and sin.   20

To vhom suld I preis to appeill
To seik redres if thou wold work me wrong?
It is too dangerous to deall
Or stryve with ane vhom I persave too strong.
 Far rather had I ȝeild   25
 Nor feght and tyn the feild.
  Vnequal is that match,
 Ane Cative with a King.
 If euer I thoght sik thing,
  Forgive me, wofull wretch.   30

Quhair I haif reklest I recant.
In tyms to cum I promise to be true.
Laith wes I to begin, I grant,
To love bot nou my reklesnes I rue.
 Ou'r rashly I rebeld   35
 Quhill Cupid me compeld
  Quhais force I find thairfor.
 Will he my ȝongnes ȝit   30
 With mercy once remit,
  I trou to faill no more.   40

30

Lyk as Aglauros, curious to knau
Vhat Mercurie inclosit within the creell
(Suppose defendit), ceist not till sho sau
The serpent chyld that Juno causit to steell,
5   Quhilk to hir sisters willing to reveill
Or she wes war, evin with the word, anone
Sho wes transformit in a marble stone,

Or as Psyches (by her Mother mov'd
Hir sleeping Cupid secreitly to sie)
10   Resav'd the lamp to look him vhom sho lov'd
Quhais hevenly beutie blind't hir amorous ee
That sho forȝet to close the Lamp till he
In wrath auok and fleu sho wist not vhair
And left his deing Lover in dispair,

15   Even so am I o wareit by my weird
For wondring on a Deitie divyne,
The Idee of Perfectione in this eird
Quhilk sorie sight oft gart me sigh sensyne.
I sau tua sunnis in semicircle shyne
20   Compelling me to play Actæons pairt
And be transformd into a bloody hairt.

For lurking Love (vha lang had lyne in wait,
30ᵛ   Persaving tym), he took me at a stot.
Fra he beheld me broudin on the bait,
25   He tuik a shaft and suddently me shot
Quhais fyrie heid brint in my harte so hot
I gave a grone as I had givin the ghost
And with a look my Liberty I lost.

My qualities incontinent did change
30   For I that somtyme solide wes and sage
Begouth to studie, stupefact and strange,
Bereft of Resone, reaving in a rage,
No syrops sueet my sorou culd assuage
For cruell Cupid to revenge his wroth
35   First made me love, and syn my Lady loth.

8 Psyches] Pysitches K

Lo I that leugh in Liberty at Love
And thoght his furie bot a fekles freet
Am nou compeld that pastym for to prove
Quharof the sour I sie exceeds the sueet.
That poysond pest perplexis so my spreet   40
I sitt and sighis all soliter and sad
Half mang'd in mynd, almost as I war mad.

Meit, drink and sleip and Company I hait.
I leive most lyk ane Hermit allone.
Bot as the Buk vhare he is bund mon blait   45
Becaus delyverance he persaifis none,
So must I needs nou mak my mirthles mone
And wair my words with weiping all in vane
Quhair nane bot Echo ansueirs me agane.

Hir modest looks with Majestie so mixt   50   31
Bad me be war if I had not bene blind.
Hir purpose grave, more pithie nor prolixt,
Prognosticat my wrasling with the wind,
3it foolish I (vhose folie nou I find)
Forc't by Affectione, sau not vhat I soght.   55
Bot Negligence, alace, excuisis nocht.

So long as I my secreit smart conceild
It seimd I wes a gaituard in hir grace
Bot welauay hou soon it wes reveild
Then I persaivit that pitie had no place.   60
Hou soon sho kneu my languishing, allace,
I gat Command hir Company to quyt
And not to send hir nather word nor wryt.

O sentence sharpe, too suddan and seveir,
O bailfull bidding bitter to obey,   65
O wareit Orange willed me to weir,
O wofull Absence ordande me for ay,
O duilfull dume delyvrit but delay
(The worst is ill if 3e be bot the best),
I grant 3e ar weill grevous to digest.   70

Proud ee that looked not befor thou lap
Distill thy teirs of murning evermair.
Proud hart vhilk haȝard't vhair thou had no hap,
To drie thy Penance patiently the prepair.
75 Cast of thy Comfort, cleith thy self with cair.
Sen thou art thrald, think thou mon thole a thrist.
To plesur hir thou may be blyth to brist.

31ᵛ **31** ## The sacrifice of Cupid

Hou oft throu compass of the Christall skyis?
Hou oft throu voyd and watrie vaults of air?
Hou oft throu cluds vhair exhalations lyis?
Hou oft, Cupido, vnto thyn auin repair
5 For sacrifice haif I sent sighing sair?
Accompanied with sharpe and bitter teirs
Hou oft haif I (thou knauis hou, vhen and vhair)
Caus'd my complante ascend into thy eirs?
Suppose thou sees not, ȝit I hope thou heirs
10 Or otherwyse but dout I suld dispair.
Releiv my breist that sik a burthen beirs
And thou sall be my Maister evermair,

And I sall be thy seruand in sik sort
To merit thy mantenance if I may.
15 My pen thy princely pussance sall report.
Ȝea I sall on thyn alter evrie day
Tua Turtle Douis for ane oblatione lay,
A pair of Pigeons vhyt as ony flour,
A harte of wax, a branch of Myrhe and ay
20 The blood of sparouis thairon sprinkle and pour.
Ȝea I sall for thyn honour evrie hour
In songs and sonets sueetly sing and say
Tuyse or atanes, 'Vive, vive l'amour',
And sa my Voues I promise for to pay.

30.73 hap] h... K 75 cair] c... K 76 thrist] thr... K

Triumphantly thy Trophee sall I trim   25
Quhair I sall brave and gallant buitings bring
And wryt thairon: 'Behold the spoills of him
Quha for his Conqueis may be calde a King'.   32
My happy harte thair highest sall I hing
In signe that thou by Victorie it wan,   30
A rubie rich within a Royal ring
Quhilk first I got vhen I to love began.
Als willing nou as I ressav't it than,
To thee my self with service I resigne.
Quhat wald a Maister wish mair of his man   35
Then till obey his thoght in evry thing?

Bot oh! as one that in a rageing ravis
Bereft of baith his resone and his rest
Compeld to cry, bot knauis not vhat he craivis
Impatient throu poysone of his pest,   40
So do I nou, mair painfully opprest,
Hope help at him vhais help culd nevir heall
Bot be the contrair martyr and molest.
Forgive me Cupid, I confes I faill,
To crave the thing that may me not availl,   45
3it to the end I may my grief digest
Anis burne hir breist that first begouth my baill
That sho may sey vhat sicknes me possest.

32   The Secreit prais of Love

As evirie object to the outuard ee
Dissaivis the sight and semis as it is sene
Quhen not bot shap and cullour 3it we se
For no thing els is subject to the ene,
As stains and trees appeiring gray and grene,   5
Quhais quantities vpon the sight depends,
Bot qualities the cunning Comprehends.

32.7 Comprehends] C...h...d... K

53

32ᵛ   Euen sa vha sayis they sie me as I am,
I mene a man, suppose they sie me move,
10   Of Ignorance they do tham selfis condam.
By syllogisme this properly I prove.
Quha sees (by look) my loyaltie in love,
Quhat hurt in hairt, vhat hope or hap I haiv?
Quhilk ressone movis the senses to consaiv.

15   Imaginatione is the outuard ee
To spy the richt Anatomie of mynd
Quhilk (by some secreit sympathie) may see
The force of love vhilk can not be defynd,
Quharthrou the hairt according to his kynd
20   Compassionat, as it appeirs plane
Participats of plesur or of pane.

Of hevins or earth some sim'litude or shape
By cunning craftismen to the ees appeir,
Bot vho is he can counterfutt the Ape
25   Or paint a passion palpable, I speir,
Quhilk enters by the organ of the eir
And bot, vhen it is pithilie exprest,
And ȝit I grant the gritest pairt is gest?

Suppose the heuins be huge for to behold,
30   Contening all within thair compas wyde,
The starris be tyme (thoght tedious) may be told
Becaus within a certan bounds they byd.
The Carde the earth from waters may devyde,
Bot vho is he can limit Love, I wene,
33   35   Quhom nather Carde nor Compas can contene?

Quhat force is this subdeuing all and sum?
Quhat force is this that maks the Tygris tame?
Quhat force is this that na man can ouircum?
Quhat force is this that rightlie nane can name?
40   Quhat force is this that careis sik a fame?
A vehemency that words can not reveill
Quhilk I conclude to suffer and conceill.

33

Ressave this harte vhois Constancie wes sik
Quhill it wes quick, I wot ȝe never kneu
A harte more treu within a stomak stik
Till tym the prik of Jelousie it sleu,
Lyk as my heu (by deidly signis) furthsheu,   5
Suppose that feu persav'd my secreit smart.
Lo heir the hairt that ȝe ȝour self ou'rthreu.
Fairweill, adeu, sen death mon vs depart.

Bot lo hou first my Legacy I leiv.
To God I give my Spirit in heuin so hie.   10
My Poesie I leave my Prince to preiv
(No richt can reiv him of my Rhetorie).
My bains to be bot bureit vhair I die.
I leiv to thee the hairt wes nevir fals
About thy hals to hing vhare thou may sie.   15
Let thyn to me then be so constant als.

Remember vhair I said once eftir none
Or March wer done that thou thy cheeks suld weet   33ᵛ
And for me greet or endit war that Mone,
I sie ouer soon my Prophesie compleit.   20
O Lady sueet, I feir we neuer meet.
I feill my spreet is summond from above
For to remove. Nou welcome windin sheet.
Death givis decreet that thou must lose thy Love.

This sentence som thing I persaiv too sair   25
To meit na mair with thee my Love, alace.
God give the grace that na vnkyndlie cair
Do the dispair nor thy gude fame deface.
Give Patience place. Considder weill the cace.
This is the race that euery man must rin.   30
Thoght I begin (vha had no langer space
Thee to imbrace) once, god, if I micht win!

Sen for thy saik Death with his darte me shot
That I am bot a carioun of clay
35 Quha quhylome lay about thy snauie throt,
Nou I must rot vha some tym stood so stay.
Quhat sall I say? This warld will auay.
Anis on a day I seimd a semely sight.
Thou wants the wight that neuer said the nay.
40 Adeu for ay, this is a lang guid nicht.

34

Melancholie, grit deput of Dispair,
With painfull pansing comis apace acompanyde with Cair
Quhais Artalʒie is Angvish shooting sair,
Of purpose to perseu the place   vhair Plesvr maid repair.
34 5 Presuming to prevaill,   A muster grit they mak.
Amids thair Battell bitter Bail   Displayis his baner blak
Quhais colours do declair   to signifie but smart,
Quharin is painted cold Dispair   Quha wrings a hopeles hart,
        Quhilk armes on far
10   So vglie ar
            And ay
            Convoyd with Dolovr and with Dvil
        That Hope micht skar
        If they come nar,
15   And fray
            Ane hairt perhaps out of his huill,
For sighis and sobbis of shooting hes not ceist
Quhill they haif brasht the buluark of my breist
        And cryis, 'Go to, the hous is win!
20   Melancholie, cum in!'
Thoght Rigovr then be rekles rash
ʒit Cvrage bydis the brash
And then the hairt (vhilk never ʒeild)
Of Constancie hes maid his sheild,
25 Quharon thair shaftis and sharpest shottis
Lyk hailstanes aff ane studie stottis.

34.8 a hopeles hart] a hop... K 18 breist] bre... K

ȝit pairties proudlie baith pretend
The Victorie in end
And so the tyme but treuis thay spend
T'assaill and to defend.   30

The rendring reid vhilk bouis with euerie blast
In stormis bot stoupis vhen strongest treis Ar to the ground douncast
Bot ȝit the rok vhilk firmer is and fast   34ᵛ
Amidst the rage of roring seas,   he nevir grouis agast.
The busteous blast he byds   With watring wauis and huge
Quhilk ramping ouer his rigging ryds   Bot can not caus him budge.
Quhat reks then of the reid   Or of the trees vhat reks?
The Rok remanes a Rok indeid   Quhilk nather bouis nor breks.
      So sall my harte
      With patient parte   40
            Remane
         A rok all rigour to resist,
      And sall not start
      To suffer smart
            For ane   45
         Quhom to obey I count me blist.
ȝea thoght I had a hundreth thousand hairts
And euiry hairt peirc't with als mony dairts
      And euirie dairt thairof also
      Als mony shafts and mo,   50
And eviry shaft thairof must needs
To haif als mony heeds
And euirie head als mony huikis
And evirie huik als mony fluiks
And evirie fluik in me war fast,   55
So long as breath of lyf micht last
         I suld not seme for shame to shrink
         For hir of death to drink,
         Quhais Angels ees micht ay, I think,
         Revive me with a wink.   60

29 spend] spe... K 33 blast] blas... K 32 Ar to the ground douncast] ... K 46 me
blist] me (pl; *del.*) blist 60 Revive me] Revive (wt; *del.*) me K

35

The cruell pane and grevous smart
That I endure baith day and nicht
Hes so bereft my woundit hairt
That I am lyk nane other wight.
5   With pansing sair I am opprest
In absence of hir I love best.

Sometym I buir ane hairt was frie
Quhilk nevir will be so agane.
Thoght Cupid markit oft at me
10   He wastit monie a shot in vane,
3it fortun broght me in that place
Quhare I might sie hir plesand face.

A burning darte of hot desyre
That Bearne buir aluayis at his belt
15   Quhairwith he set my breist on fyre
And maid my woundit hairt to melt.
Fra I the force thairof did feild
I wes constraned for to 3eeld

To hir, the lustiest on lyve
20   That euer was or euer will be,
Quhais Beutie does with Venus stryve
And in the end gettis Victorie,
Hir colour does exceid als far
As Phœbus does the Morning star.

25 Hir hair above hir forheid grouis
By Natur curling bright and shene.
Hir brouis they are lyk bendit bouis,
Hir ees Lyk pearcing Arroues kene
Quharuith sho hes me woundit so.
30   I want a harte and she hes tuo.

58

It is a thing most evident
Quhilk Natur dois to all men give.
It folouis also Consequent
No man without a hart can live.
    Sen 3e posses my hairt all hours,   35
    3e bruik it weill and len me 3ours.

Then freshest Phœnix, freind and fo
Both fremmd and freindly, nou fair weill.
Quhen I sall be full far the fro,
My Verse before thy feet sall kneill   40
    To caus thee tak this hairt to thee
    Quhilk wald no more remane with me.

36

On Love and fortun I complene,
On 3ou and on my hairt also
Bot most of all on my tuo ene
(The gritest workers of my wo)
    All vhilks hes causit so my smart   5
    That I must live without a hairt.

First to the eyis committit war   36
The keepers of the hairt to be
To spy and to persaiv on far
The comming of the enemie   10
    Bot they that had this watch to keep
    In Beuties bosum fell on sleep.

Then fra the pairty adversar
Persav't the fortres but defence,
They clam the Buluark soft and fair   15
Quharas the hart maid residence,
    Bot 3it I wyt the harte be sake
    It 3eild't to Love without a strake.

The blindit Archer als I blame,
20 Beginner of my grevous grains
Quhilk shameles shooter thoght no shame
To smyll and shute me baith at ains.
    Bot sen he took me vnder trest
    He band me bundman to the best,

25 To wit vnto ʒour womanheid,
Quhilk worst I wyt of all my woes
Quhais beutie (be it homicide?)
I feir it most of all my foes,
    Quhilk Natur set so far above
30   The rest vhill that it vanquisht Love.

I wyt Dame fortun, not that sho
Hes set ʒou highest in degrie
36ᵛ Bot rather that sho wald not do
The lyk in all respects to me.
35   Had our Estates bene weill compaird
    I had not vterlie dispaird.

37   **37**

ʒong tender plante in spring tym of ʒour ʒeirs
Quhais fame mot floorish fresh and never faid,
Clene polisht pearle vnspottit as appeirs
On vhom my Love is (if ʒe lyk it) laid,
5 Not that I grene ʒour honour to degraid
Bot rather wald ʒour weilfair ay advance,
ʒit I must say as sooth men oft hes said
Love maks the choyce bot fortun maks the chance.

36.36, *infra*: My fansie feeds vpon the sugred gall K; *see Introduction*
37.6 advance] advanc... K 8 chance] cha... K

Quhare weirds will work, vha may withstand thair will?
Nane dou reduce the Destinies decreit.   10
Bot vhat they ordane, ather gude or ill,
Force is to suffer ather sour or sueit.
Quhat they determe, no sentence can retreit.
Not as men wald bot as they will they vote.
Thoght some hold fortun for a fekles freit,   15
Luk as it lyks, I look bot for my lote.

Quhair I haif chosen I culd be content
If that my luk war vhair I love to light.
If I come speid I think my tyme weill spent
And if I mis to mend it as I micht   20
I can reteir vhan resone thinks it richt.
Thair is no match bot vhair tuo mutuall meits.
Men mettall tryis by sey and not by slight
For 3e mon grant all is not gold that gleits.

Some flours may shoot suppose they haif no seed   25   37ᵛ
Als trees may floorish and bring furth feu fruit,
Not that in 3ou sik doublenes I dreid
Suppose 3e seme to shift me vhen I suit.
I can forbeir if once I get rebuit
I will not bind bot vhair I bound to byde.   30
At syndrie marks if that 3e shaip to shoot
3e may shoot short or sometym far asyde.

Dreigh river marks with hights and hidden houis
Ar perrillous and not as they appeir.
Beguyling bairnis that shoots with brissall bouis   35
And dou not drau thair arrouis to thair eir,
Short butts ar better vhair thair bouis may beir.
Far foullis hes ay fair fethers sum will say.
Quhen 3e haif lost, it is too lait to leir.
A turne in tyme is ay worth other tuay.   40

9 will] ... K 14 vote] vot... K 22 meits] ... K 24 gleits] (gle; *del.*) gleits. K

Tak tym in tyme vhill tyme is to be tane
Or ʒe may wish and want it vhen ʒe wald.
Ʒe get no grippe agane if it be gane
Then vhill ʒe haif it best is for to hald.
45 Thoght ʒe be ʒong ʒit once ʒe may be ald.
Tyd will not tarie. Speid or it be spent.
To prophesie I dar not be so bald
Bot tyn ʒe tyme perhaps ʒe may repent.

Houbeit ʒour Beuty far on breid be blaune
38 50 I thank my God I shame not of my shap.
If ʒe be guid, the better is ʒour auin
And he that getis ʒou hes the better hap.
I wald not sik men in ʒour credit crap
Quha heght ʒou fairer nor I feir ʒe find,
55 Thairfor I wald ʒe lookit or ʒe lap
And waver not lyk Widdercok in wind.

If ʒe be constant I sall neuer change.
If ʒe be fickle I am forc't to flitt.
If ʒe be stedfast I sall not be strange.
60 If ʒe be wylie I wald leirne a wit.
Ay as ʒe wse ʒou I agrie with it.
Be doing on, I dout not ʒe ar wyse.
Baith heft and blead ar in ʒour hand as ʒit,
Then barlacheis or barlachois advyse.

65 Can ʒe not play at nevie nevie nak,
A pretty play whilk Children often wse
Quhair tentles Bairnis may to thair tinsall tak
The neiv with na thing and the full refuse?
I will not skar ʒou sen ʒe mynd to chuse
70 Bot put ʒour hand by haʒard in the creill,
Ʒit men hes mater vharvpon to muse
For they must drau ane adder or ane eill

Thoght 3e be as I mon confes 3ou, fair,
I wald not wish that fra 3our freinds 3e ran.
Houbeit 3e think me to 3ou no compair,   75
I haif the moyan lyk ane other man.
I neid not waist it that my Elders wan.   38ᵛ
I hope to help it if I had my helth.
Gar 3e me gang from 3ou, vhair I began,
If I wald vant, I wot, of griter welth.   80

3it I am not so covetous of kynd
Bot I prefer my plesur in a pairt.
Thoght I be laich I beir a michtie mynd.
I count me rich, can I content my hairt.
3it or I enter in ane other airt   85
3our vter ansueir courteously I crave,
Quhom 3e will keep or vhom 3e will decairt.
Sa fair 3e weill vhill I the same resave.

38

Quhen folish Phaeton had his course outrun
And plung'd the fyrie Phlægon in the sea
And bright Diana had bot neu begun
Vpon the grund to cast hir watrie ee,
Quhat tyme the bluid vnto the hairt does flie   5
As sojouris sure thair Capitan to keep,
At that tyme Morpheus sent to summond me,
Quhom I obeyde and sa I fell a sleep.

Quhair in my dreme I sau anone appeir
A Naiked boy vha bure a Turkish bou.   10
He nok't ane arrou longer nor a speir.
The heid wes gold vhilk brint lyk ony lou.
His Countenance begouth ay for to grou
Mair vncouthlyk, vharof I wox afrayde.
Quod he, 'Defend thee gallant if thou dou,   15   39
For thou sall be no longer vnassayit'.

37.74 ran] r... K 88, *infra*: finis K
38.3 Diana] (*om.*) K

63

With that he shot and hat me on the breist
(The sheirand shaft soon slippit to my hairt)
Syne bad me cum to ʒou and mak requeist
20 Quhair I suld find the salue to heall my smart.
Vpon my feet incontinent I start
And stagring stood astonisht with the straik.
Haiv pitie thairfor on my painfull harte
And saif the man that suffers for ʒour saik.

25 My harte wes ay at libertie till nou
That I did sie ʒour cumly cristall ene
Quhais luifsum looks so peirc't my body throu
That ay sensyn ʒour bondman I haif bene.
I pray thairfor with sighing from my splene
30 ʒour womanheid for to be treu and kynd.
This Paper in my Absence sall obtene
To hold me aluay present in ʒour mynd.

Fra I be gane I knau thair ar aneu
Quha wald be glade ʒour favour to procure.
35 Be permanent houbeit they perseu.
Let not sik louns with leasings ʒou allure.
Sua our tua Loves for evir sall indure
Conjoynd in ane as fyr is in the flint.
Found ay ʒour bigging vhair the grund is sure
40 Sa nather Tyme nor Travel sall be tint.

39ᵛ Tak heed thairto I hairtlie ʒou exhort
And keep in mynd the Counsel I ʒou give.
If that perchance some ʒonkiers cum athort
With facund words and preissis ʒou to prieve
45 Luik this my letter, it sall ʒou relieve
In absence alsueill as I war in sight.
I will not stand with mo words ʒou to deiv
Bot for this tyme I bid ʒou haif guidnicht.

---

20 smart] smar... K 24 saik] sa... K 27 throu] th... K 28 bene] be... K 29
splene] splen... K 30 kynd] ky... K 34 procure] proc... K 39 sure] sur... K 38
But] (To; *del.*) But K

39

O Cleir
Most deir
Give eir
Vnto my cry,
   Sueit thing   5
Bening
And ȝing
Of yeiris grene,
   But sleuth
   Haiv reuth.   10
   My treuth
The tym sall try.
   Remeid
   With speid
   Or Deid   15
I must sustene
   For thoght
   Hes wroght
   And broght
Me to dispair   20
Becaus no signe is shaune
That ȝe held me ȝour aune
That I micht it haif knaune
   To comfort me of cair.

   My hairt   25
   Inwart
   Does smart
Within my breist.
   My mynd
   Most kynd   30
   Is pynd
But recompence.
   Of ȝou
   I trou
   Wha nou   35
Regardeth leist
   My wo

But ho
To slo
40 Me but offence
40 That am
Ane lam.
The sam
3e may persaive
45 For I am innocent
And eik obedient.
If I be permanent
Some pruif thairof I haif.

3our ee
50 May se
In me
Is no deceit.
3our eir
Perqueir
55 May heir
My Constance als.
Espye
If I
Applye
60 Ane vther geat
Or oght
Hes soght
Quhilk moght
Be to 3ou fals
65 Bot ay
I stay
Aluay
Vpon 3our grace.
In esperance I byd
70 And firmely do confyd
That fortun sall provyd
For us baith tym and place.

72 place] pl... K

Secreit
To meit
My spreit   75
To recreat
And pleis
My eis
Quhilks deis
For laik of sight   80
And kisse
With blisse
For this
May mitigat
My quent   85
Torment,
Consent
Sen it is richt
And do
Thairto   90
As sho
That may alone
My persone saiv or spill.
To grant me lyf or kill
All lyes into ȝour will   95
As ȝe list to dispone.

Restore   40ᵛ
Thairfore
To glore
Precordiall   100
My lyf
From stryf
Or knyf
Of Atropus
With noy   105
Destroy
My Joy
Terrestriall
To blame
ȝour Name   110
With fame

Most odious
          If ȝe
          Sall be
115   To me
     Without respect
So strange to let me sterv
Except ȝe sie me suerv
Then do as I deserv
120   Bot causles not correct

          For that
          Ȝe wat
          May lat
     A man to love
125   And hald
          Him cauld
          Vha wald
     To ȝou obey.
          Be war
130   Ou'r far
          Ȝe gar
     Me not remove
          Bot give
          Me leiv
135   And greiv
     Me not I pray
          For out
          Of dout
          About
140   Vs ar aneu
Quha deadly hatred haith
That we love other baith.
God keep vs from thair skaith.
          Fairweill my Lady treu.

113 3e] 3e (sa; *del.*) K

40

Quhy bene ȝe Musis all so long
    On sleep this mony a day?
Let not ȝour harmony and song
    In silence thus decay.
Distill by influence   5
Ȝour stremis of Eloquence
That throu your heuinlie liquor sueit   41
My Pen in Rhetoric may fleit
        For till expres
        The comlines   10
        Of my Maistres
            With ioy repleit.

To kythe hir cunning, Natur wald
    Indeu hir with sik grace,
My spreit rejosis to behald   15
    Her smyling Angels face
Lyk Phœbus in the south
To skorne the rest of youth.
Hir curling loks lyk golden rings
About hir hevinly haffats hings   20
        Quhilks do decore
        Hir body more
        Quhom I adore
            Above all things.

Hir brouis ar brent lyk golden threeds,   25
    Hir siluer shyning brees
The bony blinks my Courage feeds
    Of hir tua christall ees
Tuinkling illuminous
With beams Amorous   30
Quhairin tua naikit Boyis resorts
Quhais Countenance good hope reports
        For they appeir
        Vith smyling cheir
        As they wald speir   35
            At me some sports.

41ᵛ Hir comelie cheeks of vive colour
    Of rid and vhyt ymixt
Ar lyk the sanguene Jonet flour
40   Into the lillie fixt.
Hir mouth mellifluous,
Hir breathing savorous,
Hir rosie lippis most eminent,
Hir teeth lyk pearle of Orient,
45   Hir halse more vhyt
    Nor I can wryt,
    With that perfyt
    And sapient.

Hir Vestall breist of Ivorie
50   Quhairon ar fixit fast
Tua tuins of clene Virginitie
    Lyk boullis of Alabast.
Out throu hir snauie skin
Maist cleirlie kythes within
55 Hir saphir veins lyk threids of silk
Or Violets in vhytest milk.
    If Natur sheu
    Hir hevinly heu
    In vhyt and bleu
60   It wes that ilk.

Hir Armes ar long, hir shulders braid
    Hir middill gent and small.
The mold is lost vharin wes maid
    This A per se of all.
42 65 The Gods ar in debait
Concerning hir estait.
Diana keeps this Margarit
Bot Hymen heghts to match hir meit.
    Deserve let sie
70   Amount from thrie.
    Go merie she
    That is so sueet.

61 braid] brai... K   69 let sie] let (thrie; *del.*) sie K

Quhat can both shoot and open loks
As can the only kie?
Persaiv this pithie Paradox   75
    And mark it weill in me.
Quhais Beutie hes me burt?
Quhais Beutie healls my hurt?
Quhais Beutie blythnes me bereivis?
Quhais Beutie gladnes to me givis?   80
      Quhais beutie lo
      Dois me vndo?
      Quhais Beutie to
        My spreit revivis?

41

O lovesome Lady, lamp of light,
    Freshest of flours fair,
Thy beutie and thy bemes bright
    Maks me to sigh full sair.
My noy reneueth evirie nicht   5
    And kendlis all my cair
          And so
I sigh suppose I may na mair   42ᵛ
    Sen fortun is my fo.

Somtyme I had gude confidence   10
    That plesur suld succeid
Quhill in the tyme of our Absence
    Good fortun did me leid
But nou I find my esperance
    Almaist ou'rcome with dreid   15
          Also
I feill the fatal Nymphis threid
    Sen fortun is my fo.

41.7] ... K

Is this ȝour Lau ȝe Gods of Love
20   Or do yee so consent
Into ȝour counsels from above
       All Lovers to torment?
Better it war for our behove
       We had not bene acquent
25   Nor go
To love and na way be content,
       Sen fortun is our fo.

I put no doubt bot ȝe wald do
       Ȝour pouer me to saive
30   Bot tym will not consent thairto
       So grit vnhap we haif
Ȝit be ȝe sure that ȝe ar sho
       Quhome to my harte I gaive
              But mo.
43 35 Grant me some kyndnes vhen I crave
       Thoght fortun be our fo.

Let not my Treuth and constancie
       For euer be forȝet
Nor tak no plesur for to sie
40   Me fettrit in ȝour net
Bot grant me als grit Libertie
       As first vhen we tua mett,
             My Jo.
I grene for it I can not gett
45   Sen fortun is my fo.

Alace these golden houris ar gone
       Quhen nane did vs debar
That nou sik licience haif we none
       Skantlie to speik a far
50   Ȝit wicked peple will suppone
       We do the thing we dar,
             Both tuo.
My Curage prikis me to ryd nar
       Thoght fortun be my fo.

32 ar sho] ar (sure; *del.*) sho K

42

O plesand plant passing in Pulchritude
O lillie lude of all the Muses nyne
I laik Ingyne to shau thy Celsitude.
A tearie fluid does blind thir ees of myne
  ...   5
Thyn eirs inclyne vnto my Cairfull cry
Sen nane bot I hes for thy Person pyne   43ᵛ
Let me not tyn vhom thou intends to try.

Tak tym in tym for tym will not remane
Nor come agane if that it once be lost.   10
Sen we ar voc'd, vhairfor suld we refrane
To suffer pain for ony bodies bost?
My vexit ghost, quhilk rageing Love dois roste
Is brint almost, thrugh heit of my desyr
Then quench this fyre quhilk runneth ay the poste   15
Out throu my cost, consuming bain and lyre.

Nou if this heit descend into my Levir
A fervent fevir sall soon my harte infect.
Thairfor correct this humor nou or nevir
Or we dissevir (Suppose we be suspect,   20
Go to, vhat rek?) and gar the bealing brek
For fra it lek I hald the danger done.
Then speid 3ou soon that we no tym neglect
To tak effect in waning of the Mone.

4 thir] th(a; *del.*)ir K 5] *om.* K

43

Before the Greeks durst enterpryse
In Armes to Troy toun to go
They set a Counsell sage and wyse
Apollo's Ansueir for to kno
5   Hou they suld speid and haif succes
In that so grit a busines.

44   Then did they send the wysest Grekis
To Delphos vhare Apollo stode
Quha with the tearis vpon thair Cheeks
10   And with the fyrie flammis of wod
And all such rites as wes the guyse
They made that grit God sacrifyce.

Quhen they had endit thair Requests
And solmnely thair service done
15   And drunke the Vyne and kild the beists
Apollo made them Ansueir soon
Hou Troy and Trojans haiv they suld
To vse them hailly as they wold,

Quhilk Ansueir maid thame not so glad
20   That thus the Victors they suld be
As evin the Ansuer that I had
Did gritly ioy and comfort me
Quhen lo thus spak Apollo myne,
'All that thou seeks it sall be thyne'.

1 Before] When as Fo durst] did Fo 2] To Troyes town in armes to goe Fo 3 set] choosed Fo 8] Apollos answer for to know Fo 10 And with] But and Fo 11 And] With Fo 12 made that] did their Fo 13 endit thair Requests] done thus their request Fo 13–18] *om.* Fo 15] And drank the wine and slew the beast Fo 16 made] gave Fo 17 Hou] That Fo 18 hailly] fully Fo 19 Quhilk] Quhais Ja 20] That they sould thus the victors be Ja; That they should thus victorious be Fo 21 that] quhilk Ja; which Fo 22 gritly] also Fo 23] For thus then said Apollo myne Fo thus] this Ja

44

Adeu O Desie of delyt,
Adeu most plesand and perfyt,
   Adeu and haif gude nicht.
Adeu thou lustiest on lyve,
Adeu suete thing superlatyve,   5
   Adeu my lamp of licht.
Lyk as the lyssard does indeid   44ᵛ
   Leiv by the manis face,
Thy Beutie lykuyse suld me feid
   If we had tyme and space.   10
         Adeu nou, be treu nou
            Sen that we must depairt.
         Forȝet not and set not
            At light my constant hairt.

Albeit my body be absent   15
My faithfull hairt is vigilent
   To do ȝou service treu
Bot vhen I hant into the place
Quhair I wes wont to sie that face
   My dolour does reneu.   20
Then all my plesur is bot pane,
   My cairis they do incres.
Vntill I sie your face agane
   I live in hevynes.
         Sair weeping but sleeping   25
            The nichts I ouerdryve.
         Quhylis murning, vhylis turning
            With thoghts pensityve.

Somtym good hope did me comfort
Saying the tym suld be bot short   30
   Of Absence to endure
Then Curage quickins so my spreit
Quhen I think on my lady sueet
   I hald my service sure.
I can not plaint of my estait,   35   45
   I thank the Gods above,

For I am first in hir consait
    Quhom both I serve and love.
        Hir freindis ay weindis
40   To caus hir to revok.
    Sho bydis and slydis
        No more then does a Rok.

O Lady for thy Constancie
A faithfull servand sall I be
45   Thyn honour to defend
And I sall surelie for thy saik,
As doth the Turtle for her maik,
    Love to my lyfis end.
No pane nor travell, feir nor dreid
50   Sall caus me to desist,
Then ay vhen ʒe this letter reid
    Remember hou we kist
        Embracing with lacing
            With others teiris sueet.
55   Sik blissing in kissing
        I quyt till we tua meit.

45

Quha wareis all the wicked weirds bot I?
Or vha bot I suld curse the thrauard faits?
To vhom bot me does destinies deny
Some kynd of Comfort to thair auin estaits?
45ᵛ 5   For vhom bot me doth Love in ambush ly
With hidden huiks in his beguyling baits
    Of sugred sueet dissaitis?

Weill ward thou weep o ou'r audacious ee
Sen with a sight thou wes so soon ou'rsyld.
10   I sent the forth as Centinall to see
Bot with a blink dame Beutie thee begyld,

44.51 Then ay] Then (ʒ; *del.*) ay K

Fra thou wes fast and had no force to flie.
My wofull hairt, auay with thee. Thou wyld
          Fra me to be exyld.

To follou thee Affectioun tuk the feeld,   15
Fair-heghting hope wes laith to byd behind,
Then Curage with a stomok stoutly steeld
Bad will ga wave his baner with the wind,
Last, Reson rais ay shotfrie vnder sheeld
Bot fantasie fast follou'd him behind   20
          And bleu him bravelie blind.

Then lyk a neu maid Mariner in mist
Quha saillis the seas but compasse, lead or Carte,
By change of wind wes wrong befor he wist
As prentise proud, mair peirter nor expert,   25
Evin so did I, als Ignorant, insist
As Novice neu, vnvsit in that art
          Till I had hurt my harte.

Or I wes war I had resauit the wound   46
So dangerous, so deidly and so deip   30
The strenth vharof gart all my stomok stound.
From vein to vein I felt the Canker creep.
The poysound poynt had peirc't me so profound
That (welauay) I culd bot waill and weip
          And sigh vhen I sould sleep.   35

Love maid my chose, bot fortun maid my chance.
Love follou'd fast bot fenȝeid fortun fled.
Love perseveird in hope of recompance
Bot fortun fals ay shorde that we suld shed.
Love willing wes my labour to advance   40
Bot Fortun ay my Brydall bakuard led
          Quhilk all my baill hes bred.

18 the] thee K 21 And] (Then Curag; *del.*) And K 31 stound] stou... K 33 pro-
found] profou... K 36 chance] ch... K

3it not a vheet my thraldome I forthink.
War I to chuse, I wald not change my chose.
45 I shaip not for no suddan shours to shrink
Sen peircing pyks ar kyndlie with the Rose.
Houbeit mishap be in my harte a hink
3it I will on hir Permanence repose
           In spyte of fortuns nose.

50 The highest hillis mair thretnit ar with thunder
And tallest Trees with Tempest ofter tryde
Nor hilloks small or bramble bushis vnder.
Vnworthie things ar aluay leist invyde.
46ᵛ Quhat Natur works we may not think it wonder.
55 Love longer lastis the derer that we by it.
           This dou not be deny-it.

Let weirds rin wod, let furious faits be fearce,
Let Absence vrne, let Cupids Arrou peirce,
Let fortun froun, Let destinies despyte,
60 Let tratling tongues, let bablers ay bakbyte,
Let Enemies my haples hap reheirce,
I cair not by thair malice all a myte.
           In Love is my delyte.

46

Hay nou the day dauis,
The jolie Cok crauis,
Nou shrouds the shauis
           Throu Natur anone,
5 The thissell-cok cryis
On Louers vha lyis,
Nou skaillis the skyis,
           The nicht is neir gone.

The feilds ou'rflouis
10 With gouans that grouis
Quhair Lilies lyk lou-is
           Als rid as the rone,

45.44 chose] ch... K

The Turtill that treu is
With nots that reneu-is
Hir pairtie perseuis,   15
     The night is neir gone.

Nou hairts with hynds   47
Conforme to thair kynds,
Hie tossis thair tynds
     On grund vhair they grone,   20
Nou hurchonis with hairs
Ay passis in pairs
Quhilk deuly declairs
     The night is neir gone.

The sesone excellis   25
Thrugh sueetnes that smellis,
Nou Cupid Compells
     Our hairts echone
On Venus vha vaiks
To muse on our maiks   30
Syn sing for thair saiks,
     The night is neir gone.

All curageous Knichts
Aganis the day dichts
The breist plate that bright-is   35
     To feght with thair fone,
The stoned steed stampis
Throu Curage and Crampis
Syn on the land lampis
     The night is neir gone.   40

The freiks on feildis
That wight wapins weildis
With shyning bright sheilds   47ᵛ
     As Titan in trone,
Stiff speirs in reists   45
Ouer cursors crists
Ar brok on thair breists,
     The night is neir gone.
19 tossis] tursis K 20 grone] gᵣone K 44 As] At K

So hard ar thair hittis
50   Some sueyis, some sittis
And some perforce flittis
        On grund vhill they grone,
Syn grooms that gay is
On blonks that bray-is
55   With suords assayis,
        The night is neir gone.

47

A bony No with smyling looks agane
I wald ʒe leirnd sen they so comely ar.
As touching ʒes, if ʒe suld speik so plane
I might reprove ʒou to haif said so far,
5   Noght that ʒour grant in ony wayis micht gar
Me loth the fruit that Curage ocht to chuse
Bot I wald only haif ʒou seme to skar
And let me tak it fenʒeing to refuse

And warsill as it war against ʒour will,
10   Appeiring angrie thoght ʒe haif no yre
For haif ʒe heir is haldin half a fill.
48   I speik not this as trouing for to tyre
Bot as the forger vhen he feeds his fyre
With sparks of water maks it burne more bald
15   So sueet denyall doubillis bot desyr
And quickins curage fra becomming cald.

Wald ʒe be made of, ʒe man mak it nyce
For dainties heir ar delicat and deir
Bot plentie things are prysde to lytill pryce,
20   Then thoght ʒe hearken let no wit ʒe heir
Bot look auay and len thame ay ʒour eir.
For folou Love, they say, and it will flie.
Wald ʒe be lov'd, this Lessone mon ʒe leir.
Flie vhylome Love and it will folou thee.

47.6 that Curage] that (fort; *del.*) Curage K

48

Aualk Montgomries Muse
    And sey vhat thou can say,
Thy long and just excuse
    Mæcenas taks auay
        Quhais high heroique actis   5
        His Name immortall maks.

Then welcome hame my Lord,
    Suete Semple welcome hame
Quhais Vertues wan the word
    That formest flies with fame   10
        Quharof all Cuntreyis crakis
        And the Immortall maks.

Thou wan the flour in France   48ᵛ
    With eviry kynd of Armes
As dager, suord and Lance   15
    In Pastyme and alarmes.
        Thy leiving no man laks
        Bot the Immortall maks.

Thy body, mynd and spreit
    Disposd, resolu'd and quik   20
Thy hairt, thy hands, thy feit
    Magnanime, strong and sik
        As Curage all contracts
        Quhilk the Immortall maks.

Thy meeknes into moues   25
    And aufulnes in yre
From sik a fontan floues
    As springs for till aspyre.
        Sik frute thy Travell taks
        And the Immortal maks.   30

12] And th... I...ll... K

Thy Cuntrie, King and Kin
    Thy qualities decoird.
All pairts vhair thou wes in
    Thinks long for thee my Lord.
35   So wyd thy word does waxe
          That the Immortall maks.

Sen Poets maist profound
    Thy praysis do proclame
49 My Trompet (to) sall sound
40   The famphar of thy fame,
          Quod he vhom siknes wraks
          And the Immortall maks.

Then happy travell tane
    Sen thou hes boght the best.
45 Thoght pairt of gold be gane
    Thy honour is increst.
          Men weill imployes thair paks
          That thame immortall maks.

49

Remember rightly vhen ȝe reid
The wo and dreid
But hope to speid
    I drie into dispair.
5 My hairt within my breist does bleid
Vnto the deid
Vithout remeid.
    I'm hurt I wot not vhair.
Alace   Vhat is the caus, think I,
10 But grace   That I in langour ly?

The more I drink, more I desyr.
As I aspyre
The fervent fyre
    My cairfull Corps consume.
15 Me to torment no tym ȝe tyre,

Baith bane and lyre
Throu Cupids yre,   49^v
        To dead but ony dome.
I burne   I frei3e in yce also.
I turne   For freindship to my fo.   20

In prison sen 3e hald my hairt
Releiv my smart,
Drau out this darte
        Furth of my bailfull breist.
Haif pitie on my painfull parte.   25
As by the Carte
Men knoues the Arte
        Both south, north, west and eist
3e may   Persave my wounds are grene
I say   And look bot to my ene   30

Quhais longsum looks my lyf beuryis.
Wo to the spyis
First did suppryis
        My hairt within 3our hald
Quhilk fast into 3our fetters lyis   35
In dout vhat wyse
That feirfull syse
        Pronunce thair sentence wald.
I quake   For feir my puncis lope.
I shake   betuixt Dispair and hope.   40

To crueltie if 3e consent
I am content
As patient
        3our plesur to fulfill
Or pleis 3our pitie to prevent   45   50
My grit torment
Or I be shent,
        Chuse 3ou to spair or kill.
I stand   of death no vhitt affrayde,
Command And 3e sall be obeyde.

16 lyre] l... K

50

The wofull working of my woundit hairt
Quhilk Danger hes neir drivin in Dispair
Is sorer to sustene then is the darte
Of Death vhilk suld dissolve my cruell cair
5   ...
Thrugh fortun frail vhais vnfelicitie
Hes wroght in me sik caus of sighing sair
That Death suld be no lothsum thing to me.

Come gentill Death and that with suddentie
10   And mak dispatch of this puir hairt of myne.
Thy sterving straik with force thou let outflie
And light on me to end my peirles pyne.
Sen sho vhom I do serve will not inclyne
Nor grant me grace my pains for to deploir
15   Bot will for want of pitie sie me tyne,
Come gentle Death and let me die thairfor.

Alace that euer sik perfyte beütie
As is in ʒou my lovesome lady deir
Suld haif bene plac't thair vhair as pietie
20   Might not most frelie in hir place appeir.
Alace that Danger with hir deidly cheir
Such Lordship had vhair ...
50ᵛ   Alace that ever a ʒoldin Prisoneir
Suld feill the peirles painis that I nou prove.

25   Alace suld I for hairtie Love be hated
Or suld I find for freindly favour fead.
Alace suld my treu service thus be quated
With hir that is the chose of womanheid.
Alace suld sho that suld of right remeid
30   The deidly dolour daylie I sustene.
Be merciles, then wish I to be deid
And so be quyt of all my cairs clene.

5] *om.* K 22] *cropped* K

51

Displesur with his deadly dairt
So horriblie hes hurt my hairt
   With sik ane heid
   That no remeid
   Saiv only Deid   5
    Can cure my smart.
  The poysond poynt me priks
  Quhilk in my stomok stiks
    Profound
  Quhais venom rains   10
  Thrugh al my vains.
No salue can mak me sound.

I count not of my lyf a cute.
My hairt hes biddin sik rebute
   That it wald evin   15
   (God knauis in hevin)
   Wish to be revin
    Out be þe ruitt.
  It is so crost with cair   51
  That it may nevir mair   20
    Revive.
  Cum thairfor Death
  And cut my breath.
I list not longer live.

The Destinies my lyfe despytis   25
And bitter baill my bouells bytis.
   These thrauard thrie
   (Curst mot they be
   To martyr me)
    Laughis and delyts   30
  For they haif wroght my weird
  Vnhappiest on eird
    And ay

6 Can] May Ti 15–16] *rev.* Ti 16 God] Gods Ti 18] Ti; ... K 20 may] can Ti
22] Then velcum Deth Ti 23 And] to Ti 24 not] no Ti 25–36] *om.* Ti

Continues still
35   To work my ill
With all mishief they may.

Hes hevins? hes earth? hes God? hes air
Determinat that I dispair?
     Hes all in ane
40   My contrare tane?
For me allane
       They ar too sair.
Sen thair is no remorce
My Patience perforce
45   Hes bene
Of illis I wse
The leist to chuse.
I may not mend bot mene.

51ᵛ   Might my misluk look for relief
50   Or ȝit doght I digest my grief
     Then wer I wyse
It to disguyse
Bot lo vhair lyis
     My maist mischief.
55   I smore if I conceill,
I wrak if I reveill
     My hurt.
Judge ȝe vha heirs
Quhat burthene beiris
60 My stomok stuft with sturt.

For from Carybdis vhill I flie
I slyde in Sylla ȝe may sie.
     I saill, it semes,
Tuixt tua Extremis
That Danger demes
     My ship sall die.

---

37 God] gods Ti 46 illis] evils Ti 48 mend] murne Ti 50 Or ȝit doght] ȝit culd Ti 54] all my mischeiff Ti 55–56] *rev.* Ti 58 vha] þat Ti 60 with sturt] with (stryfe; *del.*) sturt K; with stourt Ti 61] For quhill I fra Caribdis flee Ti

Nou (Sone) since I must smart
Thou of my Age that art
      The staffe
Evin MURRAY myne   70
Len me a Lyne
To end my Epitaph.

52   THE ELEGIE   52

Now SINCE the day of our depairt appeirs
Guid Resone wald my hand to ʒou suld wryt
That vhilk I can not weill expres but teirs,
Videlicet, adeu my Lady vhyt,
Adeu my Love, my lyking and delyt   5
Till I returne for vhilk I think so lang
That Absence els does all my bouells byt,
Sik gredie grippis I feell befor I gang.
Resave vhill than A harte lyk for to mang
Quhilk freats and fryis in furious flamis of fyre.   10
Keep it in gage, bot let it haif no wrang
Of sik as may perhaps his place desyre.
This is the summe of that vhilk I requyre:
If it hes ocht offendit, let it smart,
If it be true, then let it haif the hyre.   15
Oh! wold to god ʒe might behold this harte
Quharin a thousand things ʒe suld advert:
Thair suld ʒe sie the wound vhilk ʒe it gaiv,
Thair suld ʒe sie the goldin deadly darte,
Thair suld ʒe sie hou ʒe bereft it haiv,   20
Thair suld ʒe sie ʒour Image by the Laiv,
Thair suld ʒe sie ʒour hevinly Angels face,
Thair suld ʒe soon my permanence persaiv,
Thair suld ʒe sie ʒour Name haif only place,
Thair suld ʒe sie my languishing alace   25 52ᵛ
For our depairt, bot since ʒe knou my painis

51.68 Age] edge Ti
52.2 wryt] wr... K 10 fyre] fy... K 13 requyre] requy... K 18 gaiv] g... K 24 place]
pl... K

I hope if ȝe considder weill the cace
And spyis the teirs vhilks ouer my visage rains
If in ȝour breist sik sympathie remanis

30 Then sall ȝe suffer som thing for my saik.
Quhair constant Love is, aluay it constranis
In weill or wo coequall pairt to take,
Lyk as my members all begins to quake
That of ȝour duill the half I do indure

35 Quhilk I suppone ȝe for my Absence mak.
Then haif no dout that ony Creature
Can dispossesse ȝou of my hairt, be sure,
Nor ȝit remove from ȝou my constant mynd
Since I am ȝours quhom Love culd not allure

40 Sen I wes borne till nou that I enclynd
To ȝou allone for whom my hairt is pynd.
Of Lovis fyr befor I nevir kneu
Nor ȝit acquent with Cupid in this kynd
Bot look hou soon gude fortun to me sheu

45 Ʒour sueet behaviour and ȝour hevinly heu
As A per se that evir Natur wroght
Then vncouth cairs in me began aneu
Both in my spreit and in my trublit thoght.
My Libertie vhilk I in bondage broght

50 Sa that my frank and frie desyr or than
Ane hunder places for my plesur soght
...

53 And ay sall do vhill I am leving man.
Sall ȝe then eftir our depairt forȝet

55 That vhilk is ȝours and change on na wyse can?
Hou soon myn ee no sight of ȝours culd get
It weeping said, 'O deidly Corps defet,
Quhair bene these lamps of light, these cristall ees
Quhilks maid ws ay so mirrie vhen we mett?'

60 Quod I agane with sighing voce, 'Thou sees,
Thoght thou for dolour vnder shadou dees.
Be not abaisd suppose thou haif no sight.
Thy sun is hid and keeps no more degrees

---

39 not allure] not (*indecipherable*; *del.*) allure K 52] *cropped* K 58 cristall ees]
crista ... K 63 degrees] degre... K

Bot for thy sake goes to at none for night.
That is to say that hevinly Visage bright   65
Quharon thou wont thy fantasie to feid
Is far fra thee, vhair throu thou laikis thy sight'.
So lustie Lady, well of womanheid,
Myne ee and I but Comfort ar indeed
And do bewaill thy wofull Absence ay.   70
Regrating 3ou my woundit hairt does bleed
And than I think vhen I am far auay
Leist that meintym blind Love suld thus assay
All meins he micht by craft or 3it ingyne
To open vp his blindit ees that they   75
Might clerelie see these gratious ees of thyn
And so beholding sik a sight divyn,
His mynd to love the shortly suld be mov'd   53ᵛ
And caus me at ane instant for to tyne
The thing quhilk I sa lang and leall haif lov'd.   80
Be 3e not constant vhen 3e sall be prov'd,
Love sall ou'rcome 3our honest ansueirs all
That 3e sall think to 3eild it 3ou behov'd.
Love is so slie vhais fairdit language sall
Peirce and get entrie throu a stony wall.   85
I wish 3ou thairfor with him to be war
His mouth is hony, bot his hairt is gall.
On kitlest huiks the sliest baits they ar.
If he the heght or slilie drau the nar
Thou ansueir him, 'Go Love, reteir the hence   90
For I Love one vho hes my hairt so far
He merits not to tyne him but offence'.

67 thy sight] th ... K 73 assay] as... K 86 him to] him (w; *del.*) K 89 if he] if (t; *del.*) he K

53   THE NAVIGATIOUN

Haill bravest burgeoun brekking to the Rose,
The deu of grace thy leivis mot vnclose,
The stalk of treuth mot grant the nurishing,
The air of faith support thy florishing.
5   Thy noble Counsell lyk trees about thy grace
Mot plantit be, ilk ane into his place
Quhais ruiting sure and toppis reaching he
Mot brek the storme befor it come to the.
54   They of thy bluid mot grou about thy bordour
10   To hold thy hedge into ane perfyt ordour
As fragrant flouris of ane helthsome smell
All venemous beistis from the to expell.
The preachers treu mot ay thy Gardners be
To clense thy root from weeds of heresie.
15   Thy gardene wall mak the neu Testament
So sall thou grou without impediment.
All lands about sall feir thy Excellence
And come fra far to do thee reverence
As I my self and all the rest ȝe se
20   From Turkie, Egypt and from arabie.
      As for my self I am ane german borne
Quha ay this fasion vhilk ȝe se hes worne
Quhilk lenth of tym culd nevir caus me change
Thoght I haiv bene in mony cuntrey strange.
25   Thrugh all Europe, Afrik and Asia
And throu the neu fund out America,
All thair conditiouns I do vnderstand
Baith of the peple and also of the Land
Quhais trim attyre wer tedious to tell.
30   Something ȝour grace sall shortly sie ȝour sell.
In contrare clething ȝour Excellence sall ken
The Turk, the More and the Egyptien.
      Nou sall I shau vnto ȝour Majestie
Hou they and I fell first in Company.
54ᵛ 35   CONSTANTINOPIL, sometym of Christendome,
Pertening to ane Empreour of Rome

10 into ane] into (th; *del.*) ane K   13 be] b... K

Quho as we reid wes callit Constantyn,
Eftir his Name he callit the Citie syn
Becaus he lov't it best of tounis all.
Euen thair he sat into his Tribunall   40
As in the Metropolitan of Grece
Quhilk his successours bruikit lang in peace
Till tym that they throu thair Iniquitie
Wer givin ouer vnto the Enemie
As for ane prey al hail to be devoird.   45
Thair 30ng men slayn, thair Virgins war deflorde,
Thair tender babis 3it on the nurish knee
Tane by the feet and cast into the see.
Let vther lands a mirrour of this mak
And by thair Nichtbours example let thame tak   50
I will not Judge vhairfor that god so did
Becaus his secreits ar to all men hid
Bot weill I wot the Lord did so permit.
For vhy? the Turk does bruik this Citie 3it
And much of Grece he hes into his hands.   55
Bot for to tell 30u hou the Citie stands
Hard by the syde of the auld PONTUS sea.
Fornent it lyis the land of NATALIE.
Quha in these pairts pleisis for to hant,
The Turks pasport neids not for to want.   60
Sa I my self as ane among the laiv
Requyrit ane vhilk he me glaidly gaiv
That I micht come and sie this noble toun   55
Quharof befor I hard so grit renoun
Quhilk vhen I come my fortun wes to be   65
Ludgit perchance with this same Companie
Soupit togither in ane Chalmer lay
Crackand ouer heid vhill it wes neir hand day.
I speird at thame vhair that they last come fra
And eftiruard vhair they myndit to ga.   70
'We duell', say they, 'vnder the star ANTARTIC.
Nou wald we sie the Vrses and pole ARTIC.
We shaip to saill neir the Septentrion
Touards the North and helthsome regione

68 day] ... K 69 come fra] com... K 71 Antartic] Antar... K 72 Artic] Arti... K

75 Nou callit Scotland, as we haif hard report
Of wandring fame vhilk fleeth ay athort
Quhair presently beginneth for to ring
So sapient a 3ing and godly King,
A Salomon for richt and judgment.
80 In eviry langage he is Eloquent.
All Lands about do beir of him record.
He is the chosen vessell of the Lord.
To sie this king nou glaidly wald we go
And (if 3e pleis) to tak ane pairt also
85 3e ar bothe welcome and richt necessar
Vnto his grace our comming to declair.
For 3e haif travellit throu mony lands
And eviry language also vnderstands'.
55ᵛ 'Content', quod I and so we wer agreit.
90 ...
...
Fraughtit our ship and syne our Anker weyde.
    Phœbus nou rysing with his laughing grace
Smylit on Neptuns still and calmit face.
95 Vpuent our saillis tauntit to the huins.
The Trumpets soundit tuentie mirrie tuins.
Vp went our boyis to the Toppis abone
And ou'r the bordour shook our Topsaill soon.
Some went before for to shaik out the blind.
100 Wp went our bonnets, our Missens vp behind.
Some to the gueit fattis for to bedeu the saills.
Bothe foir and eft our Taikle drauis and haillis.
Our bottisman our geir perfytlie neits.
Fair wes the wind and roum betuene tua sheits.
105 Maisters and Pilots cunning in that Arte
Went to the Compas for to prik the Carte
For to persaiv the dangers vhair they lay.
We Passingers went to the chesse to play
For in that Airt we no thing vnderstude
110 Thairfor we did thame nather ill nor good.
    Our ship wes clene and saillit very fast.
Of Hellespont or we the straits had past,

75 report] repor... K 90–91] *om.*

We struik at Cestus and at Abydon
Quhair passing ships are rypit euery one
To sie if they haif goods that ar forbiddin   115
So from thair presence ʒe may haif no thing hiddin.
For these tua Castells ar the only kees
Of all Turkie and do divyde the sees
Pontus Euxinus from the Mediterran.   56
On Asia syd appeirs ʒit most plane   120
The wals of the old and famous Troy
Quhilks long ago the Greeks did destroy.
The Poets wryts that in that place also
Leander died suimming to Hero.
Sik Pleonasmus figurs I refuse.   125
I shape a shorter Syncopa till vse
And to my purpose quicklie for to cum.
We entred nixt in Mediterraneum.
Vnto the Rhods we saild the redy way
Quhilk wes shortsyne of Christendome, they say.   130
To Creta nixt our course directit we
Quhair that they mak this noble Malmesie.
Betuixt the Malt and Cicill lay our rout.
The wind come skant, we docht not double out.
Fra that we sau thair micht no better be   135
We plungit vp the coast of Calabrie.
Our Maister soon his lyttill vhissell cheird
His Mariners incontinent compeird
And eviry man did by his taikling stand
To haill and drau as he gaiv them command.   140
     'To saill vp Sigeum (mates) we ar assuird.
Thairfor tak on ʒour babert luif abuird.
Out with ʒour boulings, the wind is south southwest.
Wp with ʒour sheats and haill thame to the best.
Come no lauer bot luif a lytill we   145
For ʒon is Sicill with his heads thrie
Quhais shape ʒe sie is lyk to Cerberus   56ᵛ
And for to deall with no les dangerous.
ʒon is mount Ætna vhair the fyre comis out,

114 passing ships] passing (ar; *del.*) ships K 120 Asia syd] Asia (ʒ; *del.*) syd 134
out] ... K 137 cheird] cheir... K 141 assuird] assuir... K 144 best] bes... K

93

150 ʒon is Charybdis that vhirlis ay about
And ʒon is Sylla on the other shore
Resisting Neptun, making him to rore.
Steir studdie (mate) fra ʒe ʒour self hes sene thame.
Thair is bot dead or we mon throu betuene thame'.
155 　 Fra that we come this gredy gulf within
We micht not heir ane other for the din,
On baburdsyde the vhirling of the sand,
On steirbuirdsyd the Roks lay off the land.
Betuixt the tua we tuik sik taillʒeweis
160 At hank and buick we shippit syndrie seis.
As ane is done, another neu begins.
Quhill we war past our hair stude widdirshins.
God saifed our ship and ruled our noble ruther
And helpt vs throu as he hes mony vther.
165 Fra we wer past, I wot if we were fane.
We will not grene to gang that gait agane.
　　 We entrit nixt in the Tyrrhenum sea
And sailit to tua ylis in Italie,
Sardinia not far from Corsica.
170 We wat ane Anchor evin betuixt they tua.
We weyde fra thyn and peyde our Anchor custum
And entrit nixt into the sea Liguscum
By Minork and Majork in the Mediterran
And so alongst all the coast of Spane.
57 175 Gebraltars straits at length syn passit we
And entred in the wyd and Ocean sea
Quhais moving maks (as writs PLVTARCHVS)
Into the mone ane face appeir to vs.
I will not dippe into Astronomie
180 For feir I fall in cace I clim so hie.
It is the Arte that I did nevir leirne.
Belyve we left all Aragon a sterne.
　　 Be we had saillit four and twenty hours
The lift begouth for to ou'rcast with shours.
185 The cluds blak ou'rquhelmit all the skyis.
Neptunus ryders begouth also to ryis,
The bouand Dolphin tumbland lik a vhele

177 PLVTARCHVS] PLVTARCH... K 183 twenty] xx K

Quharby our Maister vnderstude right weill
That Eolus wes kindling vp in yre.
The hevins all vox rid as ony fyre,   190
The cluds rave in shours of grit hailstanis,
Doun with a clappe come all our saillis at anis,
From the Northeist thair come an vgly blast,
Maid vp our Takill and ou'r buird went our mast.
The storme increst four dayis mair and mair.   195
Our Maister also begouth for to dispair
Quhill the fyft day that it began to cleir
Then as we micht we mendit vp our geir
Quharof the leist pairt wes remanit haill.
ʒit at the last we come to Portingaill.   200
Glaid wes our fellouis fra that they sau the shore
And bettir hairted nor they wer before.   57ᵛ
They tuik some Curage and begouth to crak.
First the Egyptian he began and spak,
'Wes it not heir vhair Pharaos dochter landit,   205
First of the Scots as we do vnderstand-it?'
The Turk alledgit Gathelus wes a Greke
So evirie man did his Opinione speke.
ʒit baith thair menings wes, I vnderstude,
ʒour grace wes cumming of thair Ancient blude   210
Quhilk wes the caus that they so willinglie
Had cum so far to se ʒour Majestie.
Thus cracking on we did the way ou'rdryve
Quhill we at lenth in Ireland did aryve,
Quhilk wes begun, they said, be thair forbears.   215
Some held thame treu and others held thame lears,
Some wald say ʒea and others some said nay,
With Pro and Contra so shortnit we the way
    Of Osshane syne we passit soon the yle.
In Jarsay and Grinisay within a pretie vhyle.   220
Alongst Ingland within the yle of wight
In at the Nedles our Pilot tuke vs right,
Furth at Sanct Ilands and entrit in pace

188 weill] wei... 192 anis] ani... K 193 an vgly blast] an (e; *del.*) vgly blas... K 194
mast] ... K 195 mair] ma... K 198 geir] gei... K 201 shore] sho... K 222 Nedles
our] Nedles (t; *del.*) our K

Then to the Douns vhair that we raid a space.
225 Fra they persaiv'd the hils high of calk
One to another they begouth to talk.
'Thir ar the Hils, surely we suppone,
Quharthrou this land is callit Albion'.
58 They daskand farther, 'Vhat if the Quene wer deid?
230 Quha suld be nixt or to the Croun succeid?'
They follouit furth this Argument so far,
Syndrie wes sibbe bot ay ȝour grace wes nar.
'Quha wat', quod they, 'bot his grace may pretend?
The thing is ȝit far of that God may send.
235 Becaus heirin we na thing vnderstand
We will not haȝard for to go a land
Leist they perchance micht find some falt in vs
As Inglishmen ar very captious'.
We weyd from thyn and wald no langer byde
240 Bot saild alongst the Inglish haill cost syde
The vhilk to vs appeird very fair
Thoght notwithstanding all wes ind and bair
ȝet fertill baith for bestiall and Corne
Houbeit or than that all wes win and shorne
245 Quharas no rare thing in our way we fand
Quhill we aryvit hard heir at the hand
Quhar that we sau evin standing in the see
The strongest Craig we thoght in Christentie
Baith high and stay vhen we wer to it come.
250 Thair wes no way vharby it might be clum
And als it stude tua mylis of from the land.
Euen thair perchance ane fisher boat we fand.
We speirit at thame vhat kynd of Craig it wes.
They ansueird vs that it wes cald the basse.
58ᵛ 255 They sheu us als vha wes thairof the Lord
And hou that men went vp it in a corde
And als hou tua might keep it weil aneugh.
We said na mair bot come our way and leugh.
'ȝe sall', quod they, 'sie mony stranger thing
260 If that ȝe chance to trauell with our King'.

---

229 deid] de... K 233 pretend] prete... K 237 vs] ... K 239 byde] b... K 240
syde] sy... K 244 shorne] shor... K 252 fand] fa... K 253 wes] w... K

Then we come sailing to the Porte of Leith.
To come right in we thoght it very eith
For other shippis ather sax or sevin
Had come befor ws thair in to the hevin.
Becaus that we wer nevir thair afore   265
We tuke the Ludging nerest to the shore.
I haif bene far bot ʒit in all my lyfe
I neuer sau a mirrier hartsum wyfe.
'Be blyth', quod sho, 'for ʒe sall se our King,
God blisse his Grace and mak him long to ring'.   270
Becaus she saw that it wes groune lait
Sho gart hir boyis come with vs all the gait
Quho broght vs heir vnto ʒour highnes ʒett
Quharas the Court with torches all wes sett
To shau the way vnto ʒour graces hall   275
That eftir supper we might sie the ball.
My fellouis comes nou. I mon mak auay.
God blisse ʒour grace, I haif no more to say.

54   A Cartell of the thre Ventrous Knichts   59

As ydilnes is mother of all vyce
And sluggishnes the very sone of shame
So honour is that only pearle of pryce
That leivis to men ane Everlasting Name
Quhen they ar dead to live agane by fame   5
Quharof the gredy Curage evir gloirs,
Quhilk wes the caus we come so far from hame
To knau this Court vhilk all the world decoirs,
Quhilk for to sie we saild by syndry shoirs
And past the perillous gredy gulfe of Perse   10
And levir sees that syndry shippis devoirs
Quhare is no fish bot Monsters fell and feirse
Quhais vgly shappis wer tyrsum to reherse
And mairatou'r we come not to that end
To wery ʒou and wast the day in Verse,   15
Quhilk otheruyse we purpose for to spend
As pairtly by our clething may be kend

54.7 hame] ha... K   8 decoirs] de... K   9 shoirs] shoir... K   12 feirse] feir... K

97

And vncouth Armes that errant knichts were
Of forrein lands vhom fortun heir hes send
20   To find thy grace vhom we haif soght so far
Than grant thou vs befor that we come nar
Thy saiv sure conduct that we may be frie
To prove thy Knights. We dout not bot they dar
59ᵛ   In play or ernest be bold to brek a tre
25   And so, I trou, dar ony of 3on thre
Bot they ar not come heir for sik a thing
Bot rather for thair Ladyes sake to se
Quha fairest runis and oftest taks the ring.
Go to than shirs and let vs streik a sting.
30   (Cast crosse or pyle, vha sall begin the play?)
And let the luifsome ladyis and the King
Decerne as Judges vha dois best this day
So for my pairt I haif no more to say.
God speid 3ou weill and keip the timber haill.
35   Wait on 3our fortun vhill sho say 3ow nay.
I wish 3ou weill if fortun may availl.

55   Epitaph of R. Scot

Good Robert Scot, sen thou art gone to god
(Cheif of our souerane Colledge Justice clerks
Vho vhill thou liv'd for honestie wes od
As wryt beirs witnes of thy worthy werks)
5   So faithfull formall and so frank and frie
Sall nevir vse that office eftir thee.

54.18 were] w... K 20 we haif] we (s; *del.*) haif K far] ... K 21 nar] n... K 23 dar]
d... K 36 *infra, within two horizontal lines, the heading* Epitaphs K

56 Epitaph of the Maister of work Drummond of Carnok

60

Stay Passinger thy Mynd, thy futt, thy ee,
Vouchsaif a we his Epitaph to vieu
Quha left bot feu, behind him sik as he
Syn leirnd to de, to live agane aneu.
    All knoues this treu, vho noble Carnok kneu.   5
This Realme may reu that he is gone to grave.
All buildings brave bids Drommond nou adeu
Quhais lyf furthsheu he lude thame by the laiv.
Quhair sall we craiv sik policie to haiv?
Quha with him straiv to polish, build or plante?   10
These giftis I grant god lent him by the Laiv
Quha mot resaiv his saull to be a Sante
    To regne with him in evirlasting glore
    Lyk as his Corps his Cuntrey did decore.

57 Epitaph of Jhone and Patrik Shaues

If ethnik ald by superstitious stylis
(Quhilk poyson 3it of Paganisme appeirs)
Wer stellified to rule the rolling spheirs
(As Pagnisme Poets and profane compylis,
    Quhais senceles sences Satan so ou'rsylis   5
By Oracles illuding all thair eirs
In double speches ansuers sik as speirs
Quhilk godles gods the graceles Grekes begylis)
Then more praisuorthie Pelicans of SHAWIS   60ᵛ
Quhais saikles bluid wes for 3our souerane shed.   10
Lo blissit brether, both in honours bed,
His sacred self 3our Trumpet bravely blauis.
    By CASTOR and by POLLUX 3ou may boste,
    Deid SHAWIS 3e live, suppose 3our lyfis be loste.

56.title Drummond of Carnok] (Sir Robert; *in another hand*) Drummond of Carnok (knight; *in another hand*) K

58   Epitaph Robert Lord Boyd

Heir lyis that godly, noble, wyse Lord Boyd
Quha Kirk, the King, and commounweill decorde
Quhilks war vhill they this Jeuell all injoyd
Defendit, Counseld, governd be that Lord.
5   His Ancient hous oft perreld he restord.
Tuyse sax and saxtie ʒeirs he liv'd and syne
By Death the thrid of Januar devord
In Anno thryse fyve hundreth auchtie nyne.

59

Supreme Essence, beginning Vnbegun,
Ay Trinall ane, ane vndevydit thrie,
Eternall Word vha Victorie hes wun
Ou'r Death, ou'r hell Triumphing on the Trie,
5   Forknaulege, Wisdome and All-seing ee,
JEHOVAH, ALPHA, and OMEGA all,
Lyk vnto nane, nor nane lyk vnto thee,
Vnmov't vha movis the rounds about the Ball,
61   Contener vnconteind, is, was and sall
10   Be Sempiternall, Mercifull and Just,
Creator, vncreatit, nou I call.
Teich me thy treuth since into thee I trust.
         Incres, confirme, and kendill from above
         My faith, my hope, bot by the lave my Love.

58.2 the King] and king Po 3 Quhilks] Vich Po 4] Maintend Gouernd and councelled by þat Lord Po
59 title] *supra:* SONETS 1 beginning] Beginner C3 2 ane, ane] ane and C3 3 Eternall] Eternally C3 vha] that He C2 C3 4 ou'r] and He Triumphing] triumphand He C2 7 nor] and C3 nane] none like He C2 C3 8 vha] quhilk He; moving C3 the rounds] He C3; thee round K 12 since into] since (v; *del.*)into K 13 kendill] He C2 C3; strenthen K 14 bot] C2; and K by] with *LH margin, 19c hand* K

60

High Architectur, vondrous-vautit-rounds,
Huge-host of Hevin in restles-rolling spheers,
Firme-fixit polis vhilk all the axtrie beirs,
Concordant-discords, suete harmonious sounds,
    Boud-ʒodiak (circle-belting-Phoebus bounds),   5
Celestiall signis, of moneths making ʒeers,
Bright Titan to the Tropiks that reteirs
Quhais fyrie flammis all chaos-face confounds,
    Just balanc'd ball amidst the hevins that hings,
All Creaturs that NATUR creat can   10
To serve the vse of most vnthankfull man,
Admire ʒour maker, only King of Kings.
    Prais him (o man) his mervels that remarks,
    Quhais mercyis far exceids his wondrous warks.

61

Iniquitie on eirth is so increst
All flesh bot feu with falset is defyld,
Givin ou'r of God with gredynes beguyld
So that the puir but Pitie ar opprest.
    God in his Justice dou na mair digest   5   61ᵛ
Syk sinfull suyn with symonie defyld
But must revenge, thair vyces ar so vyld
And pour doun plagues of famin, suord and pest.
    Aryse o Lord, delyuer from the lave
Thy faithfull flock befor that it infect.   10
Thou sees hou Satan sharps for to dissave
If it were able, euen thyn auin elect.
    Sen Conscience Love and Cheritie all laiks,
    Lord short the season for the chosens saiks.

60.4 Concordant-discords] Concords discordant Ti 5 circle] circles Ti 7
Tropiks] Ti; Topiks K 8 all] auld Ti 9 hings] Ti; hin... K 10 Creaturs] crea-
ture Ti 13 mervels] merceis Ti remarks] Ti; remar... K 14 warks] Ti; war... K
61.7 But] (Givin ou'r of God; *del.*) But K 7 vyld] vy... K

62   To Maister Dauid Drummond

I

As Curious Dido Ænee did demand
To vnderstand vha wrakt his Toun and hou
Him self got throu and come to Lybia land,
To vhom fra hand his body he did bou
5   With bendit brou and tuinkling teirs I trou
(He said, 'If thou O Quene wald knau the cace
Of Troy, alace, it garis my body grou
To tell it nou, so far to our disgrace
     Hou in short space that somtym peirles place
10 Before my face in furious flammis did burne,
Compeld to murne and than to tak the chace
I ran this race, bot nevir to returne')
     Sa thou lyk Dido, Maister Dauid Drummond
Hes me to ansueir, by thy sonet summond.

II

The hevinly furie that inspyrd my spreit
Quhen sacred Beughis war wont my brouis to bind
62 With frostis of fashrie, froȝen is that heet.
My garland grene is withrit with the wind.
5   Ȝe knau Occasio hes no hair behind.
The bravest Spreits hes tryde it treu I trou.
The long forspoken Proverb true I find,
No man is man and man is no thing nou.
     The Cuccou flees befor the Turtle dou.
10 The pratling Pyet matchis with the Musis.
Pan with Apollo playis, I wot not hou.
The Attircops Minerva's office vsis.
     These be the grievis that garris Montgomry grudge
That Mydas not Mecenas is our Judge.

II.13 grudge] gr... K

63   To Maister Patrick GALLOWAY

Sound, GALLOVAY, the Trompet of the Lord,
(The blissit brethren sall obey thy blast)
Then thunder out the thretnings of the word
Aganst the wicked that auay ar cast.
    Pray that the faithfull in the fight stand fast.   5
Suppose the Divill the Wickeds hairts obdure,
ʒit perseveir as in thy Preichins past
For to discharge thy Conscience and cure.
    Quhat Justice sauld! vhat pilling of the pure?
Quhat bluidy Murthers ar for gold forgivin?   10
God is not sleipand thoght he tholde, be sure.
Cry out, and he shall heir the from the Heuin,
    And wish the King his Court and counsell clenge
    Or then the Lord will in his wrath revenge.

64   To his Majestie   62ᵛ

Shir, clenge ʒour Cuntrie of thir cruell crymis,
Adultreis, witchcraftis, incests, sakeles bluid.
Delay not, bot (as David did) betymis
ʒour Company of such men soon secluid.
    Out with the wicked, garde ʒou with the gude.   5
Of mercy and of Judgment sey to sing.
Quhen ʒe suld stryk I wald ʒe vnderstude.
Quhen ʒe suld spair I wish ʒe wer bening.
    Chuse godly Counsel, leirne to be a King.
Beir not thir burthenis longer on ʒour bak.   10
Jumpe not with justice for no kynd of thing.
To just Complantis gar gude attendance tak.
    Thir bluidy sarks cryis alwayis in ʒour eiris.
    Prevent the plague that presently appeirs.

63.6 the Divill] the (wicked; *del.*) Divill K 13 clenge] cleng... K

65   In praise of his Majestie

Support me sacred Sisters for to sing
His Praise vhilk passis the Antartik Pole
Quha fand the futsteppe of the fleing fole
And from Parnassus spyd the Pegase spring,
5   The hundreth saxt by lyne vnconqueist King,
Quhais knichtlie Curage kindling lyk a Cole
Maks Couarts quaik and hyde thame in a hole.
His brand all Brytan to obey sall bring.
     Come troup of tuinis, about his Temple tuyn
10   Ʒour laurell leivis with palmis perfytly plet
Wpon his heid Cæsarean to sett.
Immortaliʒe ane Nobler nor the Nyne,
63   A Martiall Monarch with Minerva's spreit,
     That Prince vhilk sall the Prophesie compleit.

66   In Praise of Maister John Maitland chanceller

Of Mars, Minerva, Mercure and the Musis
The Curage, Cunning, Eloquence and vain
Maks maikles Maitland mirrour to Remane
As Instrument vhilk these for honour vsis,
5   Quhais fourfald force with furie him infusis
In battells, Counsels, Orisones and brain.
It neids no proofe, experience is plane.
A Cunning King a Cunning Chanceller chuisis.
     Quhat happines the hevins on him bestoues
10   Hes trimlie at this trublous tyme bene tryde.
Thoght worthynes of wreches be invyde
Ʒit wonted Verteu ay the grener grouis.
     Then lyk his Name the Gods for Armis him gives
     Suord, Pen and wings in croun of laurel leives.

65.3 Quha] And K 5 King] K... K 7 hole] hol... K 14 compleit] comp... K
66.13 gives] giv... K 14 leives] lei... K

67   In prais of the Kings Vranie

I

Bellona's sone, of Mars the chosen Chyld,
Minerva's wit and Mercuris goldin tung,
Apollo's light that Ignorance exyld,
From Jove ingendrit and from Pallas sprung,
    Thy Vranie o second Psalmist sung   5
Triumphis ouer Death in Register of fame
Quharfor thy Trophee trimlie sall be hung
With laurell grene Eterniȝing thy Name
    Bot euen as Phœbus shyning does ashame
Diana with hir boroude beimis and blind   10   63ᵛ
So vhen I preis thy praysis to proclame
Thy weghtie words maks myne appeir bot wind
    ȝit (worthy Prince) thou wald tak in gude pairt
    My will for weill. I want bot only arte.

II

Of Titans harp sith thou intones the strings
Of Ambrose and of Nectar so thou feeds
Not only vther Poets thou outsprings
Bot vhylis also thy very self excedes,
    Transporting thee as ravishd vhen thou redes   5
Thyn auin inventione, wondring at thy wit,
Quhat mervell than thoght our fordullit hedes
And blunter brainis be more amais'd at it
    To sie thy ȝeirs and age vhilks thou hes ȝit
Inferiour far to thy so grave ingyne,   10
Quha haȝard at so high a mark and hit
In English as this Vranie of thyne,
    Quharfor thy name (o Prince) eternall ringis,
    Quhais Muse not Jove bot grit JEHOVA sings.

title] *adjacent, RH*: Son K

III

Can goldin Titan shyning bright at morne
For light of Torches cast a gritter shau?
Can thunder reird the higher for a horne?
Craks Cannouns louder thoght a Cok suld crau?
5   Can our waik breathis help Boreas to blau?
Can Candle lou give fyr a griter heet?
Can quhytest Suanis more quhyter mak the snau?
Can Virgins Teirs augment the Winters weit?
64   Helps pyping Pan Apollo's Musik sueet?
10 Can fontans smal the Ocean sea incres?
No: they augment the griter not a quheet
Bot they thame selfis appeir to grou the les.
      So (peirles Prince) thy Cunning maks the knoune.
      Ours helps not thyn. We stenȝie bot our aune.

IV

As bright Apollo staineth eviry star
With goldin rayis vhen he begins to ryse
Quhais glorious glance ȝit stoutly skaillis the skyis
Quhen with a wink we wonder vhair they war
5   (Befor his face for feir they faid so far)
And vanishis auay in such a wayis
That in thair spheirs they dar not interpryse
For to appeir lyk Planeits as they ar,
      Or as the Phœnix with her fedrum fair
10 Excels all foulis in diverse hevinly heuis,
Quhais Natur contrare Natur sho reneuis
As ONLIE, but Companione or compair,
      So, Quintessenst of Kings, vhen thou Compylis,
      Thou stanis my Versis with thy staitly stylis.

III.2 shau] shau Ja; schaw Mx 4 crau] cr... K 5 breathis] breath Ja Mx 8 Winters weit] Winter ... K; Vinters weit Ja; winteris weit Mx 8–9] reversed Mx 12 they thame] they (s; *del.*) thame K appeir] appears Ja Mx 13 peirles] worthy Ja Mx Cunning maks] works sall mak Ja Mx
IV.3 skyis] sk... K 4 war] wa... K 13 Compylis] Compy... K 14 stylis] sty... K

68   To his Majestie for his Pensioun

I

Help (PRINCE) to vhom, on vhom not, I complene
Bot on, not to, fals fortun ay my fo
Quha but, not by a resone reft me fro
Quho did, not does, ʒit suld my self sustene.
    Of Crymis not cairs since I haif kept me clene   5
I thole, not thanks thame Sir vho serv'd me so,
Quha heght, not held to me and mony mo   64ᵛ
To help, not hurt, bot hes not byding bene
    Sen will not wit, to lait vhilk I lament
Of sight not service, shed me from ʒour grace.   10
With, not without ʒour warrand ʒit I went
In wryt, not words, the papers ar in place.
    Sen chance not change hes put me to this pane
    Let richt, not reif my Pensioun bring agane.

II

If lose of guids, if gritest grudge or grief,
If povertie, imprisonment or pane,
If for guidwill ingratitude agane,
If languishing in langour but relief,
    If det, if dolour and to become deif,   5
If travell tint and labour lost in vane
Do properlie to Poets appertane,
Of all that craft my chance is to be chief.
    With August Virgill wauntit his reuard
And Ovids lote als lukles as the lave.   10
Quhill Homer liv'd his hap wes wery hard
ʒit vhen he died sevin Cities for him strave.
    Thoght I am not lyk one of thame in Arte
    I pingle thame all perfytlie in that parte.

title *adjacent, RH:* 4 Son... K
I.1 complene] comple... K

III

If I must begge it sall be far fra hame.
If I must want it is aganis my will.
I haif a stomok thoght I hold me still
To suffer smart, but not to suffer shame.
5   In spyt of fortun I shall flie with fame.
65   Sho may my Corps bot not my Curage kill.
My hope is high houbeit my hap be ill
And kittle aneugh and clau me on the kame.
      Wes Bishop Betoun bot restord agane,
10   To my ruin reserving all the rest
To recompence my prisoning and pane,
The worst is ill, if this be bot the best.
      Is this the frute Sir of your first affectione,
      My Pensioun perish vnder your protectione?

IV

Adeu my King, Court, Cuntrey, and my kin,
Adeu suete Duke vhose father held me deir,
Adeu Companiones Constable and Keir
(Thrie treuar hairts I trou sall neuer tuin).
5   If byganes to revolve I suld begin
My Tragedie wald cost 3ou mony a teir
To heir hou hardly I am handlit heir
Considring once the honour I wes in.
      Shirs, 3e haif sene me griter with his grace
10   And with 3our vmquhyle Maister to and myne
Quha thoght the Poet somtyme worth his place
Suppose 3e sie they shot him out sensyne.
      Sen wryt nor wax nor word is not a word
      I must perforce ga seik my fathers suord.

III.14 protectione] protectio... K
IV.13 word] wor... K

69   To the Lords of the Session

I

Quhare bene ȝe brave and pregnant sprits becum?
Quik vive inventionis ar ȝe worne auay?
I am assuird by simpathie that sum   65^v
Wald never wish that Cunning suld decay.
    If ony be, your Lordships must be thay   5
Whose spreits ȝour weeds of Verteu hes you spun.
Then mak the Poet Pensioner I pray
And byde be justice as ȝe haif begun.
    Sen I haif richt vhy suld I be ou'rrun?
Incurage me and able I can carpe.   10
Hald evin the weyis, the Victory is wun,
As I confyde in King and solid Sharpe
    Quhom I culd len a lift, your Lordships knauis,
    War they in Love as I am in the Lauis.

II

Alace my Lords, hou long will ȝe delay
To put the Poets Pensione out of plie?
ȝon shifting Sophists hes no thing to say,
Their fekles flyting is not worth a flie.
    Mak Bishop Betone vhat they lyk to be,   5
He must perforce be ather quik or deid.
If he be deid, the mater maks for me.
If he be quik then they can cum no speid.
    By Consequence it can not bot succeid.
For laik of forces they must tyn the feild.   10
And for the Bishope, I defy his feid.
ȝok vhen we will, I hope to gar him ȝeild.
    So good, My-Lords, I crave no more of ȝou
    Bot shift me not vhill ȝe haif slane my sou.

title *adjacent, RH:* 4 So... K

66   III

How long will ȝe the Poet's Patience prove?
Shaip ȝe to shift him lyk a pair of Cartis?
Look vp my Lords, thair is a Lord above
Quha seis the smallest secreit of ȝour hairts.
5   He vnderstands ȝour offices and ȝour airts.
He knauis vhat is committit to ȝour Cure.
He recompencis as ȝe play your pairts.
Once, soon or syne, ȝour Lordships must be sure
      For he respects no Princes more then pure.
10   Quhat evir ȝe do then, hald the Ballance evin,
Sa to do Justice, I ȝou all conjure,
As ȝe will merit ather hell or hevin.
      Deserv not de- (befor ȝour Lordships) -fames
      For I may able eterniȝe your Names.

IV

My Lords, late lads, nou leidars of our Lauis,
Except ȝour gouns some hes not worth a grote.
Your Colblak Conscience all the Cuntrey knauis.
Hou can ȝe live except ȝe sell ȝour vote?
5   Thoght ȝe deny, thair is aneu to note
How ȝe for Justice jouglarie hes vsit
Suppose ȝe say ȝe jump not in a jote.
God is not blind, he will not be abusit,
      The tym sall come vhen ȝe sall be accusit
10   For mony hundreth ȝe haif herryit heir
Quhare ȝe sall be forsakin and refusit
And syn compeld at Plotcok to appeir.
      I hope in God at lenth thoght it be late
      To sie sum sit into ...

III.4 hairts] hairt... K 5 airts] (C; *del.*)airt... K 13 Deserv] Deserv(is; *del.*) K
IV.3 knauis] knau... K 9 accusit] accu... K 14] *cropped* K

70   # To his Aduersars Lauyers   66ᵛ

Presume not Prestone, Stirling is no strenth
Suppose ȝe come to cleik auay my King.
Beleiv me baith, ȝe sall be lost at lenth.
Assure your selfis and think nane other thing.
    Byde ȝe the brash vhill I my battrie bring,   5
For all your CRAIG vhar in ȝe so confyde
Experience will play ȝou sik a spring,
Sall pluk your pennis and pacifie ȝour pryde.
    I sall beseige you sa on euirie syde
Ȝour baggage buluarks sall not be na buit.   10
Ȝe sall not haif ane hoill ȝour heids to hyde
Fra tym ȝe caus my Cannoun royal shuit.
        Haif at ȝour Rocks and Ramparts with a rattill,
        Sho suits so SHARPE ȝe dou not byde a brattill.

71   # Of Maister John SHARPE

I

If gentle blude ingendrit be by baggis
Then culd I ges vho wer a gentle Jhone.
If he be wysest with the world that waggis
Ȝit culd I wish ȝou to a wittie one.
    If he be all vha thinks his Nichtbours none   5
Then surely I suld shau ȝou vho wer all.
If he be Cæsar vho doth so suppone
Then I conjecture vhom I Cæsar call.
    If he be sure vho sueirs and sayis he sall
Then certanly I wot weill vho wer sure.   10
If he be firme vho neuer feirs to fall
I doubt not then vhose dayis suld lang indure.
        Sed quæritur, vhat Lau he leivis at leist?   67
        He wald not preich, he can not be a preist.

70.10 sall not] sall (b; *del.*) not K
71.title *adjacent, RH:* 2 Son. K

II

A Baxters bird, a bluiter beggar borne,
Ane ill heud huirsone lyk a barkit hyde,
A saulles suinger seuintie tymes mensuorne,
A peltrie pultron poyson'd vp with pryde,
5   A treuthles tongue that turnes with eviry tyde,
A double deillar with dissait indeu'd,
A luiker bak vhare he wes bund to byde,
A retrospicien vhom the Lord outspeud,
       A brybour baird that mekle baill hes breud,
10   Ane Hypocrit, ane ydill Atheist als,
A skurvie skybell for to be esheu'd,
A faithles, fekles, fingerles and fals
       A turk that tint Tranent for the Tolbuith:
       Quha reids this riddill he is sharpe forsuith.

72   To Robert Hudsone

I

My best belouit brother of the band,
I grein to sie the sillie smiddy smeik.
This is no lyfe that I live vpaland
On rau rid herring reistit in the reik,
5   Syn I am subject somtyme to be seik
And daylie deing of my auld diseis,
Eit bread, ill aill and all things ar ane eik.
This barme and blaidry buists vp all my bees.
       3e knau ill guyding genders mony gees
10   And specially in Poets, for Example
67ᵛ   3e can pen out tua cuple and 3e pleis.
       3our self and I, old Scot and Robert Semple,
              Quhen we ar dead that all our dayis bot daffis,
              Let Christan Lyndesay wryt our Epitaphis

72.title *adjacent, RH*: 5 Son. K

II

With mightie maters mynd I not to mell
As copping Courts or Comonwelthis or Kings.
Quhais Craig ȝoiks fastest, let thame sey thame sell.
My thoght culd nevir think vpon sik things.
    I wantonly wryt vnder Venus wings.   5
In Cupids Court ȝe knau I haif bene kend
Quhair Muses ȝit some of my sonets sings
And shall do aluayis to the worlds end.
    Men hes no caus my Cunning to commend
That it suld merit sik a Memorie   10
ȝit ȝe haif sene his Grace oft for me send
Quhen he took plesure into Poesie.
    Quhill Tyme may serve perforce I must refrane
    That pleis his Grace I come to Court agane.

III

I feid Affectione vhen I sie his grace
To look on that vhairin I most delyte.
I am a liȝard fainest of his face
And not a snaik with poyson him to byte
    Quhais shape's alyk, thoght fashonis differ quyt.   5
The one doth love, the other hateth still.
Vhare some taks plesur, others tak despyte.   68
One shap, one subject, wishis weill and ill.
    Euen so will men (bot no man judge I will)
Baith loue and loth and only bot ane thing.   10
I can not skan these things above my skill.
Loue vhome they lyk, for me I loue the King
    Vhose highnes laughed som tym for to look
    Hou I chaist POLWART from the chimney nook.

III.9 I will] I ... K 12 King] K... K 14 nook] ... K

IV

Remembers thou in Æsope of a taill?
A louing Dog wes of his Maister fane.
To faun on him wes all his Pastym haill.
His courteous Maister clappit him agane.
5   By stood ane Asse, a beist of blunter brane.
Perceiving this bot looking to no freet,
To pleis hir Maister with the counterpane
Sho clambe on him with hir foull clubbit feet
    To play the Messan thoght sho wes not meit.
10 Sho meinit weill, I grant hir mynd wes guid
But vhair sho troude hir Maister suld hir treit
They battound hir vhill that they sau hir bluid.
    So stands with me vho loues with all my hairt
    My Maister best, some taks it in ill pairt.

V

Bot sen I sie this Proverbe to be true,
Far better hap to Court nor service good,
Fairueill (my brother HUDSONE) ...
68ᵛ Vho first fand out of PEGASE fut the flood
5   And sacred-hight of PARNASE-mytred hood
From vhence somtyme the son of DELOS sent
Tua seuerall shaftis vher he of DELPHOS stood
69 With PENNEVS dochter hoping to acquent.
    Thy HOMER's style, thy PETRARK's high Invent
10 Sall vanquish Death and live Eternally,
Quhais boasting Bou thoght it be aluayis bent
Sall neuer hurt the sone of Memorie.
    Thou onlie Brother of the Sisters Nyne
    Shau to the King this poor Complant of myne.

IV. 9 not meit] not ... K 11 hir treit] hir ... K 12 bluid] b... K 13 my hairt] my ...
K 14 pairt] pa... K
V.3] *cropped* K

72a Christen Lyndesay to Robert Hudsone

Oft haive I hard, bot ofter fund it treu
That Courteours kyndnes lasts bot for a vhyle.
Fra once ȝour turnes be sped, vhy then Adeu,
Ȝour promeist freindship passis in exyle.
  Bot (Robene) faith ȝe did me not beguyll,   5
I hopit ay of ȝou as of the lave.
If thou had wit thou wald haif mony a wyle
To mak thy self be knaune for a knaive.
  MONTGOMRIE, that such hope did once conceave
Of thy guid will, nou finds all is forgotten.   10
Thoght not bot kyndnes he did at the craiv
He finds thy freindship as it rypis is rotten.
    The smeikie smeithis cairs not his passit trauel
    But leivis him lingring deing of the gravell.

73 To Maister J. Murray   69ᵛ

Flie louer (PHŒNIX): feirs thou not to fyre
Invironing the aluayis-upuard ayr
Vhich thou must pas before that thou come thair
Vharas thy Sprit so spurris thee to aspyre,
  To wit, aboue the Planetis to impyre   5
Behind the Compas of APOLLO's Chayr
And tuinkling-round of burning rubies rare
Quhair all the Gods thy duelling do desyre?
  Bot duilfull Doom of Destinies thee Dammis
Before thy blissit byding be above   10
The mortal from Immortall to remove
To sacrifice thy self to Phœbus flammis.
    I prophecye when so sall come to passe
    We nevir sie such one come of thy Asse.

72a.13 trauel] trau... K
73.3 thair] ... K 8 the] th(y; *del.*)e K 9 Dammis] Damm... K 13 passe] pa... K 14
Asse] A... K

74 To Maistres Lily Ruthuen Duches of Lennox

I love the Lilie as the first of flours
Vhose staitly stalk so streight vp is and stay
To vhome the laive ay lowly louts and couers
As bund so brave a beuty to obey.
5   Amongs thame selfis (it semes) as they suld say,
'Sueet Lillie, as thou art our Lamp of light
Resave our Homage to thy Honours ay,
As kynd commands to render thee thy right.
Thy blisfull beams with beutie burnisht bright
10   So honours all the Gardein vhair thou grouis
For suetest smell and shyning to the sight
(The Heuins on the sik happy grace bestouis)
69ᵛ   That vho persaivis thy Excellence by ours
Must love the Lillie as the first of flours'.

75 A Ladyis Lamentatione

I

Vhom suld I warie bot my wicked weard
Vha span my thriftles thrauard fatall threed?
I wes bot skantlie entrit in this eard
Nor had offendit vhill I felt hir feed.
5   In hir vnhappy hands sho held my heed
And straikit bakuard wodershins my hair
Syne prophecyed I suld aspyre and speed,
Quhilk double sentence wes baith suith and sair.
For I wes matchit with my match and mair,
10   No worldly woman neuer wes so weill.
I wes accountit Countes but compair
Quhill fickle fortun vhirld me from hir vheell.
Rank and Renoun in lytill Roum sho rang'd
And Lady Lucrece in a Cressede chang'd.

74.2 stay] st... K 3 couers] ... K 5 say] ... K 9 bright] brig... K 10 grouis] grou...
K 12 sik happy grace bestouis] sik h ... pp ... b...st... K
75.title *adjacent, RH*: 3 son. K

II

MELPOMENE my mirthles murning Muse
Wouchsaiv to help a wrechit Woman weep
Vhose chanch is cassin that sho can not chuse
Bot sigh and sobbe and soun vhen sho suld sleep.
    More hevynes within my hairt I heep   5
Nor Cative Cresside vhair sho lipper lay.
Dispair hes dround my hapeles hope so deep
My sorie song is oh and welauay,
    Euen as the Oul that dar not sie the day
For feir of haukis and lurkis in dark and doull.   10
So am I nou exyld from honour ay   70
Compaird to Cresside and the vgly Oull.
    Fy lothsome lyfe, fy Death that dou not ...
    Bot quik and dead a Bysin thou must ...

III

LORD for my missis micht I mak a mends
By putting me to Penance as thou pleas'd?
Good God forgive offenders that offends
And heall the hurt of sik as are diseasde.
    Hou soon they murne with mercy thou appeasde   5
As thou hes said and surely so it semes.
Suppose my silly saull with sin be seasde
3it the Reversiones rests that it redemes.
    Destroy me not that so of the estemes.
My suete Redemer let me neuer die   10
Bot blink on me euen with thy blisful beames
And mak ane other Magdalene of me.
    Forgive my gylt sen nane bot God is gude
    So with Peccavi Pater I conclude.

II.10] for feir of h...kis ...d l...k... k...ll K 13, 14] *cropped* K
III.2 pleas'd] pleas... K 5 appeasde] a... K 11 beames] b... K 13 gude] gud... K

76

I

Fane wald I speir vhat spreit doth me inspyre.
I haif my wish and 3it I want my will.
I covet lyfe and 3it my Corps I kill.
I vrne for Anger 3it I haif no yre.
5   I flie the flammis 3it folouis on the fyre.
I lyk my lote and 3it my Luk is ill.
I 3oldin am and 3it am stryving still.
I dreid Dispair 3it hope he heght me hyre.
70ᵛ   My bluid is brunt and 3it my breist does bleid.
10 I haif no hurt and 3it my hairt hes harmes.
I am ou'rcome but enimie or armis.
The Doctours doubtis if I be quik or deid.
     If that I kneu of vhome I culd inquyre
     Fain wold I speir vhat spreit does me inspyre.

II

My plesuris past procures my present pain,
My present pain expels my plesurs past,
My languishing alace is lyk to last,
My greif ay groues, my gladenes wants a grane,
5   My bygane joyes I can not get agane
Bot once imbarkit I must byde the blast,
I can not chuse, my kinsh is not to cast.
To wish it war, my wish wald be bot vane
     3it vhill I sey my senses to dissaive
10 To pleis my thoght I think a thousand things
Quhilks to my breist bot borou'de blythnes brings
(Anis hope I had thoght nou dispair I haive),
     A stratagem (thoght strange) to stay my sturt
     By Apprehensioun for to heill my hurt.

I.1 me inspyre] me ... K 5 the fyre] the ... K

III

I wyt myne ee for vieuing of my wo,
I wyt myn earis for heiring my mishap,
I wyt my senses vhilks dissavit me so,
I wyt Acquentance that in credit crap,
    I wyt the trane that took me with a trap,   5
I wyt Affectione formest to the feild,
I wyt misluk that suld me ...
I wyt my youth that but a promeis ʒeild,   71
    I wyt my stomoch wes not stoutly steild,
I wyt hir looks vhilk left me not alane,   10
I wyt my wisdome suld haif bene my sheild,
I wyt my Tongue that told vhen I wes tane.
    Had I my Counsell keepit vndeclairde
    I micht haif dred bot deidly not dispairde.

77

I

Bright Amorous Ee vhare Love in ambush lyes,
Cleir cristal tear distilde at our depairt,
Sueet secreit sigh more peircing nor a dairt,
Inchanting voce beuitcher of the wyse,
    Quhyt Ivory hand vhilk thrust my finger ...   5
I challenge ʒou, the causers of my smarte,
As homiceids and murtherers of my harte
In Resones Court to suffer ane assyse.
    Bot oh I feir: ʒea rather wot I weill,
To be repledg't ʒe plainly will appeill   10
To Love vhom Resone never culd command.
Bot since I can not better myn estate
    ʒit vhill I live at leist I sall regrate
    Ane ee, a teir, a sigh, a voce, a hand.

76.III.7] *cropped* K 9 steild] stei... K 12 tane] ta... K
77.I.1 lyes] l... (lyes; *19c hand, LH margin*) K 5] *cropped* K 11 Resone never]
Resone (vhome; *del.*) never K command] comm... (command; *19c hand, LH*
margin) K

II

Thyne ee the glasse vhare I beheld my hart.
Myn ee the windo throu the vhilk thyn ee
May see my hairt and thair thy self espy
In bloody colours hou thou painted art.
5   Thyne ee the pyle is of a murthereris dart.
71ᵛ Myne ee the sicht thou taks thy levell by
To shute my hairt and nevir shute aury.
Myn ee thus helpis thyn ee to work my smarte.
     Thyn ee consumes me lyk a flamming fyre.
10 Myne ee most lyk a flood of teirs do run,
Oh that the water in myne ee begun
Micht quench the burning fornace of desyre
     Or then the fyr els kindlit by thyn ey
     The flouing teirs of sorou micht mak dry.

III

So suete a Kis ʒistrene fra thee I reft
In bouing doun thy body on the bed
That evin my lyfe within thy lippis I left.
Sensyne from thee my spirits wald neuer shed.
5   To folou thee it from my body fled
And left my Corps als cold as ony Kie
Bot vhen the Danger of my Death I dred
To seik my spreit I sent my harte to thee
     Bot it wes so inamored with thyn ee
10 With thee it myndit lykuyse to remane.
So thou hes keepit Captive all the thrie
More glaid to byde then to returne agane.
     Except thy breath thare places had suppleit
     Euen in thyn Armes thair doutles had I deit.

II.1 my hart] my ... K 5 murthereris dart] murth... K 10 do run] do (rin; *del.*)
run K
III.2 on the] in ʒour Ro 3 thy lippis] ʒour mouth R 7 Bot vhen] ʒitt from Ro 8]
I send my hairt to fetche my spirite from thee Ro 9 with thyn ee] ewin with thee
Ro 10–11] And still with the and likwayis does remaine / And keipeth captiwe of
all theise thrie Ro 11 the thrie] the (e; *del.*) thrie K 12 then to returne] nor to
turne back Ro 13 Except thy breath thare] Were not ʒour breath theise Ro

78   James Lauder I wald se mare

I wald se mare nor ony thing I sie.
I sie not ȝit the thing that I desyre.
Desyre it is that does content the ee
The ee it is vhilk settis the hairt on fyre.   72
    In fyr to frye tormentit thus I tyre.   5
I tyre far mair till tyme these flammis I feid.
I feed affectione spurring to aspyre.
Aspyre I sall in esperance to speid.
    To speid I hope thoght danger still I dreid.
I dreid no thing bot ouer long delay.   10
Delay in Love is dangerous indeid.
Indeid I shape the soner to assay.
    Assay I sall, hap ill or weill, I vou.
    I vou to ventur, to triumph I trou.

79   Issobell yong by loving so

I trou your Love by loving so vnsene
Vnsene siklyk I languish for your Love
Ȝour Love is comely, constant, chaste and clene
And clene is myne, Experience sall prove
    Prove vhen ȝe pleis, I mynd not to remove   5
Remove vho may, if Destinies decreit
Decreit is givin by Hymen high above
Aboue all bands that blissed band is sueet
    Sueit is that ȝok so mutuall and meet
And meit it war we met if that we might   10
We might perhaps our purpose then compleit
Compleit it quickly Reson thinks it right.
    Right beiring Rule, the righteous suld rejose,
    Rejose in God, and on his will repose.

78.4 hairt on] hairt (i; *del.*) on K   5 fyr] fry K   9 dreid] dr... K
79.5 remove] rem... K   13 rejose] rejos... K

72ᵛ **80** **Eufame wemis**

Treu fame, we mis thy Trumpet for to tune
To blau a blast a beuty for to blaise,
A Paragone vhilk Poets oght to praise.
Had I that Science I suld sey it sune
5   ʒit as I dar my Deutie sall be done
With more Affectione nor with formall phrais.
I seme, vhill I vpon hir graces gaʒe
Endymion, enamor'd with the Mone.
    My Muse, let Mercure language to me len
10 With Pindar pennis for to outspring the spheirs
Or Petrarks pith surpassing all my peirs
To pingill Apelles pynsell with my pen
    And not to say as we haif said abone
    TREW FAME, WE MIS thy trumpet for to tone.

81 **Johne Jhonsone Jane Maxuell**

Sueit soull perceive hou secreit I conceill,
Rad to reveill that peirtly I propone.
Look ony one befor me lov'd so leill.
Examene weill, oh, oh we se't in none.
5   Good love is gone except my Love alone,
Thoght gromes can grone as they wald give the ghost
Half mang'd almost, als stupefact as stone,
Lyk Treuth in Throne they look as they wer lost,
    They turne, they tost, they rave, they rage, they rost
10 As Catives crost, vhill they your fauour find.
To bid ʒou bind thair purpose runs the post
Bot bund they bost hov thay thamselfis are blind.
73   ʒit trying tyme, the touchstone of my treuth,
    As resone wold, requests you to haif reuth.

81.12 hov thay thamselfis are blind] hov tha... th... s ... lf ... K

82   His Maistres Name

Quhat pregnant sprit the Letters can espy
My Ladyis Name and surname that begins?
Betuixt thame (ay) in ordour is bot I
And only I these lovely Letters tuins.
    Thoght rekles redars rashly ouer this rins   5
ʒit sharper shuters ner the mark will shute.
Shute on, lat sie vho first my wedfie wins
For I will wed ane Apple and a Nute.
    To brek ʒour brains (ʒe bunglers) is no bute,
The mair ʒe muse the mare ʒe misse the mark.   10
I count ʒour Cunning is not worth a cute
That can not kyth ʒour self to be a Clark.
    Or ʒe this find I feir ʒe first be fane
For to begin ʒour A.B.C. agane.

83   To his Maistres Messane

Ha! lytill Dog in happy pairt thou crap
If thou had skill thy happynes to spy
That secreit in my Ladyis Armis may ly
And sleip so sueitly in hir lovely lap.
    Bot I alace in wrechednes me wrap   5
Becaus ouer weill my misery knou I.
For that my ʒouth to leirne I did apply
My ouer grit skill hes maid my oune mishap.
    Vhy haif I not (o God) als blunt a brane
As he that daylie worbleth in the wyne   10 73ᵛ
Or to mak faggots for his fuid is fane?
Lyk as I do I suld not die and duyn.
    My pregnant spreit the hurter of my harte
    Lyk as it does suld not persave my smarte.

82.2 Name and] Name (t; *del.*) and K 7 wins] w... K 10 the mark] the... K 12
Clark] Cl... K
83.8 mishap] misha... K 9 brane] b... K

84   To M.D. For Skelmurley

I

Sweet Philomene with cheiping chyrris and charris
In hauthornes vher thou hyds thy self and hants
Beuailing thy Virginitie thou wants,
My harte to grone for very grief thou garris,
5   Thy mirthles mone my melody so marris
Vhill as thy changing chivring nots thou chants.
The peircing pyks groues at thy gorge thou grants.
So neir is skaith suppose thou skantly skarris.
      For murning I may be thy mirthles match,
10   As thou art banishd so am I exyld,
As thou art trumped so am I begyld,
Thou art vnweirdit, I a woful wrech,
      Thou art asham'd to shau thy secreit smart,
      My Ladyis bagie beirs my bluidy hart.

II

Thoght peirlis give pryce and Diamonds be deir
Or royall rubies countit rich and rare
The Margarit does merit mekle mare
As Jem of Jeuels, paragone but peir.
5   Wald god if it wer gettible for geir,
Culd it be coft for cost I wald not care.
Both lyfe and goods to win it wold I ware
74   Provyding I war worthy it to weir.
      Nixt wald I wish, my purpose broght to pas,
10   That I micht tak and tame the turtle Dov
And set hir syne vhare that I micht sie throu
Ane costly Cage of cleirest cristall GLAS
      Vhilks with my Jeuell micht I joyne, I grant,
      I culd not wish in world that I want.

title *adjacent, RH*: 2 Son. K
I.9 I may] I (b; *del.*) may K 12 vnweirdit] vᵃnweirdit K
II.7 ware] ... K 9 pas] p... K 10 Dov] Do... K 11 throu] th... K 13 grant] gra... K

85   Of my Lady Seyton Margaret Montgomerie

O happy star at evning and at morne
Vhais bright aspect my Maistres first outfand,
O happy credle and o happy hand
Vhich rockit hir the hour that sho wes borne,
    O happy Pape, 3e rather nectar horne   5
First gaiv hir suck in siluer suedling band,
O happy wombe consavit had beforne
So brave a beutie, honour of our Land,
    O happy bounds vher dayly 3it sho duels
Vhich Inde and Egypts happynes excells,   10
O happy bed vharin sho sall be laid,
O happy babe in belly sho sall breid,
    Bot happyer he that hes that hap indeid
    To mak both wyfe and mother of that maid.

86   To the for me

I

Suete Nichtingale in holene grene that hants
To sport thy self and speciall in the spring,
Thy chivring chirlis vhilks changingly thou chants
Maks all the roches round about the ring   74ᵛ
    Vhilk slaiks my sorou so to heir the sing   5
And lights my louing langour at the leist.
3it thoght thou sees not, sillie saikles thing,
The piercing pykis brods at thy bony breist.
    Euin so am I by plesur lykuyis preist,
In gritest danger vhair I most delyte.   10
Bot since thy song for shoring hes not ceist
Suld feble I for feir my Conqueis quyt?
    Na, na, I love the freshest Phœnix fair,
    In beuty, birth, in bounty but compair.

85.1 star at] star (b; *del.*) at K 2 outfand] outf... K 4 borne] b... K 5 horne] hor... K
14 maid] ... K
86.title *adjacent RH*: 3 Son K
86.I.1 hants] han... K 2 spring] spri... 3 changinglie thou chants] changin...l...
thou ... K 12 Conqueis quyt] Conqueis (tyne; *del.*) quyt K

II

Love lent me wings of hope and high desyre
Syn bad me flie and feir not for ane fall
3it tedious trauell tystit me to tyre
Vhill Curage come and culd me Couart call
5   ...
As Icarvs with wanton waxit wings
Ayme at the only A per se of all
Vhilk staynis the sun, that sacred thing of things,
    And spuris my spreit that to the heuins it springs
10 Quyt ravisht throu the region of the air
Vhair 3it my hairt in hoping ha3ard hings
At poynt to speid or quikly to despair.
    3et shrink not hairt, as simple as thou semes.
    If thou be brunt, it is with beuties bemes.

III

75

Go Pen and Paper, publish my Complantis,
Waill weghtie words, becaus 3e cannot weep.
For pitthie Poemis prettilie outpaintis
My secreit sighis as sorouis gritest heep
5   Bred in my breist, 3e rather dungeon deep
As prisoners perpetually in pane
Vhilk hes the credit of my harte to keep
In martyrdome but mercy to remane.
    Anatome3e my privie passionis plane
10 That sho my smart by sympathie may sie,
If they deserve to get some grace agane
Vhilk if they do not I desyr to die.
    Go sonet, soon vnto my soveran say,
    'Redeme 3our man or dam him but delay'.

II.5] *om.* K ...he said ...(quod I)... *in cropped LH margin* K
III.9 plane] plan... K 10 may sie] may S... K

87

I

Vhat subject, sacred sisters, sall I sing?
Vhase praise, Apollo, sal my pen proclame?
Vhat Nymph, Minerva, sall thy Novice name?
The bravest blossome beutie can outbring
    On staitly stalk neu sprouting furth to spring.   5
Hou sall I sound the fanphar of hir fame
Vhais Angels ees micht mak the sun think shame
As half eclipsed in the heuins to hing?
    Bot hola Muse! thou mints at such a mark
Vhais merit far excedes thy slender skill.   10
3it if hir grace for weill accept gude will
Then war thou well reuardit for thy wark.   75ᵛ
      Bot since to mount thy Maistres the commands,
      With hope once ha3ard for to kis hir hands.

II

Hir brouis, tuo bouis of Ebane ever bent,
Hir Amorous ees the aufull Arrouis ar,
The Archer Love vho shoots so sharpe and far,
My breist the butt vhairat hir shots ar sent,
    ...   5
My lyf the wageour, if I win the war,
My Patience pleids my proces at the bar,
My bluid the long expensis I haif spent,
    My secrete sighis solisters for my sute,
My trinkling teirs the presents I propyne,   10
My Constancie hir Councellours to enclyne.
But Rigour ryvis the hairt out by the root.
      Hope heghts me help bot feir finds no refuge.
      My pairties ar my Javellour and my Judge.

I.2 proclame] proclam... K 3 name] n... K 5 to spring] t... K 7 think shame]
thin... K 9 mark] ma... K 11 gude will] gude ... K
II.5 *om.* K

III

Excuse me Plato if I suld suppone
That vnderneth the heuinly vauted round
Without the world or in pairts profound
By Stix inclos'd that emptie place is none,
5   If watrie vauts of Air be full echone
Then vhat contenis my teirs, vhich so abound
With sighis and sobbis which to the hevins I sound
Vhen Love delytis to let me mak my mone?
     Suppose the solids subtilis ay restrantis
10   (Vhich is the maist, my Maister, ʒe may mene),
76   Thoght all war void ʒit culd they not contene
The half, let be the haill of my Complaintis.
     Vhair go they then, the Question wald I crave,
     Except for ruth the hevins suld thame ressave?

IV

Vha wald behold him vhom a God so grievis,
Vhom he assaild and danton'd with his dairt,
Of vhom he freiʒis and Inflams the hairt,
Vhais shame siclyk him gritest honour givis,
5   Vha wald behald a ʒouth that neuer leivis
In vain to folou the Object of his smarte,
Behold bot me persaiv my painfull pairt
And th'Archer that but mercy me mischeivis.
     Thair sall he sie vhat Resone then dar do
10   Against his bou, if once he mint bot to
Compell our hairts in bondage basse to beir,
     ʒit sall he se me happiest appeir
     That in my hairt the Amorous heid does lie
     Vith poyson'd poynt, vhairof I glore to die.

III.13 crave] c... K 14 ressave] ... K
IV.2 dairt] d... K 5 leivis] l... K 8 th'Archer] th'(e; *del.*) Archer K mischeivis]
mischei... K 9 sall he] sall (ʒe; *del.*) he K dar do] d... K 11 beir] be... K 13 does
lie] does ... K 14 to die] t... K

V

Hou long sall I in languishing lament?
Hou long sall I bot duyne and dou not die?
Hou long sall Love but mercy murther me?
Hou long against me sall his bou be bent?
    Hou long sall pane my plesur so prevent?   5
Hou long sall weping blind my watrie ee?
Hou long sall baill my bedfelou ʒit be?
Or vhen sall I with Comfort be acquent?   76ᵛ
    Hou long sall hope be hindrit be mishap?
Hou long ʒit Love will thou my Patience prove?   10
Hou long sall wo in wrechitnes me wrap?
Vp once and my Melancholie remove.
    Revenge, Revert, Revive, Revest, Reveall
    My hurt, My hairt, My hope, My hap, My heall.

88   Of the Duleweid

The burning sparkis of Helens Angells ee
But missing any, woundit eviry wicht
That come within the boushot of her sicht.
Bot Love vhose harte Compassion had to see
    Sa many Lovers but Redemption dee   5
Vha war attraptit with so sueet a slicht,
In murning blak he cled this Beutie bricht
As funerall mark and handsenʒie to be.
    But all in vane (alace) I must confes.
For vhy? a thousand Lovers not the les   10
Thoght they persaiv'd that Burrio Death to bost
Within hir eyis and sau him vhar he sat
ʒit feirles ran they notwithstanding that
To se these eyis, and syn gaiv vp the Ghost.

87.V.2 die] d... K 5 prevent] preven... K
88.12 hir] his K

129

89

Had I a foe that hated me to dead
For my Reuenge I wish him no more ill
77   Bot to behold hir eyis vhilk euer still
Ar feirce against me with so sueet a feid.
5   Hir looks belyve such horrour suld him breid
His wish wold be his Cative Corps to Kill.
Euen plesurs self culd not content his will.
Except the Death no thing culd him remeid.
      The vgly looks of old MEDUSA's eyis
10   Compaird to hirs ar not bot Poets leyis
For hirs exceids thame in a sharper sort.
The GORGON bot transformit men in stanis
Bot she inflammis and frei3is both at anis.
To spul3ie hairt that Minion maks hir sport.

90

Quhat suld I wish? if wishing war not vane,
Gold? siluer? stones? or precious peirlis of Inde?
No, no: I carie not a misers mynd,
I wish no more bot to be borne agane
5   Provyding that I micht a man remane
And sho that bure me euen of sik a kynd
That in hir birth hir persone war not pynd
Bot ay the plesur to exceid the pane,
      Then to be borne into a bonie bark
10   To saill the seyis in sik tym of the 3eir
Vhen hevy hartis it helthsum halds to heir
The mirthful Maveis and the lovesome Lark.
      In end I wold, my Voyage being maid,
      ...

89.5 breid] b... K 7 will] wi... K 8 remeid] reme... K 9 eyis] eyi... K 12 stanis]
sta... K 14 sport] sp... K
90.1 vane] va... K 2 Inde] I... K 5 remane] rema... K 6 kynd] kyn... K 7 pynd]
py... K 11 heir] he... K 12 Mavis] Mav(*indecipherable*) K Lark] ... K 14] *cropped*
K

91   The Poets Apologie to the Kirk of Edinburgh   77ᵛ

I wonder of ȝour Wisdomes that ar wyse
That baith miskennis my Method and my Muse.
Quhen I invey, such Epithets I wse
That evin ALECTO laughing at me lyis.
    My Trumpets tone is terribler be tuyis   5
Nor ȝon Couhorne vherof ȝe me accuse,
For fra the fureis me with fyr infuse
Quhom Bautie byts he deir that Bargan byis,
    For if I open wp my Anger anes
To plunge my pen into that stinking styx   10
My tongue is lyk the Lyons vhair it liks,
It brings the flesh lyk Bryrie fra the banes.
    I think it scorne besyd the skaith and sklander
    To euin an Ape with aufull ALEXANDER.

92   That he wrot not aganste the Madins of Edinburgh

Quhat rekles rage hes armde thy Tygirs tung
On sueit and simple soulis to speu thy spyte?
Quhat Syren suld such poysond songs haif sung?
Quhat Deuill such Ditties devysit to indyte?
    Quhat madnes mov'd such venemous vords to write?   5
Quhat hellish hands hes led thy bluidie pen?   78
Quhat furious feynd inflam'de thee so to flyte,
Thee, no wyse nou to numbred be with men?
    Quhat euer thou may be, thou art a knave I ken,
So leudly on these lassis to haif leid   10
And if thou pleis appoint hou, vhair and vhen
And I sall mak thee, beist, not to byde be-it,
    That nather they ar sik as thou hes said
    Nor I am he these rascall raylings maid.

91.7 with fyr] with (feir; *del.*) fyr K
92.2 to speu] to (spill; *del.*) (speu; *LH margin*) K 4 devysit] devysi K 5 to write
to] ... (write; *19c hand, LH margin*) K 7 flyte] fl... (flyte; *19c hand, LH margin*)
K 8 men] me... K 9 thou may be] thou (caret; *19c hand*) (may; *19c hand, LH
margin*) K knave I ken] knave ... K 12 be-it] be-... K

93   To his Majestie that he wrote not against vmquhill Maistres Jane Cuninghame

Sir, I am sorie that ʒe suld suppone
Me to be one in lucre to delyte
Or speu despyt against hir vho is gone.
No nevir none culd fee me so to flyte.
5   I war to wyt the bureit to bakbyte
Or to indyt hir families defame
Thoght Cuningham. In Conscience I am quyte
By word or wryt, aneugh nou for my Name.
I sueat for shame besyd the blot and blame.
10   Men suld proclame it wer Montgomries Muse.
Fy, I refuse sik filthie these or theam
Hou beit at hame mair vncouthnes we wse.
I must confes it war a fekles fead
Quha docht do nocht bot to detract the dead.

94   From LONDON to William Murray

Belouit Brother, I commend me to ʒou.
Pleis you resaiv this lytil pretie ring
With all the rest of goodnes I may do ʒou
Quhan I may vaik fra service of the King
5   Sen for ʒour saik I keepit sik a thing,
I mene the pece of lether from ʒour spur.
If I forʒet, in hemp god nor ʒe hing,
Vncourtessie comes aluayis of a Cur,
Bot ʒe sall find me byding lyk a bur
10   Quhilk lichtlie will not leiv the grip it gettis
And am right dortie to come ou'r the Dur
For thame that by my kyndnes no-thing settis
Thus haif I bene as ʒit and sal be so,
Kynd to my freind, bot fremmit to my fo.

93.title not] no... K 7 quyte] quy... K 8 Name] N... K 9 blame] bl... K 10
Montgomries Muse] Montgomrie... K 14 dead] ... K

95

I   Ladyland to Captain Alexander Montegomrie

My best belouit Brother of the craft,
God if ȝe kneu the stait that I am in.
Thoght ȝe be deif, I knou ȝe ar not daft
Bot kynd aneugh to any of ȝour kin.
    If ȝe bot sau me in this Winter win   5
With old bogogers hotching on a sped
Draiglit in Dirt, vhylis wat evin to the skin
I trou thair suld be tears or we tua shed.   79
    Bot maist of all that hes my bailis bred
To heir hou ȝe on that syde of the Mure   10
Birlis at the Wyne and blythlie gois to bed
Forȝetting me, Pure Pleuman, I am sure.
    So sillie I, opprest with barmie Juggis
    Invyis ȝour state that's pouing Bacchus luggis.

II   Eȝechiel Montgomerie's Ansueir to Ladyland

Beloved Brother, I haif sene your bill
And smyld to sie the sonet that ȝe send
I sie ȝow skornfull thoght ȝe haif no skill
Becaus to play the Poet ȝe pretend.
    Bot sen ȝe craiv ȝour cunning to be kend,   5
Come on Companion, I becall ȝour craks
For all the Poeme (Pleuman) ȝe haif pend,
I am ou'r sair for ȝou and other sax.
    To match Montgomerie thoght a mint thou maks
Thou menes be me, thy Maich and mair nor match.   10
Hou beit thou brave vs (bour) behind our baks,
No man invyis our weilfair bot a wrech.
    Mell not with vs vhose heads weirs laurel plaits.

I.7 skin] s...i... (chin; *supra, 19c* hand) K 10 of the Mure] of (t; *del.*) the M... K
11 to bed] to ... K 13 Juggis] Jug... K 14 Bacchus luggis] Bacchu... K
II.3 skill] sk... K 5 kend] ... K 6 craks] crak... K 7 pend] pe... K 9 thou maks]
th... m... K 13 laurel plaits] l... K

79ᵛ Our Muse drinks wyne vhen thyn bot suims in suaits.
15 If I haif shod ʒou strait or on a vane
Gar Peter Barkley drau the naill agane.

III Ladyland to Eʒechiel Montgomerie

Sir Icarus, ʒour Sonet I haiv sene
Nocht Ignorant vhose bag that bolt come fro.
ʒe lent ʒour Name to feght against ʒour frene
Till one durst neu'r avou him self my fo.
5 I mak a vou and I heir ony mo
Such Campillmuts ʒe better hold ʒou still.
ʒe crak so crouse I ken becaus ʒe'r tuo
Bot I am dour and dou not want my will.
Grou I campstarie it may drau to ill
10 Thairfore it's good in tyme that we wer shed.
My Bee's aloft and daggit full of skill.
It getts corne drink sen Grissall toke the bed.
Come on good Gossopis, let vs not discord.
With Jhone and George ʒe must convoy my Lord.

96a

[1 To my old Maister and his yong Disciple
[2 Tua Bairnis of Beath, by Natur taught to Tipple.

80 **96 THE OLD Maister**

The LESBIAN LAD that weirs the wodbind wreath
With CERES and CYLENUS gled ʒour ging.
Be blyth KILBVRNIE with the Bairns of BEATH
And let LOCHWINNOCH Lordie lead ʒour ring.
5 Be mirrie men, feir GOD and serve the King
And cair not by Dame Fortuns fead a flea.
Syne 'Welcome hame suete SEMPLE' sie ʒe sing,

95.III.2 bag that bolt] bolt that bag K
96a.[a–b] see Notes
96.1 wreath] wr... K 4 ring] ri... K 5 King] K... K 6 flea] fl... K 7 sing] sin... K

'Gut ou'r and let the wind shute in the sea'.
 I, RICHIE, JANE and GEORGE are lyk to dee,
Four crabit crippilis crackand in our crouch.   10
Sen I am trensh-man for the other thrie,
Let drunken PANCRAGE drink to me in Douch
  'Scol frie, al out, albeit that I suld brist.
  Ih wachts, hale beir fan hairts and nych … drist'.

97 Against the God of Love

Blind brutal Boy that with thy bou abuses
Leill leisome Love by Lechery and Lust,
Judge, Jakanapis and Jougler maist vnjust,
If in thy rageing RESONE thou refuises,
  To be thy Chiftanes changers ay thou chuisis   5 80ᵛ
To beir thy baner, so they be robust.
Fals Tratur, Turk, betrayer vnder trust,
Quhy maks thou Makrels of the Modest Muses?
  Art thou a God, no, bot a Gok disguysit,
A bluiter buskit lyk a belly blind   10
With wings and quaver waving with the Wind,
A plane Playmear for Vanitie devysit.
  Thou art a stirk for all thy staitly stylis
  And these good Geese vhom sik a God begylis.

96.8 sea] s… K 9 dee] d… K 11 thrie] thr… K 12 Douch] D… K 14] *cropped*
97.11 Wind] W… K 14 *infra*: Finis. K; (ff. 81–81ᵛ) Auay vane world bewitcher of
my hairt K; *see Introduction*

98

82   Come my Childrene dere, drau neir me
      To my Love vhen that I sing.
   Mak ӡour ears and hairts to heir me
      For it is no eirthly thing
5   Bot a Love
          Far above
      Other Loves all I say
         Vhich is sure
         To indure
10   Vhen as all things sal decay.

83   O my Lord and Love most loyal,
      Vhat a prais does thou deserve.
   Thoght thou be a Prince most Royal
      With thy Angels thee to serve
15   Ӡit a pure
         Creature
   Thou hes lovit as thy lyfe.
        Thou didst chuis
        The refuis
20   Of the world to be thy wyfe.

   Whill I did behold the favor
      Of his Countenance so fair,
   Whill I smellit the sweetest savor
      Of his garments rich and rair,
25   'Oh' I said,
        'If I had
   To my Love ӡon Prince of glore
       For my chose,
       Wold I lose
30   Others all I lov'd befor'.

1–10 *set to music* K; *see Introduction* 2 vhen that] þat quhen Ta 3 ears and hairts] hearts and ears Ta 10 Vhen as] quhen þat Ta (f. 82ᵛ) *blank* K 13 Thoght] Suire Ta 17 as] Ta; al K 18–19] *rev.* Ta 21, 23, 31 Whill] When Ta 22 his Countenance] the face that is Ta 23 sweetest] Ta; suet K 27 To] For Ta 28 my] that Ta 29] I would lose Ta 30 Others all] Ta; Other (jo; *del.*) loves K

Vhill I did these thoughts within me   83ᵛ
    With a secreit sigh confes
Lo my Lord and Love espyd me
    And dreu neir me vhar I wes
        Then a ring   35
        Did he thring
    On my finger that wes fyne
        'Tak', quod he,
        'This to the
    For a pledge that I am thyne.   40

'Nou thou hes that thou desyrit,
    Me to be thy Lord and Love.
All the thing that thou requyrit
    To the heir I do approve
        Ʒit agane   45
        For my pane.
    Only this I crave of thee,
        For my pairt
        Keep thy hairt
    As a Virgin chast to me'.   50

Oh my soul therfor repent the
    Of the love thou hadst before:
Let his countenance content the
    Since he is the king of glore.
        So shall he   55
        Be to the
    All the thing that thou wouldst have.
        In his Love
        Shall thou prove
    Quhat thy heart can wish or crave.   60

31 thoughts within] Ta; words besyd K 33 Lo] Than Ta 34 wes] ... K 37 fyne]
fy... K 38–39 Tak of me this said he Ta 40 thyne] t... K 43 requyrit] reqy(*inde-cipherable*)t K 45 Ʒit] But Ta 48 my] thy Ta 50 to] for Ta 51–60] Ta; *om.* K;
see Introduction

Invectiues Capitane

Allexander Montgomeree
and
Pollvart etcetera

To his Maiestie

All reddie as alreddie I have bene
All reddie shall I be quhill lyf may lest,
All reddie evir sorrow to sustene
On land and sey, at large or fetterit fast,
In trubleous tyme, in boist of fortounes blast,
In heich estate or ȝit in Law degree,
In wealthe or woe, in healthe or seckness cast.
As I have bene alreddie shall I bee
Then if my dewtie may deserve sick fee
Forget not me quhois hart is whoillie ȝouris
Whois lyf and deathe sayis bot forget not mee
Submitting all into your Princelie Poueris.
   And since alreddie (Sir) I am your thrall
   Forget not me amangis your servantis all.

       Tullibardine

99 Invectiues Capitane Allexander Montgomeree and Pollvart

I   Ane Flytting or Invective be Capitane Alexander
     Montgomerie aganis the Laird of Pollart

Fals feckles fowlmart, loe heir a defyance,   2v
Go sey thy science, do, droche, quhat þow dow,
Gang trot in ane tow, mandrak but myance,
We will heir tyance, peild pellet, on that pow.
For mony ʒeld ʒow thow cald fra ane know   5
And hid þame in ane how, stark theif, quhen þow staw þame,
Mensweirand thow saw thame and maid bot a mow,
Syne fyld by the row quhen they come that aw þame.

Thy dittay wes deid, þow docht not deny it.
Thy trumperie wes tryd, thy falset they fand.   10
Burrio the band, cor mundum þow cryd,
Condempnit to be dryd and hung vp fra hand.
Quhill þow payit ane pand, in that stour þow did stand.
With ane willing wand þow wes weill scurgit
Syne finallie furgit quhy thow left þe land.   15
Now, Sir, I demand how this poyd may be purgit.

Title] Invectiues Capitane Allexander Montgomeree and Pollvart et cetera
Tu; The Flyting Betwixt Montgomery and Polwart F1; Polwart and Mont-
gomrie Flyting Ru
I.title] Montgomerie to Polwart F 2 sey] asay Ru 3 Gang trot in] Trot tyke to
F 4 tyance] tydance F4 pellet] Polwart F4 on that] of thy F 5 For mony]
Manie F thow cald fra] hast thou cald ouer F; hes cald over Ru 6 And] Syne F
7 Mensweirand] Mensweiring F 8 by] in F they come] the man came F; the
men come Ru 9 docht] dare F 11 Burrio] Burreau F; But reave F5 12 to be
dryd] to die Ru; to be die'd F5 hung] hang F fra] fre Ru 13 that] a F 14 þow]
thy skin F 15 finallie furgit] feinzedly forged F; feinzedly forge F5 quhy thow]
how thow F; thow Ru 16 Sir] sirs F this] his Ru may] can F

Schort mischappin schit that schuip sick ane swnȝie,
Als proud as ȝe prunȝie ȝour pen salbe plukkit.
Cum kis quhair I cuckit and change me þat cwnȝie.
20 ȝour gruntill lyk grunȝie is gracles and gukkit.
ȝour mowthe wald be mwkkit till ȝe wer instructit.
ȝour flirdome wanfuckit, ȝe tersell of ane taid,
ȝour meitter mismaid hes louslie lukkit.
Thow cwmelie conductit thy termes on ane slaid.

2ᵛ 25 Arpit angrie Ettercoip and auld vnsell aip,
Thow grenis to gaip vpon the grey meir.
Ga pley with thy peir, I sall pay the lyk a paip,
Thow will rax in ane raip or þe end of the ȝeir.
I promeis the heir to thy chaftis ill cheir
30 Till þow gang and leir to lik at the þe lowderis.
With pottingeris poulderis except þow ovrsmeir,
That scab that ȝe beir will scall the to þe schoulderis.

Tusche, twyscheillit trumpour, with tratling þow trowis
Makand vane vowis to mache þe with me.
35 With þe poynt of ane kie weill brunt on thy browis,
Now god salve kowis quhairfra come ȝe.
I tell þe, bumbie, ane doggis deid þow will die
Quhen I sall syne sie the hung be þe heillis
For stuff þat þow steillis into þe cuntrie.
40 Na man may save the for þow art past the seillis.

17 Schort mischappin] Yet wanshapen F that] thou F 18 pen] pennes F 19 me
þat] that Ru 20 gruntill lyk] gryses grunzie F 21 wald be] most be F; must me
Ru till ȝe wer] while ye be F 22 ȝour] Foule F flirdome] frildome Ru ȝe tersell]
tersell F 23 louslie lukkit] lousilie lucked F 24 Thow cwmelie] I grant thow F
on] in F4 slaid] staid Ru 25 Arpit] Little F 26 Thow grenis] Throw grenis Tu;
Ye grein for F 27 Ga pley] Play F I sall pay] or I'll pull F 28 Thow will rax] Go
ride F or þe end of the] for this noble new F 30 Till þow gang and] Except thou
go F lowderis] lowder F 31 poulderis] powder F except] thy selfe F 32] The
Castell ye weir weill seiled on your shoulder F 33 Tusche] This F with] with his
F þow trowis] he trowes F; trowes F3 34 Makand] Making F þe] him F 35
poynt] print F 36 salve] sen Tu; salbe F kowis] crowes F; witness F5 37 I tell þe]
For all your F bumbie] bombill F; bombling F4 ane doggis deid þow will die]
ye'r war'd a little wee F; ȝe warred a little wie Ru 38 Quhen I sall syne] I think for
to F the] you F; thee F3 39 stuff] termes F into þe cuntrie] of ald poetrie F 40]
Now wha soud trow thee, that's past baith the seilis F

Proud poysonit pykthank pervers and puir,
I dow not induir to be dobbit with ane duik.
I'se fell the lyk ane fluik flat on þe fluir.
Thy scrowis obscuir ar borrowit fra sum buik.
Fra lyndsay þow tuik, þow art chawceris cuik   45
Ay lyand lyk ane ruik if na man wald scar the.
Bot I sall debar the þe kingis kitching nuik.
Thow art fleyit for ane luik bot I sall ryd nar the.

Stif stridand stikdirt, Ise gar þe stink
To teiche þe to think with thy maister to mel.   50
On sick as thy sell, pert pratling prink,
Culd þow not wair ink thy tratlingis to tel?
Hy, ȝe huirsone, to hel amangis þe feyndis fel
And drink of þat wel that poysonit thy pen
Quhair devillis in þair den dois ȝammer and ȝell.   55
Heir I the expell from all christinit men.

II The Secund Invective

Vyld, venymous vipper, wanthreivinest of thingis,   3
Half ane elph, half ane aip, of nature denyit,
Thow flyttis and þow freittis, þow fartis and þow flingis,
Bot this bargane, vnbeist, deir sall þow by it.
'The kuif is weill wairit þat twa home bringis',   5
This proverb, peild pellet, to þe is applyit.

I.41 puir] periured F 42 induir] indure it F dobbit] bitten F 43 fluik] duik F5
flat] flatlingis F 44 scrowis] sorrowes Ru are borrowit] ar borrow Tu; are bor-
rowed F 45 art bot] art F 46 Ay] Still F na man wald] gif men wald not F 47 I
sall] beist I F kitching] chimney F 48 art fleyit] flees F 49 Stif] False F I'se] I
will F 50 To teiche þe to think] How durst thou mint F 51 pert] little F prink]
pink F pick F5 52 Culd þow not] Could not F4 tratlingis] tratling F 53 Hy ȝe]
Hoy F; How Ru 54 And] To F drink] (drik) drink Tu 56 christinit] Chris-
tian F 56 infra: Finis be Apollois poet / Of his first reply to Pollart Tu
II.title] Montgomeries answer to Polwart F 1 Vyld] Vyle F; Wyld Ru wan-
threivinest] wanthriftiest F 3] Thow flait with a countrey, the quhilk was the
Kings F Thow] Throw Tu 4 this] that F 6 peild] foull F3 Ru pellet] Pelt F;
pett Ru

Sprung speidder, of spyt thow spewis furth springis.
Wanschaippin wowbat, of þe Weirdis invyit,
I can schaw how, quhair and quhat begate the
10   Quhilk wes nather man nor wyf
        Nor humane creature on lyf.
        Fals stinkand steirar vp of stryf,
            Hurkland howlat, have at the.

Into the hinderend of harvest on ane alhallow Evin
15   Quhen our goode nichtbouris ryddis, if I reid richt,
        Sum buklit on ane bwnwyd and sum on ane bene,
        Ay trippand in trowpis fra the twie licht.
        Sum saidlit ane scho aip all grathit into grene,
        Sum hobling on hempstaikis, hovand on hicht,
20   The king of pharie with þe court of the elph quene
        With mony alrege incubus ryddand that nicht,
Thair ane elph on ane aip ane vnsell begate.
        In ane peitpot by powmathrone
        That brachart in ane bus wes borne.
25   They fand ane monstour on the morne
            War facit nor ane cat.

7 Sprung] First F furth] furt Tu; furth F; out F3 Ru spyt] spit F; spite F5 8 Wanschaippin] Yet, wanshapen F 9 schaw] tell thee F quhair, and quhat begate] when, where, and quha gat F; Quhen, or quhere, and quha gat Ru 10 Quhilk] The quhilk F 12 Fals] Thou F 13 Hurkland] False F 14 Into] In Ja F on ane] on Ja F 15 ryddis] dois ryde F if] nou gif Ja 16 bwnwyd] benwod Ja; bunewand F 17 trippand] trottand Ja F in] into Ja 18 saidlit] sadland Ja F; sadled F3 19 hobling] hotcheand Ja; hobland F hempstaikis] ane hempstalk Ja F on] on a Ja; to þe F 20 with þe] and his F of] with F 21 elrich] elfish F5 ryddand] was ryddand F 22 on ane] Ja F1; and ane Tu; one Ru 23] Besyde a pot baith auld and worne Ja; Into ane pot by Pomathorne F 24 That] This Ja

The wirdsisteris wandering as they wer wont than   3ᵛ
Saw revinis ruge at þis rat be ane rone ruite.
They musit at þis mandrak mismaid lyk ane man,
Ane beist bund with ane bunwyd in ane auld bute.   30
How this ghaist haid bene gottin to ges they begane,
Swir sweillit in ane swyneskin and smeirit our with sute.
The bellie that it buir they bitterlie ban.
Of that mismaid mowdywart mischeif they mwte.
That cankerit camscheocht vncristnit they curs   35
     And baid þat it suld nevir be but
     The glengoir, gravell and þe gut
     And all þe plaigis þat euir wes put
       In pandorus poysonit purs.

The coche, þe connoche, the collik and þe cauld,   40
The coirdis, þe colt evill, þe claspis and the cleikis,
The hunger, þe hart euill, þe hoist mot þe hauld,
The boche and þe barbillis and þe cannogait breikis,
The ringbane, the banescheven on thy sprung spauld,
The feirsie, þe falling evill that fellis mony freikis,   45
Ourgane with angilberreis as thow growis auld,
The choikis, the charbunkill with þe wormis in thy cheikis,
The snuf, þe snoir, þe scheippisch, the schanker
     With the bleid and bellithrow,
     Thy bytting battis, the baneschaw,   50
     The mischeif on thy melt and maw,
       The scabbis and þe canker,

28 ruge] rugand F þis rat] that ratton F 29 þis] that F; the Ru F3 mismaid] vnmade
F 30 bunwyd] bonewand F 31 this] that F 32 Swir sweillit] Weil swyl'd F; Weill
sweddelled Ru 33 it buir] it first bair F they bitterlie] full bitterly they F ban] (bane;
del.) ban Tu 34 that] this F3 35 cankerit camscheocht] cruiked camschoche croyll F
36 And] They F it] baiche F; baith Ru nevir] not F 38 euir wes] first were F; first
was Ru 39 In] Into F poysonit purs] purse F 40 þe] and the F 41 þe colt evill] and
the cout-evil F; and the Goutewill Ru 42 þe hoist mot] and the hoist stil F; and the
host schall Ru 43 and þe cannogait] with the Cannigate F 44] With bockblood and
beanshaw speven sprung on thy spald F; With bokblud bainespavin sprong in þe
spald Ru 45 freikis] a freek Ru 46 with] all with F 47 choikis] kinkhost F with þe]
and F thy] the F 48 þe] and the snoir F; and the snoit F5 scheippisch] chaudpeece
F the schanker] and the chanker F 49 bleids] bleid Tu; blaids F; bladdes Ru 50
Thy bytting battis] The bleiring and F; The bleiring bats and F4 51] With the
mischief of the melt and maw F 52 scabbis] clape F and] the F5

The frenesie, the fluikis, the fykis and þe felt,
The feveris, the totteris with the spenȝie fleis,
55   The doyt and the dysmell indifferentlie delt,
The pelodie, the palsie, þe poikis lyk peis,
The neising, the snytting with swaming to swelt,
The wandevill, þe wildfyre, þe womeit, þe weis,
Þe mair, the migrum, þe mureill, þe melt,
60   The warbillis, þe wood worme that doggis of deis,
  The phtiseik, þe twithȝaik, þe tittis and þe tirrillis,
        The panefull poplasie, the pest,
        The rottin roup, þe auld rest,
        With paines and parlasie opprest
65   And nippit with þe nirrilis,

The bruik, þe byllis with blisteris and blainis,
Baith beld and bleirit, brokin bakit, staneblind,
Wirriand on wind flaiffis and windie wainis,
The hoikis in þi choikis, hakkit heillis ay behind,
70   Thy swyne poikis, þe poistrume and pisching with pane,
Hydropasie, herschaw and hyves sall the bind,
The skunnering cattaris and hartskaid remanis,
Baith kruikit and crampit and chitterrit to the chin,
  The stayne and þe studie, the stane and þe sturdie,
75   Lipper lispane of the lidder ill
        Of dubbis and dreggis to drink thy fill:
        No wyf will wische the wors with hir will
          For þow art not wurdie.

53 fluikis] fluxes F fykis] fyk F felt] fele F 54 totteris] fearcie F 56 pelodie] powlings F þe poikis] with pocks F 57] The swerf and the sweiting with sounding to swelt F 58 wandevill] weame-ill F; wonbill Ru þe weis] and the vees F 59 the migram] and the migrame F; and the ingrame (mygrame LH margin) Ru þe mureill] with meathes in F þe] thy Ru 60 þe wood-worme] and the wood-worme F that doggis of] wherof dogs F 61 þe tirrillis] and tirles Ru 62 the pest] and pest F 63 rottin roup þe] rot the roup and the F 64 paines and parlasie] parles and plurisies F 66–91] om. F

The messillis, the mwillis, þe mallange mak þe mantane,
The fumyng, þe flewme, þe foothing, the flame,   80
The gelling, þe gulsocht, þe gall hauld þe gauntane,
The stane worme, þe ringworme not slaiking of swame,
The wirsome, þe wraittis, not wormis be thow wantane,
The pluirasie, þe pluckeuill ay dwynand in ane dwame,
Hoikis, hoillis in thy heillis with the fyre of Saint Antane, 85
The louslie phirasie, the Tarrie vncame,
Ay ryvand of ane reif of venymeous water,
    The lymphat, lunscheocht lithargie,
    The aikand aixis extasie,
    Desyrand daylie for to die   90
        Bot nevir the better.

'Wo worth', quod the Weirdis, 'the wichtis that the wrocht.
Threid bair be thair thrift as thow art vanthrewin.
Als hard be thair hansell þat helpis þe to ocht.
The rottin rim of thy womb with ruikis salbe revin.   95
All boundis quhair þow byddis to baill salbe brocht.
Thy gall and thy gwysorne to þe glaidis salbe gevin,
Ay schort be thy sollace, with schame be thou socht.
In hell mot þow hawnt and hyd the from heavin,
And ay as þow growis auld, So eik in anger   100
    To live with lymmeris and outlawis,
    With hurcheonis aittand haipis and hawis,
    Bot quhen þow cumes quhair þe cok crawis
        Tarie no langer.

4ᵛ

92 Weirdis] wordes Ru wichtis] wicht Tu; wights F wrocht] brocht F4 94 þe
to ocht] þe ocht Tu; thee to ought F 95 thy] my F4 ruikis] rockes Ru 97 to
þe] to F 98 be thou socht] be socht Tu Ru; be thou sought F 99 hawnt] haunt
thee F 100 growis auld] auld growes F eik in] eikand be thy F 103 quhen]
where F4 þe cok] cockes F 104 Tarie no] Tary there na F

105 'Botht schame and sorrow on hir snowt that sufferis the
  to sowk,
  Or scho þat cairis for thy creidill, cauld be hir cast,
  Or bringis onie bedding for thy blae bowk
  Or lowsis af thy ludʒeotis so long as they lest
  Or offerris the ony thing all the lang oulk
110 Or first refreschis þe with fuide albeit þow suld fast
  Or quhen thy duddis ar bedirtin þat givis thame ane dowk.
  All gromes quhair thow grainis at thy gruntill be agast.
 Als freamit be thy fortoune As foule is thy forme.
   First sewin ʒeir be thow dum and deif
115   And eftir that a commoun theif.
   Thow art markit for a meischeif,
    Foule vnworthie worme.

  'Vntrowit be thy tounge ʒit tratling all tymes,
  Ay fals be thy fingeris bot laith to confes,
120 All cuntreis quhair thow cwmes accuse þe of crymes,
  Ay þe langer that thow live thy luk be the les,
  ʒit still be þow reivand bot rude of thy rymes.
  All ill be þow vsand and ay in exces.
  Ilk moone be þow mad fra past be the prymes,
125 Syne plaigit with povertie thy pryde to oppres,
 With wolfis and wilcattis thy weird be to wander
   Draiglit throw dirtie dubbis and dykis
   Taigilt and towsilt with toun tykis.
   Say, lowsie lowne, quhat evir þow lykis,
130   Thy tounge is no sclander'

105 Botht schame] Shame F the to] þe Ru 108 ludʒeotis] lingals F; lingʒeiles Ru lest] may lest F 109 all the] all Ru 110 albeit] howbeit F 111 bedirtin] beshitten Ru thame] the F 112 All] As Tu; grainis] greits F gruntill] ganting F 113 freamit] froward F is] ill Ru 114 ʒeir] ʒears F 115 a] ay a Ru 116 Thow art] Thus art thou F 118 Vntrowit] 119] fourth line of stanza F Ay] And F 121] second line of stanza F that thow] that Ru 122] Ay raving, and rageing, [reaving and raigne Ru] in rude rat rymes F 124 prymes] pryme Tu 125 Syne] Still F 126 wolfis] warwolfes F 128 Taigilt and towsilt] Tousled and tuggled F 129 lowne] lyar F quhat evir] what F 130 is] it is F5

Fra þe weirdsisteris saw the schaip of that schit,   5
'Littill luk be thy lot', quod they, 'quhair þow lyis'.
'Thy fowmart face', quod þe first, 'to flyt salbe fit'.
'Nikniven', quod þe nixt, 'sall nureische þe thryse.
To ryde post in Elphin none abiller nor it'.   135
'To dryve doggis furth to dryt', þe third did devyse,
'All thy dayis sall þow be of thy bodie bot a bit.
As suche as þow seames, als scharp be thy syse'.
Then dewlie they deimit quhat deid it suld die.
    The first said, 'suirlie of a schot'.   140
    The nixt said, 'in a rynnand knot'.
    The thrid, 'be thrawing of þe throt
        Lyk a tyk on a trie'.

Then wilfullie voitit the weirdis in ane voce
The deid of þat daiblet and then they withdrew.   145
To let it ly þair allone they thocht littill lose
In ane den be ane dyksyde or the day dew.
Thair a cleir cumpany cum eftir close,
Nickniven with hir nymphis in nomber anew
With chairmes from cathnes and chanrie of Ros   150
Quhais cwnning consistis in casting a clew.
Sein' þat same thing, they said to þameself,
    'This maikles monstour is meit for ws
    And for our craft commodious,
    Ane vglie aip and incubus   155
        And gottin of elf'.

131 Weird Sisteris saw] sisters had seene F 132 be thy] thy Ru quod they] there F 133 fowmart] froward Ru 134 Nikneven] Nieniren Ru thryse] twyse F 135 in] to F 136 furth to] but to F; but of Ru did] can F 137 thy] they Tu of] but of Ru thy body] ane body F bot a bit] a bitt Ru 138] Als such is this sentence as sharp is thy syse F; Als suith is this sentence as sharp is thy syse F3 Ru; Als faith is this sentence as sharp is thy sile F5 139 Then] Syne F 141 nixt said in] second of F 142 þe] his Ru 143 on] ouer F; out owre F5 144] When the weird sisters, had thus voted all in ane voyce F; When all the weird sisters had thus voted in ane voyce F3 Then] The Tu 145 þat] the F and then they] syne they F; and syne then Ru; then syne they F3 146 þair] all F thocht] thoght it F 147 dyksyde] dyk F 148 cum] came soone F; and soone Ru 151 a] of a F 152 Sein' þat same thing they] They seeing this sairie thing said F þameself] themselves Ru 153 maikles monstour] thriftles thing F 156] Gotten with ane elf F

Thir venerabill virginis quhome ȝe wald call wiches
In tyme of thair triumph they tirlt me that taid.
Sum bakward on broidswis and sum on blak bicheis,
160   Sum in steid of ane staig over ane stark munk straid,
From the heavinis to the hellis sum hobbillis, sum hichis,
With þair mowthis to þe moone sick murgeonis they maid,
5ᵛ   Sum be force and effect the four windis fichis
And nyne tymes wirdersones about the thorne raid
165 And glowrand to þe ground grivouslie gaipis,
      By craft coniurand feyndis by force
      Furth of ane carne bysyde ane croce.
      Thir ladyis licht fra thair hors
      And band þame with raipis

170   Syne bairfute and bair ledgit to bapteis that barne
To ane well went they west by ane wood syde.
They saw the schit all beschyttin and soipit in charne.
On thre headit hecate in haist þair they cryit,
'As we have fund in this feild this fundlin forfarne
175   First his faith he forsaikis, in the feynd to confyde,
Be vertew of thir wordis and of this raw ȝarne
And thryse thre and threttie knottis on ane blew thred
And of deid menis memberis weill schewit in ane schoe
      Quhilk we have band from top and tae
180   Ewin of ane hundreth men and mae.
      Now grant ws, goddesse, ere ve gae
      Our dewtie to doe,

157 ȝe wald] the warld F 158 they tirlt] tirr'd F that] the F 159 bakward on] back-
ward raid on F sum on blak] some black F5 161 heavinis to the hellis] how to the
[how the F5] hight F hichis] hatches F 162 sick murgeonis] murgeons F 163
and] in F 164 thorne] throne F 165 And] Some F grivouslie] some grievously F
166 by force] perforce F 168 Thir] The F4 licht] lichted F; lichtand Ru 170
Syne] Some F2 171 To ane well went they west] Till a water they went F they]
thy Tu 172 saw the schit] fand the shit F; fand then shit F2 and soipit in] in the
awin F; in his awin F3 173 On] One ane Tu; On F in haist þair] to heir them F
174 this feild] the field F 175 faith] father F5 the feynd] thee F 176 of] *om.* F; be
Ru 177 thryse thre and] whill this thrise F; quhill their thryse Ru ane] this F
threed] threed byd F; blew threid F5 178 deid] thir F schewit in] sow'd to F 179
band] tane F and] to F 181 goddesse] devillis Tu 182 dewtie] dueties F

'Be þe moving of þe mone, mapamone and þe kingis ell,
Be phlegitoun, the sevin starnis and þe Chairlvane,
Be the hicht of þe heavin and lawnes of hell,   185
Be all the brether of belliallis buird in ane band,
Be the pollis, þe planeittis and singis all tuell,
Be þe michtis of þe moone lat mirknes remane,
Be the elementis that our craft can compell,
Be the floodis infernall and fureis of pane,   190
Be all the ghaistis of our gang that dwellis þair doun,
    In signe of stikis, that stinking strand,
    And pluto that our court command,
    Resave this harlot of our hand
      In name of Mahoun.   195

'That this worme in our wark sick wonder can wirk   6
And throw poysoun of þis poyd our practik prevaillis
To cut of our cwmmer to cum to the kirk
(For the half of our help I hauld heir is haill),
Let nevir þis vndoche of evill doing Irk.   200
All boundis quhair it bydis may brocht be to baill.
Of blis let it be als bair as þe birk
That tittest þat taidrell may tell ane ill taill.
Let no wo in þis warld to þis wrache be wantit'.
    Be they haid said the fyre flauch flew,   205
    Bothe thunder, weit and windis blew
    Quhair be the cwning cummeris knew
      Thair asking wes grantit.

183] *third line of the stanza* F: Be the hornes, the handstaff and the kings ell 184] Be the windes and the weirds and the Charlewaine F 185] *first line of the stanza* F heavin] hevins F and lawnes] hownesse F; be the hownesse Ru F3 186] Be thunder be fyreflaughts be drouth and be raine F 187 pollis þe] Poles and the F singis] the Signes F 188 þe michtis] the mirknes F; mirknes F3 189 that] all that F craft] crafts F draftis Ru 190 floodis] fiends F and fureis of] and the furies in F 191 Be] Gar F our gang] the deid F 192 signe of] Lethe and F that stinking strand] thae stinkand strands F; the sturkand strand Ru 193 our] your F 194 harlot of] howlat aff F hand] hands F 196 sick wonder can] some wonders may F 197 throw poysoun] through the poyson F þis poyd our] this pod our F; that podde our Ru; this pouder F5 practic prevaillis] pratiques prevaill F 198 to cum] fra comming F 199 I hauld heir is] and hes it heir F; and has it in their F5 200 evill] ill F 201] But ay blyth to begin all barret and baill F 202 Of blis] Of all blis F 203 þat] the F 204 wo] vice F to þis wrache] in this wanthrift F 205 fyre flauch] fireflaughts F 206–08] 232–34 Ru 206 weit] raine F 207 the cwming] their comming F; *om.* Ru 208 the] their F

Quhen þe cummeris that crab with pluto contractit
210 They promeist as parentis for thair awin pairt
Ane mother of mischeif an they micht mak it,
Ane Imp of all ill most meit for þair airt.
Nikniven as nwrische to teich it gart tak it
To saill the see in a sive bot compas or cairt
215 And milk of ane harin tedder that wyfis suld be wrakit
And þe kow give ane choppin wes wont give a quart,
That bairnis suld bane baith bloode and banis
    Quhen they haue neither milk nor meill,
    Compellit be hunger for to steill,
220   Then sall they give him to the deill
        Ofter nor anes.

Fra the dames devoitlie haid done þair devoir
In having that hurchoun, they haistit þame hame
Of that mater to mak amangis þame na moir,
225 Saifing nixt þat þe Nunes þat nirlend suld name.
Thay cowit ther kytrell the face of it bair
And Nippit it so done neir that to sie it wes schame,
Syne callit it peild pollart, they peild it so sair.
'Quhair we clip', quod þe cwmmeris, 'it cummeris na kame
6ᵛ 230 For we have to Mahoun for hansell his hair'.
    They maid it lyk a scrapit swyne
    And ay as they pold it they gart it quhryn
    And schuif as we may sie syne
        The face of it bair.

209-34] *stanzas rev.* F 209 Quhen] Fra F4 crab with] crab had with F 210 parentis for] parents syne for F 211 mother] mover F mak] for to make F 212 Ane imp] As ane imp F; As a Nimphe Ru meit] apt F 213 Nikniven] Nieniren Ru teich it] teach Ru 214 the see] sure F 215 that] thoght F 216 wont] wont to F 217] Many babes and bairnes sal blisse thy bair banes F 219 be] for F for to] to Ru 220 give him] give thee F; giv Ru 221 Ofter] Able ofter F 222-34] *om.* Ru 222 Fra the] When thae F 223 that] this F 224 amangis þame] remained F 225 nirlend] working F; worling F3; *om.* Ru 226 cowit ther] kow'd all the F; know'd all the F3 bair] before F 227 done] doones F that to] to F 228 Syne] They F peild] pull'd F 229 it cummeris] there needs F 230 have] have heght F his] this F 232 pold it] cow'd F; cowk'd F4 gart] made F 233] It shav'd the self, ay on sensyne F 234] The beard of it sa bair F; The beard was sa bair F3

Be ane eftir midnicht þair office they endit   235
For then it wes na tyme for trumpouris to tairie.
Sum bakvard on biches and broodsowis bend.
That cruikit crokadeill quyt with þame they carie.
To þe cocatrice in ane creill they send it
Quhair sevin ȝeiris it sowkit, sweillit, singit and sarie.   240
The kin of it be þe cry incontinent kend it,
Feching fude for to feid it from the field of pharie
Ilk elph of þame all broch ane almond oisteris
       Bot wes no dayntie dische,
       Ane foul phlegmatik fowsum fiche,   245
       Insteid of sawche on it they piche,
         Sic fude, sick foisteris.

And first fra þe father syne sindrie haid fed it,
Mony mwnkis and marmaidynis come with þe moþer.
'Black boiche on þair bouk', quod thay, 'that first breid it',   250
Ay offerring þat vndoche fra ane to ane vþer.
Quhair that serpent sowkit sair wes to sched it
Bot belyve it began to bwkill the brother.
In þe bark of ane bowrtrie quhyllumis they bed it.
Thair taillis with the tounge of it they lyk and ruther,   255
Sum fartand, sum flyrand, thair phisnomeis þi flyp,
       Sum schevilland þair chaftis and slavere chekis,
       Sum, luiking lyce, in þe croun of it keikis,
       Sum in thair oxteris it cleikis
         Lyk a bagpype.   260

235 Be ane] Being Ru they] was F 236 For then it] At that tyd F 237 biches and broodsowis bend] horseback brauely [breiflie Ru] they bended F 238] That cammosed Cocatrice they quite with them cary F 239] To Kait of Creif in ane creill soone they gar'd [gar F₅] send it F 240 sowkit sweillit] sat baith F singit] singlit Ru 241 kin of it] *om.* Tu; kinne of that Ru 242 Fetching] Syne fetch't F; from the feild of] fast furth of the Ja; furth fra the F 243 almond] almous house F 244 Bot wes no] Indeid it was a F 247] Sik food feed sik a foster F 248 And first] Syne F father syne sindrie] fathers side finely F 249 marmaidynis come] marmasits came F 250] Black botch [both F₅] fall the breist and the bellie that bred it F breid it] breid... Tu 251 offerring þat] offered they that F 252 serpent sowkit sair wes] smatched had sowked sa sair it was F 253 bwkill] buckie F; buckle F₃ 255] All talking [tuckine Ru] with their tongues the ane to the other F 256] With flirting and flyring their Physnome they flype F 257-58] *rev.* F 257] Some choppes the kiddes into their cheeks F chekis] chek Tu 258 luiking] luikand F; looked F₅ keikis] breikis Ru 259 oxsteris] oxster hard F 260 a] an auld F

7   With mudgeounes and murgeounis and mowing þe bane
         They leit it, they lift it, they loif it, they lak it,
         They graip it, they grip it, It greitis, they grane,
         They bind it, they baw it, they bed it, they brat it,
265   It skitterit, it squeillit, they startit ilkane,
         Quhill þe ky in the cuntrie startillit and chaisit
         Quhilkis rairing ran rid wood rowtand in a rane,
         Þe wild deir in thair den þe din hes displasit,
     The cry wes vglie of aipis, elfis and owlis
270   That geis and geislingis cryis and craikis,
             In dubbis dowkit duikis and draikis,
             All folkis for feir þe feildis forsaikis
             And the toun tykis ȝowlis,

         Sick ane mirthles music thes menstrallis did mak
275   That cattell keist capriellis behind with þair heillis
         Bot littil tent to þe toune to twne leit þame tak
         Bot rameist ran reid wood and raveld þe reill.
         Fra þe cummeris thame knew they come with a crak
         To coniure the vndoche with clewis and creill,
280   All þe boundis þairabout grew bleknit and blak,
         For the din of that daiblet raisit þe devillis.
     To coniure with a clap fra caves they came far
             And for godbarne gift they gave
             To teich that theif to steill and rave
285   Bot ay þe langer þat it live
             The warld be þe war.

261 mowing þe bane] mouing the braine F 262] They lay it they lift [last Ru] it they louse it they lace it F 263 greitis] greets and F they] the Ru 264 bind] bed F bed] bind F brat] brace F; braste Ru 265 it squeillit] and skarted F; it scarted Ru startit] skirl'd F 266 Quhill] All F startillit] skarred F 267] That roaring they [that Ru] wood-ran and routed in a reane F 268 in] F; fra Ru þe din] their din F 269 cry wes] cry was sa F; cryes so Ru aipis elfis] Elfes Aipes F 271 dowkit] douks down F; doune Ru 272 folkis] beasts F 274 mirthles] nurishles Ru thes] thir F; ther Ru 275 That cattell] Whill ky F; Whilk ky Ru 276 Bot littil] Littill F þe toune to twne] their time the toone F their tyme the tome Ru 277 rameist ran] Bot ay rammeist F; But ay remaniest F2 þe reill] in their reeles F 278] Then the cummers that ye ken came all with a clak F 279 the vndoche] that coidyoch F and creill] in their creeles F 280 All] Whill all F þairabout] them about F 281 that daiblet] thir daiblets F; theis daiblettes Ru 282] To concurre in the cause they were come sa far F 283] For they their [were Ru] god-bairne gifts wald giue F 284 that theif] the child rave] reiue F 286 warld be] warld should be F 286, *infra:* Finis quod Alexander Montgomerie contra Pollart Tu

III The First Flyting in Forme of Reply to Alexander Montgomereis First Flytting be Pollart

Despitfull speidder, puir of spreit,   7^{v}
Begune with baibling me to blaime,
Gok, wyt not me to gar the greit.
Thy tratling, trewcour, I sall taime.
Quhair þow beleivit to win a naime   5
Thow sall be blasit of ane beild
And sall resaue baith skaith and schame
And syne be forcit to flie the feild.

Thy raggit roundaillis, reifand royt,
Sum schort, sum lang and out of lyne   10
With skabrous collouris, fowsome floyt,
Proceiding from ane pynt of wyne
Quhilk haultis for fault of feit lyk myne
3it, fuuill, þow thocht na schame to wreit þame
At menis command that laik ingyne   15
Quhilkis, doytit dyvouris, gart the dyt þame.

Bot, gokit guis, I am rycht glaid
Thow art begun in wreit to flyt
Sen, loun, thy language I have laid
And put þe to thy pen to wryt,   20
Bot, dog, I sall þe so dispyt,
With priking put þe to sik speid
And caus þe, cur, that warklum quyt
Syne seik ane hoill to hyd thy heid.

title] Polwarts Reply to Montgomerie F 2 Begune] Begins F 3 not me] me not
F 5 Quhair þow beleivit] When thou beleeues F 6 blasit of ane] banish'd of all
F 7 sall] syne F resaue] receite F5 8 syne] sa F 9 reifand] raveand F 10 and out]
and Tu; some out F 12 Proceiding] Proceidand F; Proceided Ru 13 fault] laike
F 15 laik] laikes F 16 Quhilkis] quhilk F gart] gars F 19 laid] (h) laid Tu 20 þe
to] þe Tu 21 Bot] Now F 22 put þe] put Tu; put thee F 24 seik ane] ane Ru

25 Ʒit, knave, acknawledge thyne offence
    Or I grow crabit for to clair the.
    Ask merce, mak obedience
    In tyme for feir that I forfair the.
    Evill sprit, I will no langer spair the.
30 Blaid, blek þe to bring in ane gwyse
    And to mak pennance sone prepair the,
    Syne pas furth as I sall devyse.

8 First fair threid bair with fundrit feit
    Recanting thy vnseamelie sawis
35 In pilgramage to allareit
    Syne be content to quyt the caus
    And in thy teith bring in the tawis
    With bekis my bidding to abyd,
    Quhidder thow will let belt thy bawis
40 Or kis all cloffis that standis besyde,

    And of thir tua tak to thy chois
    (For thy awin profeit I procure the)
    Or with ane prik in to thy nois
    To stand content I sall conjure the,
45 Bot at this tyme think I forbuir the
    Becaus I can not trait þe fairer.
    Sit þow this charge, I will assure the
    The secund salbe sumthing sairer.

25 Ʒit] Ʒel F Yeelde F4 26 for to] and sa F 28 for feir that I forfair the] for feir that forfair the Tu; leist for feirles I forefaire Ru; for fear least I forfair thee F 29 Evill] Ill F4 30 in ane] in Ru; in a F 31 to mak] to drey F drie Ru 33 fundrit] fundeit Tu; fundred F 35 Allareit] Aller, eit F5 36 Suin] Syne F 37 in] me F 39 thy] thy belt thy Ru 41 to] thou F4 42 thy awin] thy (awin; superscript) Tu; thy Ru 45 at] all Ru 47 Sit] Sir F5

IV The secund Invective aganis Alexander montgomerie replying To his secund flytting

Blaird, baibling bystour baird, obey,
Learne, scybald knave, to knave thy sell,
Vyld vagabound, or I invey,
Cuistroun, with cuiffis the to compell,
Tryit tratling trewcour, þe trewth to tell.   5
Stowp þow nocht at the secund charge,
Mischevous mischant, we sall mell
In landward language loud and large.

Quhairfoir, loun, as þow luifis thy lyf
I bothe command and counsall þe   10
For till eschew this sturtsome stryf   8ᵛ
And with thy manlie maister grie.
For þis effect I sumound the
Be publict proclamacioune
Cum and compeir vpon thy knie   15
And kis my fair fundacion.

Bot, lord, I lawche to sie the bleitter,
Gloir in thy ragmentis rasche, and raill
With mankit, manschocht, manglit meitter
Trottand and twmbland top over taill   20
As carlingis comptis þair fartis, doyd snaill.
Thy rowstie ratryme maid but mater
I culd weill follow wald I saill
Or pres to fische within thy watter.

[IV] title] The secund Invective aganis Alexander montgomerie replying To
his secund flytting that beginis In þir wordis Tu; Polwart to Montgomerie F 4
to] *om.* Tu 5 Tryit] Yet F þe trewth] trewth F 8 In landward] With laidly F
language loud and large] langwad we sall mell Tu 9 Quhairfoir] Where F 13
For] To F sumond] counsell F2 14, *infra* (For till eschew this sturtsome stryf;
del.) Tu 15 Cum and] Gowke to F 16 fair] foull F 17 bleitter] bluiter F; bloost-
er Ru 18 and] to F 19 mankit manschocht manglit] mankit manschocht man-
kit Tu; mighty manked magled F; mingtie mankit mangleit Ru 20 Trottand
and twmbland] Tratland and tumbland F3; Tratland and traland Ru 21
comptis þair] ther F 22 ratryme] ratrymes F 23 saill] seaill F; seall Ru; saill F3

25 Onlie becaus, oule, þow dois vs it
   I will wreit vers off commune kynd
   And, swinȝeour, for thy saik refuis it
   To crab þe, bumlar, by thy mynd.
   Pudlar, I pittie the so pynd
30 To buckill him that beiris the bell.
   Iak stro, be better anes ingynit
   Or I will flyt aganis my sell.

   Bot breflie, beist, I anser the.
   In sermone schort I am content
35 And sayis thy similitudis vnslie
   Ar nawayis verie pertinent.
   Thy coyd comparisonis asklent
   Ar monstrous, lyk to the that maid thame.
   Thy barking borrowit is vnlent
40 Ȝit wer they waik let the invaid þame.

9 Also I may be Chawceris man
   And ȝet thy maister not the les.
   Bot, wolf, thow waistis in cop and Can.
   In gluttonie thy grace I ges.
45 Ga, drunkin dyvour, þe addres
   (Or borrow þe Ambassattis brekis)
   To heir me now thy prais expres,
   Knaif, if þow can vnwait thy cheikis.

27 it] that Ru 28 bumlar] bumbler F; humbler F5 29 thee so] thees a F3; thee a
F5 30 that] that him that Ru; thar F4 31 Iak stro] Jackstio F5 anes] one Ru 32
will] sall F 33 I] to F 37 coyd] tyr'd F 38 to the] the Mule F 39 barking
borrowit is vnlent] borrowed barkings violent F; borrowed barking is violent
Ru 40 waik] worse F the invaid] men out war F 42 And ȝet thy] And thy Tu;
And yet thy F; And ȝet thy Ru 43 thow] that F; what F4 in] on F; both Ru
46 Or] And F þe Ambassattis (*see note*)] thee ambassed F; the ambassed Ru;
thee embessed F3 47 thy] þei Tu 48 vnwait thy] without wat F

First of thy iust genologie,
Tyk, I sall tell þe trewth I trow. 50
Thow wes begottin, sum sayis to me,
Betuix þe devill and ane duin kow
Sa quhen the feynd wes a nicht fow
In banket birland at the beir.
Thow sowkit syne ane broid blak sow 55
Amangis þe middingis mony ȝeir.

On ruittis and ruinscheochis on þe feild
With nolt þow nurischit neir a ȝeir
Quhill that þow past both puir and peild
Into argyle sum guide to leir, 60
As þe last nicht did weill appeir
Quhill þow stuid fidging at the fyre
Fast fykand with thy hieland cheir,
My flytting forcit þe so to flyre.

Into þe land quhair þow wes borne 65
I reid of nocht bot it is scant
Of cattell, clothing and of corne
Quhair welth and weilfair bothe dois want.
Now, taidface, tak þis for na tant.
I heir ȝowr howsing is richt fair 70
Quhair howland howlattis ay do hant
With robene reidbrest but repair.

50 Tyk I] I F 51 to me] me F 52 duin] dumme Ru 53] Ane night when that the
fiend was fow F; And at nicht quhen that the fiend was fow Ru 55 sowkit] swal-
lowed Ru broid blak] sweit brod F; sweit bed Ru 56 mony] many a F 57 ruin-
scheochis on] runches in F 58 neir] was F 59 Quhill] When F 60 guide] lair F
63 with thy] with Tu 64 flytting] flyte Fȝ 66 it] (ȝow) it Tu is] was F 67] *om.*
Ru 68 Quhair] Or Tu; Where F 69 taidface] taider-face Ru na] ane Tu; na F
71 howland] howlring F 72 repair] repover Ru

9ᵛ   The cuntre folkis within the land
       I knaw ar men of meikill rent
75   And luifing as I vnderstand
       Quhilk in ane innes wilbe content
       To live and leave þair hous in lent,
       In lent moneth and long in summer,
       Quhair tuelf knichtis kichingis hes a vent.
80   It will to furnes do þame cwmmer.

       In stoir of lambes and lang taillit wedders
       Þow wattis quhair money cupple gais
       In scheilling tyit fast in tedderis
       In felloun flokis of anes and twais
85   Abreid athort ȝour bankis and brais.
       Ȝe do abound in coill and calk
       And thinkis lyk fuillis to fly all fais
       With Targettis, twilȝeis and twm talk.

       Allas puir hudpyk, hunger bittin,
90   Accustomit with scurrulitie,
       Bydand lyk bystouris all beschittin
       In feildis without felicitie,
       Bair, barrane, but fertilite,
       For fault of cattell, corne and gerss,
95   Ȝour bankettis of sick vilitie,
       Deir of þe dog brane of þe mers.

73] The lords and lairds within that land F 75 luifing] liuing F 76 wilbe] we be F 77 leave] let F 78 lent] lentron long in] the lang F 79 kichingis] chimneys F 80 it will to furnes do] Quhilk for to furnish dois F furnes] furmes Tu 81 In] For F 82 wattis] knowes F cupple] couples F 83 In scheilling] For stealing F 85 Abreid] Abyd Ru 87 lyk] as F3 fly] fley F4 89 hudpyk] hood-pikes F; hog-pyks Ru 91 Bydand] Rydand F; Bystaud Ru; Ryding F4 92 felicitie] fertilitie F 93 but fertilite] with sterilitie F; with stertily Ru 95 sick vilitie] most nobilitie F 96 dog brane] dog brawne F; dogbran Ru of] in F

Woif, witles vanter, war nor wys,
Cwstroun, þow wald cor mundum cry,
Over laidnit loune with lang taillit lyse,
Thy doyttit dytmentis sone deny,   100
Trewcour, or I thy trumperie try
And mak a legent of thy lyf.
For flyt I aneis, folk will cry fy
Then þow wilbe warreit with ilk wyf.

V   Followis ane Interludge Aganis Captain alexander   10
       montgomery Befoir pollartis thrid and last Invective

Schir swyngeour, seing I want wairis
And sawis to slaik the of thy sairis
This present from þe pottingaris
        I think meit to amend þe.
For feir thy fevir feidis on follie,   5
With fasting stomak tak oydollie
Mixt with ane mowthfull of melanchollie
        From flewme for to defend the.

Syne pas ane space and smell ane flour
Thy Invart pairtis to purge and scour,   10
Tak þe thre byttis of ane ill hour
        And rubarb baich and bitter,
This dewlie done but onie din,
Syne sup sex soipis but sumthing thin
Of the deill scad thy guttis within   15
        To haill þe of þe skitter.

IV.97 Woif witles] Witless F war nor] were thou F 98 mundum cry] mundum
Tu 99 Over laidnit] Ou'r-laden F 100 dytmentis] dytings F sone] some Ru
104 warreit with ilk] war'd with euery F
V.title] Polwarts Medicine to Montgomerie being sicke F; Polwarts Medecine
to Mountgoumry Ru 1 wairis] wars F3 2 sawis] salues F 4 I] Me F3 Ru 5 For
feir] First for F; First or Ru feidis] feid F on] in F5 10 pairtis] pairte Ru 11 ill]
black F 13 This] This is F5 14 Syne sup] Sup syne F soipis] soopine Ru 16
To] The Tu þe] thy F

Vnto ane bed syne mak þe boun,
Tak ane sweit serop worth ane croune
And drink it with þe devill ga doun
20   To recreat thy sprit,
And last of all, craig to ane coird,
Send for ane powder and pay ford
Callit þe vengence of þe lord
        For thy muuge mowthe so meit.

10ᵛ 25 Gif this preserve ȝe nocht from pane
Pas to the potticaris agane
Sum recepeis dois ȝit remane
        To haill bruik, byle and blister
As diadregma quhen ȝe dyn
30 And diagducolicum wat with wyne
With powder I drait verie fyne
        And mair ȝit quhen ȝe mister.

10ᵛ   **VI** The last and thrid flytting Aganis Captain alexander
        Montgomrie as ane reply To his third Invective

Infernall, froward, fumus fureis fell,
Curst crabit cankert Clotho, comper to quell
ȝon chairibald, ȝon cative execrabill.
Provok my pen profundlie to distell
5   Sum dour dispyt to daunt ȝon dewill in hell
And dryve with duill to deid detestabill
That mad malicious monstour miserabill,
Ane tyk tormentit, tratling out of Tun,
That rynis reidwood at ilk midis of þe moone.

V.17 ane] thy F 21 to] in F 24 so] most F 25 this] that F2 ȝe] thee F 28 and] or
F 30 diagducolicum] diabolicon F with] in F 31 verie] fellon F
[VI].title] The last and thrid flytting Aganis Captain alexander Montgomrie as
ane reply To his third Invective Beginand In thir wordis (vyld ve; *del.*) In the
hendendis Tu; Polwarts third flytting against Montgomerie F 1 fumus] feam-
ing F 2] Curst, canker'd, crabed (Clotho) help to quell F Clotho] sclawe Tu 4
Provok] Provyde F distell] (dis; *del.*) distell Tu 5 in] of F 7 That] This F 8
tratling out of tun] troting out of towne FRu 9 rynis] rymes F

Reveill ȝour rairing and eger Ire   10
Inflamit with fairfull thundring thudis of fyre
To plaig the poisonit pykthank pestalent
With fleing fyreflauchis burning bricht and schyre,
Devoir ȝon Devillish dragone, I desyre,
And waist his wareit venym violent,   15
Coniure þis beistlie begger impotent,
Suppres all power of king pluttois sprit
That byddis and barkis in him als blak as Jet.

Bot reekie rewkis and rewinis, ere ȝe ryve him,   II
Desist, delay his death quhill I discryve him,   20
Syne ryplie to his rude raving reply.
To doolfull dollour derflie or ȝe dryve him,
Throw plutois power all pleasur I depryve him.
The loun man lik his womeit and deny
His schameles sawis lyk sathanis slavish smy   25
Quhais maneris with his mismaid memberis heir
Dois correspond as planelie dois appeir.

His peild pallat and vnpleasant pow
The fowsome flokis of flaeis dois overflow
With vamis and wondis all bleknit full of blainis.   30
Out our þe nek, athort his nittie now,
Ilk louse lyes linkand lyk a large lint bow
That hurts his harnes and bruisit, birny branis.
Weill baillit, þe bluid evanischit from his wanis,
With scoiris and crakis athort his fronsit front,   35
In runkillis run ruwth in þe stewis brunt.

10 Reveill] Renew F; Resceiv Ru and] rage and F 12 the] this F 15 wareit] wea-
ried F3 Ru violent] virolent Ru 17 King Pluttois] this euill F 18 That] And
Tu 19 reikie] reikis Tu 21 rude raving] raving rude F; reauing rood Ru 22
doolfull] dreadfull F 23 all pleasur I] pleasure to F 24 deny] (his; *del.*) deny Tu
25 slavish smy] slavishing Tu 27] *om.* Ru 31 his] is Ru 32 lowse lyes linkand]
lowsie lyce lykand Tu; lous lyes lucked Ru ane large lint bow] ane lint pow Tu;
a lardge ... bow Ru 33] His hairie hair and bruisit birny branis Tu; That hurts
his harnes, and pearse them to his paines F 34] Whill wit and vertue vanish'd
fra the vaines F 35 scoiris and crakis] scarts and scores F fronsit] froisnit Tu;
frozen F 36 ruwth in] within F stewis] stewes all F3; stew brunt Ru

His luggis baith lang and lasie quha can bot lak
That to þe trone hes tane so mony tak,
With blastit bowellis boldin with bristin baill
40   And streichlie hairis blavin widdersins abauk,
For fundrit beistis for fault of humour wak
Hes not þair hairis so sned as vtheris gude.
The blairit buk and bystour, to conclude,
Hes richt trim teith sumquhat sett on ane thraw
45   Ane toppit turde richt tewchlie for to taw,

With laidlie lippis and lynning syd turnd out,
His nois weill lit in bacchus blude about,
His stinkand end, corroptit as men knawis,
Contageous cankers clairis his sneivilling snowt,
50   His schewin schoulderis schawis þe merkis, but dout,
Of tarledderis, tewch tyris and vþer tawis,
And girdis of gaylayis growand new in gawis,
11ᵛ   Swa all his fowsome forme thairto effeiris,
Quhair with for filth I will not fyll ȝour earis.

---

37 lasie] leane F can bot] cannot F3 38 hes tane] he can Tu; hes tane F mony tak] many a tacke F boldin with bristin baill] boldin with brist in baill Tu; bounden with bruised blude F 40 streichlie] hapning F; happing Ru widdersins] widders(...; *del.*) ins Tu 41 For fundrit] For fundeit Tu; Foot foundred F; For fundred Ru humour] food full F 42 totheris] other F 43 bystour] boystrous F 44 on] in F 47 lit] little Ru 48 men] men wel F5 49 clairis] (s) clairis Tu; carues F sneivilling] snasling F; snasting Ru 50 but] no F 51 tarledderis tewch] teugh tarledders F 52 new] now F 53 thairto] thair Tu; thereto F 54 Quhair with] The quhilk F; Vith whilk Ru

[VII]

Bot of his conditionis to carp for a quhyll
And compt зow his qualiteis compassit with cair,
Appardoun me, poettis, to alter my styil
And wissill my wers for fylling þe air.
Returning directlie agane to Argyle   5
Quhair last þat I left him baith bairfute and bair,
Quhen richtlie I raknit thy race verie vyld,
Discendit of a dewill as I did declair.
Bot quhilk of þe godis sall gyde me aricht
    Abhorring sa abhominabill,   10
    Sua doolfull and detaistabill,
    Sua knavishe, cankerit, execrabill
        And vareit ane wicht?

In Argyll with þe gatis he зeid amange glennis
Ay vsing þe office þair of a beist   15
Quhill blistles wes banisit for handling þe hennis
Syne fordward to flanderis fast fleid or he ceist.
From þe poore anis þe pultrie he plukit be þe pennis.
Incressing In corpis þe hart in his breist
And curage inclynit to knaverie, men kennis,   20
To pestilent purpoisis planelie he preist,
Bot trewlie to tell þe trewth vnto зow
    In nawayis wes he wyse.
    He vsis cairtis and dyce
    And fled na kynd of vyce   25
        Or few as I trow.

title] The second part of Polwarts third flytting F; *om.* Tu 4 wissel] wyslie F 7
Quhen] Where F3 Ru thy] his F 8 Discendit of a dewill] Discending of Deuils
F did declair] declare F5 9 sall] will F 12 cankerit] canker Tu; canker'd F 13
vareit] wearied F3 Ru 14 with þe gatis] with the gate Tu; amang Gaits F
amang] within F 15] Ay [All Ru] there using offices of a bruit beast F 16 þe] of
F 17 fast fleid] fast he fled F 18 From þe] From F 19 Incressing in corpis] De-
lighting in theft F in his] of his F 21 purposes] purpose F5 preist] preisis Tu
22 þe trewth vnto] all the trueth unto F; the truth that unto F5 24 vsis cairtis]
used both Cairts F; vsed both caird Ru 26 few] flew Ru

He was ane fals schismatik, notoriouslie namit.
Baith hurdome and homeceid vnsell he vsit.
For schismes and Symonie þat smachart wes schameit.
30   Pryde, Ire and Invy that vndoche abvsit,
Of caching and coweitting bitterlie blameit,
For baidrie and bordaling lukles he lusit,
Thrist, drynes and drinking that devill defamit.
Fals, fenʒeit and flytting with flatterie infusit,
35 Maist sinfull and sensuall, schame to rehers,
         Quhais feckles fuilichnes
         And beistlie brukilnes
         Can na man I ges
              Weill put in vers.

40   Ane vairloche, ane woirwolf, ane wowbat of hair,
Ane devill and ane dragoun, ane doyld dromodarie,
Ane counterfute cuistroun that clerkis dois not cair,
Ane claverand cohubie that crakis of þe farie
Quhois favourles phisnome dois dewlie declair
45   His vyces and viceousnes, thocht I wald warie.
Arcandam astrologiam, a lanterne of lair,
Affirmis his bleiritnes, to wisdome contrarie,
Betaikning bothe bobbing and beldnes in aig,
         Greit fraud and fals dissait
50   Capping with coyd conceat.
         Witnes sum vers he wreit
              Half in a rage.

27 ane] (ane) ane Tu notoriouslie] notorlie Tu 29] With all the seuen sinnes, the smatched was shamed F 30 that] this F 31 Of caching and coweitting] For greedy covetousnes F 32 lusit] lufit Tu; loued F 33 Thrist] *om.* Tu drynes] dryves Ru that devill] the dyvour F; the dytour Ru 34 fenʒeid] fenʒeir F5 and flytting with flaterie] and flytting with Tu; with flyting and flattery F infusit] refused Ru 38] *om.* Ru I ges] as I gesse F3 39 in] into F3 40 vairloch ane] warloch and F5 of] but F Tu 41 and ane] ane F5 doyld] deid F 42 clerkis dois not] does clarks not cair F2; clarcks doth cair Ru 43 crakis] cruckes F2 45 thocht] although F 46 Arcandam] Arcandam's F 47 contrarie] contrair Tu; contrary F 48 Betaikning] Betaiking Ru bobbing and beldnes in] babling and beldnes of F; baibling and boldness of Ru 49 fals] foull F 50 Capping] Cappit F coyd] quyet 52 Half] Half daft F

166

Ane Indagine also concerning that cace
Suirlie sayis it is a signe of a licherous lowne,
His pailnes mixt pairtlie with broun in the face   55
Arcandam ascryvis to baibling ay boun
And tratling intemperat, tymeles but place.
Ane cowart, ʒit cholerik and drunk in ilk toune,
And als his ass earis an signe in schort space
That frenatik fuil sall grow mad lyk mahoun,   60
Bot ʒit sall he live lang, allace quhilk wer los
     For sick ane traitling tratour   12ᵛ
     And baibling blasphimatour
     Wes nevir formit of natour,
       Sua gukit ane guise,   65

Quhois honorabill origine þe note of his name
Callit etimoligie beiris richtlie record.
His surname it flowis fra tua termes of defame
From mont and gomorath quhair dewillis, be þe lord,
His kynsmen, wes clenelie cast out to his schame   70
That is of þair clan quhome Chryst hes abhord
And beiris of þe birth place þe horribill name
Quhair sodomeit synneris with smwik wer smord.
Now sen all is suth is said of this smy,
     Vnto þe cappit clerk,   75
     A prettie peice of wark
     That bitterlie dois bark,
       I mak þis reply.

53 Ane Indagine] Ane Anagrame F; His Anagrame F3 Ru   also] also (sayis;
del.) Tu   54 Suirlie sayis] Sayes surely F   55 mixt] next F   56 ascryvis] descryues
Ru   58 drunk in] drunkin Tu; drukin in Ru   59 an] they F   60 That] The F   61
allace quhilk wer] quhilk allace were a F   62 traitling] tryed F   tratour] taitour
Ru   63 And] A F   66 honorabill origine] origine noble F   68 it flowis] doth flow
F   71 is of] this F5   72 þe horribill] their horrible F   73 smwik] stinking F   74 is
suth is] is suith that's F; his suith that's Ru   of this smy] sonʒie Tu   75 þe] that
F   76 A] And F   78 mak] may F3 Ru

VIII Ane vther

Vyle villane and war nor I have cald þe,
Thy widderit vane is dammischit, deid and dryit.
Beschittin bystour bodie, I forbaid þe
To mache with me or elis þow sall deir buy it.
5   Thy speich but purpois, sporter, is espyit
That wreitis of wichis, warlochis and of wratches
Bot Invective, aganis him þow defyit.
Rob Stene, ȝe raif, forȝetting quhom ȝe mache.

Leve boigillis, brouneis, gyr carlingis and ghaistis.
10   Dastard, þow daffis that with sic dewillrie mellis,
Thy peild perambillis als prolixtlie lastis,
Thy reasonis sawres of reik and nothing ellis,
13   Thy sentences of swit richt sweitlie smellis,
Thow sa neir the chymlay nuik þat maid þame,
15   Seik be þe ingle amangis þe oister schellis,
Dreidand my danger durst not weill debait þame.

Thy tratling, tinklar, wald gar ane taid spew
And cairl cattis veip vinager with bothe þair ene.
Thow said I borrowit blaidis, quhilk is not trew.
20   The clene contrarie, smachart, salbe sene.
I neuir haid of that making ȝe mene,
Ane vers in wreit, in print or ȝit perquere,
Quhilk I can prive and clenge me wonder clene,
Thocht singill votes no wreiter can forbeir.

title] Polwarts last flytting against Montgomerie F 1 Vyle] Wyld Ru nor] than
F5 cald þe] tauld thee F; cauld Ru 2 vane] wame F dammischit] damnified F
deid and dryit] and dryd F 3 bodie] baldly F 4 mache] mell F buy it] byit Tu
sall] should F 5 sporter] porter F5 6 and of wratches] wraiths and wratches F 7
Invective] Invectiues F þow] well F 8 ȝe raif] thou raues F ȝe mache] thou
matches F 11] *om.* F5 als] ouer F 13 richt] sa F 14 sa] sat sa F 15 Seik] Fast F 16
Dreidand my] Dreadand my F; Dread and in Ru not] no F debait] debar F5 17
ane taid] Taides F 18 bothe þair] their F 19 quhilk] that F 20 The clene] The
F smatched] fals smatched F 23 clenge me] clenge Ru 24 votes] wordes F
25 speikin] speeches F 28 þe] that F 30 speichis] speech F 32 dar] can F3 Ru 34

To prive my speikin probabill and plane,   25
Thow man confes þow vsit my inventioun.
I raknit first thy race, syne þow agane
In þe same sort maid of thy maister mentioun.
Thy wit is waik with me to have dissentioune,
For to my speichis þow nevir maid reply.   30
At libertie to ly is thy intentioun.
I ansuer ay quhilk þow dar not deny.

Thy freindis ar feyndis, of aipis þow fenȝeis myne,
With my assistance saying quhat þow can.
I compt sik kynrik better ȝit nor thyne,   35
Cheiflie of beastis þat ar most lyk to men.
Grant, guis, þat my inventioun waris the than,
Without þe quhilk þow micht haue barkit waist,
And laid the ground quhairon thow, beist, begane
To big þe barge quhairon þow braggis maist.   40

The lak of Iudgment may be als persawit
Thir tua cheif pointis of reasoun wantis in þe.
Thow attribuittis to aipis quhair thow hes ravit
The illis of hors, a monsterous sicht to sie.
Na mervell that ill wyn ill wairit be,   45
For all thir illis thow staw, I am certane
From simplis dytmentis of ane hors did die
Or porterfeildis that dwellis into dumbartane.

Amangis thes illis of aipis quhilk thow hes tauld   13ᵛ
Thocht to ane hors perteining properlie,   50
Thow puttis þe spaven in þe former spauld
Quhilk vsis in þe hinder hocht to be.
Fra horsmen anes thy cunning heir and sie

quhat] all F 35 kynrik] kindred F thyne] mine F2 36 ar most lyk to men] most re-
semble man F 37 guis] gif F the] thine F 39 And] I F 40 barge] brig F 41 The]
Thy F 43 ravit] reaued Ru 45 wyn] won F; wyne Ru 46 thir] these F; the Ru
am] am right F 48 Or] Of F dwellis] dwelt F 49 thes] the F quhilk] that F 51
former] forder F 52 Quhilk] That F
54 haue] get F 56 thow] thou's F; thow shall Ru 58 nor] than F 61 mowt tyme]

I feir auld Allane haue no moir ado.
55 Allace puir man, he may ly doun and die
Syn thow succeid to weir the siluer scho.

Forder þow fleis vith vther foulis vingis
Ourcled with cleirar collouris nor thy awin
But speciallie with sum of simpillis thingis
60 Or for ane plukit guis thow haid bein knawin
Or lyk ane cran in mowt tyme soone ourthrawin
That man tak ay nyne steppis befoir scho flie,
So in þe gut þow micht have stand and blawin
As long as thow lyis gravellit, lyk to die.

65 I speik not of ȝour viteous divisiounes
Quhair thow pronuncit bot ȝit proponit bot pairt,
Incummerit with so mony coyd infusiounes
Quhilk schawis ye rimde but rethorik or airt.
Thy memorie is schort, beschirew thyn hairt,
70 Speikand of ane thing twyse or thrys at aneis
And can not from ane proppit place depairt
Except I wer to force the with quhin staneis.

For, crokodeill, thow ...
Of ignorence. Fy, fuill, thinkis þow no schame?
75 Thy pikkillit puir paremeonis but skill,
Pykit from Irisch Italianis, ar to blame,
Beggit from poetis brokingis for to blame.
For laik of language I wat weill þow dois it
Making that vertew vice to thy defame
80 Quhair evrie minnym aucht to be refuisit.

mounting F 64 lyis] lay F 65 ȝour] thy F 66 thow] throw Tu pronuncit bot]
pronounces and F proponit] propones F 67 coyd confusiounes] coyd infus-
iounes Tu; tryed confusions F 68 ye rimde] ye rinde Tu; thy rime F 70
Speikand of ane thing] Telling ane thing ouer F 71 proppit] proper F 72 force]
frig F 73–80] *om.* F 73] *om.* Tu 80 minnym] minmyn Tu
[VIII].81 gif þow wald now] if that thou wald F 82 Weining] Meaning F5 84]

The thingis I said gif þow wald now deny   14
Weining to wry þe veritie with wylis,
Lik quhair I laid and pikill of that py.
Thy knaverie knawin, credence from þe expellis,
The feckles folie all þe air defylis,   85
I find so mony faultis ilkane our vther.
First I man tell the all thy staitlie styllis,
Hence I beteich þe to thy birkin brother.

IX   Pollart Guid Nicht

Fonnd flytter, scheittis schytter, baccoun bytter befyld,
Blunt bleitter, padok speitter, pudding eitter pervers,
Hen pluker, closet muker, hous cukker, vere vyld,
Tanny cheikis, think þow speikis with thy breikis, foul ers,
    Woode lyk hudepyk, ay lyk to live in lak,   5
    Flour þe pin, scabbit skin, eit it in þat þow spak,

Gum gait, gallit and scald, foul fallit, quhy flait þow?
Steill ȝow, fill tow, þow dow not defend þe,
Rum royt, fonnd floyt, doyld doyt, sillie fuuill,
Quhat if I wald out cry 'Fy, fy', folk wald fell the,   10
    Sweir sow, ay fow, doyld kow, foul fall thy banis,
    Richt styld defyld, woodwyld ilk mone aneis,

Thy knavery, credence fra the quite exyles F 85 The feckles] Thy feckless F;
Thy fecks Ru 88 Hence I beteich] And syne bequeath F; Henc I beteich Tu
birkin] (bir; *del.*) birkin Tu
IX. title] *om.* F 1 scheittis] shit F befyld] all defyl'd F 2 speitter] pricker F 4
think] I think F 5 Woode lyk] Wood tyk F; Woodelyk Tu 4 Tanny] (pad;
del.) Tanny Tu; Tauny F 6 it in] it F5 spak] spake F; speiks Ru 7 Gum gald]
Gum gait Tu; Gumgad F gallit and scald] bald skade F foul fawit] foull foull
faide Ru quhy flait þow] why flait thou foole F 8 tow þow] tow now thow F 9]
Quha kend thy end, false fiend [flend Ru], phantastick mule F 10] Thief smy,
they wald cry, fy, fy, to gar end thee F 11 ay fow doyld kow] doyld kow ay fow F3
Ru 12 Richt styld] Very wild F wood wyld] ay wood wyld F
13 mismaid invaid me] thou's defate; now debate [debate the Ru] F 14] Hush

Tairie taid mismaid, invaid me if þow dow,
Lik laidill, husche paidill, schyt þe saidill, þowis be drest,
15   Kreschie sowtter, scho cluitter, mensche mowter, dar þow mow?
Swamp sandie come fra candie with grandie opprest,
      Led preif, lo, theif, mischeif on thy lippis,
      Blaird baird, thy revaird is prepaird for thy hippis,

Bumbill baitie Ise defait the, now debait the if þow dar,
20   Tarmigant, and þow vant, Ise dant þe with dinging,
Taid bak, swith pak, and thow crak cum not nar,
Sillie snaik, lene raik, rak ane aik with þe hinging,
      Vnhallat, peillit pallat, ryp wallat quhen þow spotches,
      Mischanchit, ill pancit, thryse lancit of þe boches,

14ᵛ 25   Saitling slaiker, glaid glaiker, rumraiker for releif,
Lounatik, frenatik, schismatik, swinȝeour, sob.
Tuirdfacit, ay chaisit, almaist fyld for ane theif,
Meslie kyt, and þow flyt deill dryt in thy gob,
      Cruik mow, widdiesow, soone bow or I wand the,
30   Hellis ruik with thy buik, leif þe nuik I command þe,

Land lowper, licht scoipper, raggit rowpper lyk a revin,
Halland schaiker, drawcht raiker, bannok baiker beschittin,
Craig in perrell, twm barrell, quyt þe querrell or be schevin,
Rude ratler, common tratler, poore pratler out flitten,
35   Hellis spark, skald clark, and þow bark I sall belt þe,
      Scaid scald ourbald, soone fauld or I melt the,

padle lick ladle shyte sadle, [thows be drest Ru] do thy best F 15 þow mow]
thou F5 15 mow) (mai) mow Tu 16] Ragged railer, sheep stealer, double dealer,
thou's be drest F; *om.* Ru 17 Led] Fals F; Folle F5 lo] leane F on] fall F thy]
thy (mov; *del.*) Tu 19–24] *om.* F 19 dar] (...) dar Tu 24 ill] (thryse) ill Tu 25
Saitling] Erse F 26 frenatik schismatick] frematick Ru 28 deill] Ile F 29 Cruik
mow widdiesow] Tait mow, wilde [woodie Ru] sow F 30 Hellis] Hell F3 Ru
32 beschittin] all beshittin F 34] *om.* Tu 35 Hellis spark skald] Hell spark scab-
bed F; Hell sparke scalded Ru 36 I melt] melt F5
37 twm mwggis] toome the mugs F 38 man] must F 39 brek nek] widdie neck

172

Laisie luggis, leap Iuggis, twm mwggis on þe midding,
Tanny flank, reidschank, pyk thank, I man pay the,
Spew blek, brek nek, cum and bek at my bidding,
Fals loun, mak þe boun, Mahoun man have þe,   40
    Rank ruittour, scurliquitour and Iuittour, nane fower,
    Decrest, opprest, possest with plutois power,

Cappit knaif, proud slaif, ȝe raif vnrokkit,
Quhillis slaiverand, quhillis claverand and vaiferand with vyne,
Greidie, gukkit, puir, vnplukkit, ill Instructit, ȝeis be knokit,   45
Gleyit gangrell, auld mangrell, to þe hangrell vith pyne,
    Callumniatour, blasphimatour, fals tratour most vntrew,
    Thy cheiping and peiping with weiping þow sall rew,

Mad manter, vane vanter and hanter of sclavrie,
Keillie lippis, kis my hippis, in grippis þows behint,   50
Pudding prikker, bang þe bicker, nane quiker in knavrie,
Baill brewer, poysone spewer, mony trewer hes bene tint,
    Swyne keiper, dirt dreiper, throt steiper fra þe drowth,
    Lieand lymmer, mony trimmer, I man skymmer in thy mowthe,

Fleyit fwill, mad mule, die in duil on ane aik,   55
Knave kend, christ send euill end on þat mow,
Pudding wricht, out of sicht, thowse be dicht lyk a draik,
Iok Blunt, thrawin frunt, kis þe cunt of ane kow,
    Purspeiller, hen steiller, cat keiller, now I knaw þe,
    Rubiatour, fornicatour by natour, foul fa the,   60

F 40 man] must F 41 ruittour] riatoure Ru scurliquitour] surlie without Fʒ
nane] mane Ru 43 raif vnrokkit] rave [reave Ru] ay unrocked F 44 claverand
and] taverand whiles F; stamerand and Ru 45 vnplukkit] and pluked F 46
auld] (and) auld Tu vith] and sa F 47 fals tratour most vntrew] vyle creature
vntrew F; wyld traitor vntrew Ru 48 weiping] weep Ru 49 and hanter of] ay
haunter in F; ay haunting in Ru 50-51] reversed F 50 kis] kif Tu in] into F 52
hes bene tint] hes bein pind F; had bein pynd Ru 53 dirt dreiper throt steiper]
Land leiper tuird steiper F 54 Lieand lymmer mony trimmer I man] Leane
limmer steale gimmer I sall F 55 in] with F on] or Ru 56 euill end] ill end F;
om. Ru on þat mow] on thee now F 58 kis] kill Ru ane] the F 59 knaw] quell
F 60 fa] befall F
61–65] 62, 64–65 *om.* Fʒ 61 spewd] poyson'd F pot] (and; *del.*) pot Tu 62 and

15   Tyk stikker, spewd viccer, pot likker, I man pay þe,
       Feird fleir, loud leir, and gleir in þe gallowis,
       With a cunt, deid runt, I sall dunt quhill I flie the,
       Buttrie bag, fill the knag, þow will wag with thy morrowis,
65   Coyd clatterer, skin batterer, and flatterer of freindis,
       Vyld, widderit, mathie, midderit and confedderit with feyndis,

       Blind brok, kis dok, boird bloik, banischit townes,
       Allace theifis face, na grace for that grunʒie,
       Beld bissat, marmissat, lance pissat to the lownes,
70   Deid dring, dryd sting, þow will hing but a sunʒie,
       Lik butter, throt cutter, fisch gutter, fyl þe fetter,
       Cum bleitand and greitand and eitand thy letter.

gleir in] gooked gleyar on F   63 With a cunt] Jock blunt F   dunt] punt F   flie]
slay F; pay F5   64 fill the knag] fill knag F   wag] rag F   thy morrowis] the
morrowis Tu; thy fellowis F   65 Coyd] Tyr'd F   66 mathie midderit and]
misordered F   67 brok] blocke Ru   kis] loose F; lousie F5   68 Allace] Hoie F5
71 fyl] fill F   72 thy] thy laidley F   72, *infra*: Finis. Tu; Scriptum per me
iohanem rutherfurd cum manu mea et non aliena. Finnis. Amen. Ru
99a] *om*. Tu 1, 4 amongst] among F4   7 last that thou] last thou F5   13, 16 cul-

99a   Montgomerie to Polwart

Polwart ye peip like a Mouse amongst thornes,
No cunning ye keip, Polwart ye peip,
Ye looke like a Sheip and ye had twa hornes,
Polwart ye peip like a Mouse amongst thornes.

Beware what thou speiks, little foule earth Tade,   5
With thy Cannigate breiks, beware what thou speiks
Or there salbe wat cheiks for the last that thou made,
Beware what thou speiks, little foule earth Tade.

Foule mismaid mytting, borne in the Merse,
By word and by wrytting, foule mismade mytting   10
Leaue off thy flytting, come kisse my Erse,
Foule mismade mytting, borne in the Merse.

And we mell, thou sall yell, little cultroun Cuist,
Thou salt tell euen thy sell, and we mell thou salt yell,
Thy smell was sa fell and stronger than Muist,   15
And we mell, thou sall yell, little cultroun Cuist.

Thou art doeand and dridland like ane foule beast
Fykand and fidland, thou art doeand and dridland,
Strydand and stridland like Robin red-brest,
Thou art doeand and dridland like ane foule beast.   20

troun] custroun F3 14 salt] sall F4 15 was sa fell] was fell F5 than] nor Ru 18-
19] Fykand and fidland lyke Robene reid breist / Strydand and strydland doand
and dridland Ru

THE CHERRIE

AND THE SLAE.

Composed into Scottis Meeter, be

ALEXANDER MONTGOMERIE.

Prented according to a Copie corrected be

the Author himselfe.

EDINBVRGH,

Prented be Robert Walde-graue

Prenter to the Kings Majestie.

Anno 1597.

Cum Privilegio Regio.

THE
CHERRIE
AND THE

SLAE.

Compyled into meeter,
By Captaine *Alexander*
Montgomerie.

EDINBVRGH
Printed by Iohn Wreittoun.
1636.

100   The Cherrie and the Slae, Composed into
      Scottis Meeter, be Alexander Montgomerie.
      Prented according to a Copie corrected be the
      Author himselfe.

    About ane bank quhair birds on bewes
Ten thusand times thair notes renewis
Ilke houre into the day,
    The Merle and Maveis micht be seine,
5 The Progne and the Phelomene,
Quhilk caussit me to stay.
    I lay and leynit me to ane bus
To heir the birdis beir,
    Thair mirth was sa melodius
10 Throw nature of þe 3eir,
        Sum singing, sum springing
           With wingis into the Skye,
        So trimlie and nimlie
           Thir birdis they flew me by.

Title] Off the cherry and the Slae La 4] The merle the maveis, linnet and suan Wq The] Quhair La and] the C1 micht] may C1 5 The] With La the] with La 8 the] thir C1 9 mirth was] noyce are C1 12 With wingis] So heich La Wq 13 trimlie and nimlie] *vice versa* C1 La Wq 14, *infra*: The rest is in the cherrie and the slae Wq

101   The Cherrie and the Slae Compyled into Meeter, By
       Captaine Alexander Montgomery

    About a Bank with balmie bewes
Where nightingals their nots renews
    With gallant Goldspinks gay,
    The Mavise, Mirle and Progne proud,
The Lintwhite Lark and Laverock loud   5
Saluted mirthful May.
    When Philomel had sweetly sung,
To Progne she deplored
    How Tereus cut out her tongue
And falsely her deflorde,   10
        Which storie so sorie
            To shew, ashamd she seemde.
        To heare her, so neare her,
            I doubted if I dream'd.

15   I saw the Hurcheoun and the Hair
     Quha fed amangis the flowris fair
     Wer happing to and fro.
          I saw the Cunning and the Cat
     Quhais downis with the dew was wat,
20   With monie beistis mo,
          The Hart, the Hynd, the Dae, the Rae,
     The Fowmart and the Foxe
          War skowping all fra brae to brae
     Amang the water broxe,
25   Sum feiding, sum dreiding
               In cais of suddain snairis,
          With skipping and tripping
               Thay hantit all in pairis.

     The air was sa attemperate
30   But ony myst Immaculate,
     Baith purefeit and cleir,
          The flouris fair wer flurischit
     As nature had them nurischit,
     Baith delicate and deir,
35   And euery blome on branche and bewch
     So prettily wer spred
          And hang their heidis out ouir the hewch
     In Mayis colour cled,
          Sum knopping, sum dropping
40   Of balmie liquor sweit
          Distelling and smelling
               Throw Phœbus hailsum heit.

16 Quha] Quhilk La 17 Wer] That C1 20 monie] other C1 23 War skowping]
Were skippand C1; Was skippin La 27 With] Some C1 and] some C1 28 han-
tit] huntit C1 31 Baith] C1 La; Bot C2 32 flouris fair wer] feildis ower all was
La 36 wer] was C1; thay La 37 And hang] Syne hang C1; Hingang La the] ane
C1 40 Of] The C1

The Cushat crouds, the Corbie cries,   15
The Cuckow couks, the pratling Pyes
To geck her they begin.
    The Iargoun of the iangling Iayes,
The craiking Crawes, the keckling Kayes,
They deav'd me with their din.   20
    The painted Pawne with Argoes eyes
Can on his Mayock cal,
    The Turtle wailes on withered trees
And Echo answered all,
        Repeiting with greiting   25
            How faire Narcissus fell,
        By lying and spying
            His shadow in the Well.

    I saw the Hurcheon and the Hare
In hidlings hirpling heere and there   30
To make their morning mange.
    The Con, the Conny and the Cat,
Whese dainty dounes with dew were wat
With stiffe mustaches strang,
    The Hart, the Hynd, the Dae, the Rae,   35
The Fulmart and false Foxe,
    The bearded Buck clamb up the brae,
With birsie Baires and Brocks,
        Some feeding, some dreading
            The Hunters subtile snares   40
        With skipping and tripping
            They plaid them all in paires.

18 Iargoun of] largoun or C3

The Cukkow and the Cuschet cryde,
The Turtle on the vther syde
45   Na plesure had to play,
    So schil in sorrow was her sang
That throw her voce the roches rang,
For Eccho answerit ay
    Lamenting sair Narcissus cace
50   Quha staruit at the well
    Quha with the shaddow of his face
For lufe did slay him sell,
      Quhylis weiping and creiping
      About the well he baid,
55   Quhylis lying, quhylis crying
      Bot it na answere maid.

The dew as diamondis did hing
Vpon the tender twistis and ȝing
Ouir-twinkling all the treis
60   And ay quhair flowris flourischit faire
Thair suddainly I saw repaire
In swarmes the sownding beis.
    Sum sweitly hes the hony socht
Quhil they war cloggit soir,
65   Some willingly the waxe hes wrocht,
To heip it vp in stoir,
      So heiping with keiping
      Into thair hyuis thay hyde it,
      Precyselie and wyselie
70   For winter thay prouyde it.

46 schil] still La   47 throw] with La   48 For] And Cı   49 sair] fair Cı; still La   50 Quha] That Cı La   51 Quha with] Quhairthrowe Cı; Quha throw La   52 did slay] that slewe Cı   53 Quhylis] Sair Cı La   54 the] that La   58 twistis and] tuistis Cı La   60 flourischit] did flureis La   62 In swarms the] Ane swarme of Cı La   65 willingly] cunninglie Cı   66 heip] keip La   67 with] for Cı La   68 hyd it] hydit Cı La   70 prouyde it] prouydit Cı La

The aire was sober, soft and sweet,
But mistie vapours, wind and weet,
But quyet, calme and cleare   45
　　To foster Floras fragrant flowres
Whereon Apollos paramours
Had trinckled many a teare
　　The which like silver shakers shynde
Imbrodering beauties bed   50
　　Wherewith their heavy heads declinde
In Mayes colours clad,
　　　　Some knopping, some dropping
　　　　　　Of balmie liquor sweet
　　　　Excelling in smelling   55
　　　　　　Through Phœbus wholsome heat.

　　Mee thought an heavenly heartsome thing
Where dew like Diamonds did hing
Our twinckling all the trees
　　To study on the flourishde twists   60
Admiring natures alcumists,
Laborious busie Bees
　　Whereof some sweetest hony sought
To stay their lives to sterve
　　And some the waxie vessels wrought   65
Their purchase to preserve,
　　　　So heaping for keeping
　　　　　　It in their hyves they hide.
　　　　Precisely and wisely
　　　　　　For winter they provide.   70

To pen the pleasures of that Park,
How euery blossome, branche and bark
Agaynst the Sun did schyne,
 I leif to Poetis to compyle
75 In staitlie verse and lofty style.
 It passis my ingyne.
 Bot as I mussit myne allane
I saw an River rin
 Outouir ane craggie Rok of stane,
80 Syne lichtit in ane lin
 With tumbling and rumbling
 Amang the Rochis round
 Dewalling and falling
 Into that pit profound.

85 To heir thae startling stremis cleir
Me thocht it musique to the eir
Quhair deskant did abound
 With Trible sweit and Tenor iust,
And ay the Echo repercust
90 Hir Diapason sound
 Set with the Ci-sol-fa-uth cleife
Thairby to knaw the note,
 Thair soundt a michtie semibreif
Out of the Elphis throte
95 Discreitlie, mair sweitlie
 Nor craftie Amphion
 Or musis that vsis
 At fountaine Helicon.

71 pleasures] pleasur La 72 blossome] blome on C1 74 to] thir C1 75 lofty] or-
nate C1 La 76 passis] passit La 77 mussit] muffit C2 myne] me La 79 craggie]
craig and C1 La 84 that] the La 85 thae startling] the startling C1; the stertlie
La 86 Me] I C1 87 deskant] daskene La 88 Trible] trubill La 90 Hir] The C1
Diapason] Draffassoun La 91 Ci-sol-fa-uth cleife] resoll fair enttrie clewe La
92 Thairby] Quhairby C1 93 Thair soundt] Thay sownd C1; Sounding La
semibreif] sena brewe La 97 Or] Nor C1 98] That fountoun eloquon La

To pen the pleasures of that Parke,
How every blossome, branch and bark
Against the Sun did shine
    I passe to Poets to compile
In high heroick stately stile   75
Whose Muse surmatches mine
    But as I looked mine alone
I saw a river rinne
    Out our a steepie rock of stone
Syne lighted in a linne   80
        With tumbling and rumbling
            Amongst the Roches round
        Devalling and falling
            Into a pit profound.

    Through routing of the river rang   85
The Roches, sounding like a sang
Where Descant did abound
    With Treble, Tenor, Counter, Meene.
Ane echo blew a Basse between
In Diapason sound   90
    Set with the C-sol-fa-uth cleife
With long and large at list,
    With Quaver, Crotchet, Semi-briefe
And not a Minim mist.
        Compleetly more sweetly   95
            She firdoun'd flat and sharp
        Than Muses which uses
            To pin Apollos harpe.

95 more] C4 C5; and C3 96 firdound] friddound C4

Quha wald haue tyrit to heir that tune
100 Quhilk birds corroborate ay abune
Throw schowting of the Larkis?
   Sum flies sa high into the skyis
Quhill Cupid walkinnes with the cryis
Of natures chappell clarkis,
105   Quha leving all the hevins aboue
Alighted in the eird.
   Loe how that littil God of loue
Befoir me thair appeird
      So mild-lyke and child-lyke
110   With bow thrie quarteris scant,
      So moylie and coylie
         He lukit like ane Sant.

   Ane cleinlie Crispe hang ouir his eyis,
His quauer by his naked Thyis
115 Hang in ane siluer lace,
      Of gold betwix his schoulders grew
Twa pretty wingis quhairwith he flew,
On his left arme ane brace.
      This God aff all his geir he schuik
120 And laid it on the grund.
      I ran als busie for to luik
Quhair ferleis micht be fund,
         Amasit I gasit
            To see that geir sa gay,
125   Persawing my hawing
            He countit me his pray.

---

100 Quhilk birds] C1; Quhilk bidis C2; Þe birdis La 101 schowting] schuitting
La 102 Quha flies] They sprang Ja; Quha flewe C1; Sum flew La 103
walkinnes with] walknis throw Ja; walknit throw C1; walknit with La 104 na-
tures] naturall La 105 Quha] Then Ja 106 Alighted in] He lichtit on Ja; Syne
lichtit on C1; Alleichtit on La 107 Loe how] To here La 108 thair] then Ja 111]
So moylike and coylike C1; So moylie so coylie La 115 lace] cais La 116 betwix]
betwein C1 117 pretty] proper C1 119 This god aff] This god of C1; That god
of La 123 Amasit] I maisit La

Who would have tyr'd to heare that tone
Which birds corroborate ay abone   100
With layes of lovesome larks
   Which climb so high in Christal skyes
While Cupid wakned with the cryes
Of natures chappel Clarks
   Who leaving al the heavens above   105
Alighted on the eard.
   Lo how that litle lord of love
Before me there appeard
      So mild like and child like
         With bow three quarters skant,   110
      Syne moylie and coylie,
         Hee looked like a Sant.

   A cleanly crispe hang over his eyes,
His Quaver by his naked thyes
Hang in a silver lace,   115
   Of gold betweene his shoulders grew
Two pretty wings wherewith he flew,
On his left arme a brace.
   This god soone off his geare he shook
Vpon the grassie ground.   120
   I ran as lightly for to looke
Where ferlies might be found,
      Amazed I gazed
         To see his geare so gay,
      Perceiving mine having   125
         He counted mee his prey.

'Quhat wald thow giue, my freind', quod he,
'To haif thae prettie wingis to flie
To sport thee for a quhyle
130   Or quhat gif I suld len thee heir
My bow and all my schuting geir
Somebodie to begyle?'
'That geir', quod I, 'can not be bocht
Ʒit I wald haue it faine'.
135   'Quhat gif', quod he, 'it coist thee nocht
Bot randring it againe?'
His wings than he brings than
    And band thame on my back,
'Go flie now', quod he now,
140   And so my leif I tak.

His youth and stature made mee stout.
Of doublenesse I had no doubt
But bourded with my Boy,
    Quoth I, 'How call they thee, my child?'   130
'Cupido, sir', quoth he and smilde,
'Please you mee to imploy
    For I can serve you in your sute
If you please to impire,
    With wings to flee and shafts to shute   135
Or flames to set on fire.
        Make choice then of those then
            Or of a thousand things.
        But crave them and have them'.
            With that I wood his wings.   140

'What would thou give, my heart', quoth he,
'To have these wanton wings to flee
To sport thy sprite a while
    Or what if love should send thee heere
Bow, quaver, shafts and shooting geare   145
Somebody to beguile?'
    'This geare', quoth I, 'cannot be bought
Yet I would have it faine'.
    'What if', quoth he, 'it cost thee nought
But rendring all againe?'   150
        His wings then he brings then
            And band them on my back,
        'Goe flye now', quoth he now,
            'And so my leave I take'.

I sprang vp on Cupidoes wingis
Quha bow and quauir baith resingis
To lend me for ane day.
　　As Icarus with borrowit flicht
145　I mountit hichar nor I micht,
Ouir perrelous ane play,
　　Than furth I drew that deadlie dairt
Quhilk sumtyme schot his mother
　　Quhairwith I hurt my wanton heart
150　In hope to hurt ane vther.
　　　　It hurt me, it burt me
　　　　　　The ofter I it handill.
　　　　Cum se now in me now
　　　　　　The butter-flie and candill.

155　　As scho delytis into the low,
Sa was I browdin in my bow
Als ignorant as scho
　　And as scho flies quhill sche be fyrit
Sa with the dart that I desyrit
160　My hand hes hurt me to.
　　As fulisch Phaëton be sute
His fatheris Cart obteind,
　　I langt in Luiffis bow to schute
Bot weist not what it meind,
165　　Mair wilfull than skilfull
　　　　To flie I was so fond
　　　　Desyring Impyring
　　　　　And sa was sene vpond.

141 vp on Cupidoes] so heich on Cupids C1 Quha] The La 145 I] Quha C1 I]
he C1 147 I] he C1 148 schot] hurt C1 La 151 it burt] and burnt C1; and bruit
La 153 Cum] Sum La 155 delytis into] delyttyth in La 156 in] on C1; of La 160
hand] handis C1 La 163 luiffis] Cupiddis La 164 But] And C1 165 than] nor C1
La 166 so fond] forfund La 167 impyring] Inspyring La

I sprang up with Cupidos wings   155
Whose shots and shooting geare resignes
To lend me for a day.
   As Icarus with borrowed flight
I mounted higher than I might,
Ou'r perilous a play.   160
   First foorth I drew the double dart
Which sometimes shot his mother
     Wherewith I hurt my wanton heart
In hope to hurt another.
       It hurt me or burnt mee   165
         While either end I handle.
       Come see now in mee now
         The Butterflee and candle.

   As she delites into the low
So was I browden of my bow   170
As ignorant as she
   And as she flyes while she is firde
So with the dart that I desirde
Mine hands hath hurt mee to.
   As foolish Phaeton by sute   175
His fathers chaire obtainde
   I longed in loves bow to shoote
Not marking what it meande.
       More wilful than skilful
         To flee I was so fond   180
       Desiring impyring
         And so was seene upond.

To late I knaw quha hewis to hie
170 The spaill sall fall into his eie,
To late I went to Scuillis,
To late I heard the swallow preiche,
To late Experience dois teiche,
The Skuil-maister of fuillis,
175 To late to fynde the nest I seik
Quhen all the birdis are flowin,
To late the stabill dore I steik
Quhen all the steids are stowin,
To lait ay thair stait ay
180 All fulische folke espye.
Behynd so they fynd so
Remeid and so do I.

Gif I had rypelie bene aduysit
I had not rashlie enterprysit
185 To soir with borrowit pennis
Nor 3it haue saied the archer craft
Nor schot my self with sik a schaft
As resoun quyte miskennis.
Fra wilfulnes gaue me my wound
190 I had na force to flie
Then came I granand to the ground.
'Freind, welcome hame', quod he.
'Quhair flew 3e, quhome slew 3e
Or quha bringis hame the buiting?
195 I sie now', quod he now,
'3e haif bene at the schuting'.

169 hewis to] hewis La 172] *om.* La 175 to] I C1 La 176 all] as La 178] Quhan as
þe steid is stowin La 181] They find to behind to C1 they] þai La; thy C2 183
Gif I had] Bot had I C1 185 soir] flie La 189 my] the C1 195 now] weill La now]
weill La

Too late I knew who hewes too high
The spaile shal fall into his eye,
Too late I went to schooles,   185
   Too late I heard the swallow preach,
Too late Experience doth teach,
The Schoole-master of fooles,
   Too late I find the nest I seek
When all the birds are flowne,   190
   Too late the stable door I steeke
When as the steede is stowne,
      Too late ay their state ay
        As foolish folk espy.
      Behind so they finde so   195
        Remead, and so doe I.

   If I had ripely beene advisde
I had not rashly enterprisde
To soare with borrowed pens
   Nor yet had sayde the Archer-craft   200
To shoot my selfe with such a shaft
As Reason quite miskens.
   Fra Wilfulnes gave me my wound
I had no force to flee,
   Then came I groning to the ground.   205
'Friend, welcome home', quoth he,
      'Where flew yee? whome slew yee?
        Or who brings home the booting?
      I see now, quoth he now,
        Ye have beene at the shooting'.   210

218 swound] sound C4 C5

As skorne cummis commonlie with skaith
Sa I behuifit to byde them baith,
O quhat an stakkering stait!
200　　For vnder cure I gat sik chek
Quhilk I micht nocht remuif nor nek
Bot eyther stail or mait.
　　My agonie was sa extreme
I swelt and soundt for feir
205　　Bot or I walkynnit of my dreme
He spulȝeid me of my geir.
　　　　With flicht than on hicht than
　　　　　Sprang Cupid in the skyis
　　　　For ȝetting and setting
210　　　　At nocht my cairfull cryis.

　　Sa lang with sicht I followit him
Quhill baith my feiblit eyis grew dim
Throw stairing on the starnis
　　Quhilk flew sa thick befoir my ein,
215　Sum reid, sum ȝellow, blew and grein,
Sa trublit all my harnis
　　Quhill euery thing apperit two
To my barbuilȝeit braine,
　　Bot lang micht I lye luiking so
220　Or Cupid come againe
　　　　Quhais thundring with wondring
　　　　　I hard vp throw the air,
　　　　Throw cluddis so he thuddis so
　　　　And flew I wist not quhair.

199 O quhat an] And þat in La 201 Quhilk] That C1 La nocht remuif] neither
muife C1; nowther deme La 203 My] Myne C1 204 swelt and soundt] swate
and swound C1; swet and sownit La on] oure La 208 Sprang] Spran La 211
sicht] flycht La 212 baith] that La 213 Throw] For La stairing] C1; staruing
C2 215 blew and] sum blew sum La 216 Sa] Quhilk C1; That La 219 lye
luiking so] lye luiking tho C1; haiff luikit so La 221 Quhais] Quha La 224
And] He La

As scorne comes commonly with skaith
So I behovde to bide them baith,
So staggering was my state
    That under cure I got such check
Which I might not remove nor neck   215
But either staile or mait.
    Mine agony was so extreame
I swelt and swound for feare,
    But ere I wakned off my dreame
He spoild me of my geare.   220
        With flight then on hight then
            Sprang Cupid in the skyes,
        Forgetting and setting
            At nought my carefull cries.

So long with sight I followed him   225
While both my dazeled eyes grew dimme
Through staring of the starnes
    Which flew so thick before mine eyne—
Some red, some yellow, blew and greene,
Which troubled all mine harnes—   230
    That every thing appeared two
To my barbuilied braine.
    But long might I lye looking so
Ere Cupid came again
        Whose thundring with wondring   235
            I heard up through the aire,
        Through clouds so he thuddes so,
            And flew I wist not where.

232 barbuilied] barboyled C4

225 Fra that I saw that God was gane
 And I in langour left allane
 And sair tormentit to,
  Sum time I sicht quhill I was sad,
 Sum time I musit and maist gane mad,
230 I wist not quhat to do.
  Sum tyme I ravit halfe in a rage
 As ane into dispaire.
  To be opprest with sic ane page
 Lord gif my heart was saire.
235   Like Dido, Cupido
    I widill and I warye,
   Quha reft me and left me
    In sic ane feirie-farye.

  Then felt I Curage and Desyre
240 Inflame my hairt with vncouth fyre
 To me befoir vnknawin
  Bot now na bluid in me remaines
 Vn-brunt and -boyld within my vaines
 Be luiffis bellies blawin.
245 To quenche it or I was deuorit
 With siches I went about
  Bot ay the mair I schape to smor it
 The baulder it brak out,
   Ay preising but ceising
250   Quhill it may breik the boundis,
   My hew so furth schew so
    The dolour of my woundis.

225 Fra that] Bot fra C1 228 quhill I was sad] quhan I wald fane La 237 reft] left C1 left] reft C1 240 Inflame] Inflamyng La hairt] breist La 243] Vnbrunt and bruilȝeit throw my vaines C1; Bot brunt and bould within my wanis La 244] And all away was blawin La 245 it or] me soir La 246 siches] schiftis La 247 smor it] smorit C1 C2 La 250 may] mycht La

196

Then when I saw that god was gone
And I in langour left alone
And sore tormented too,   240
    Sometime I sigh'd while I was sad,
Sometime I musde and most gone mad,
I doubted what to doe.
    Sometime I rav'd halfe in a rage   245
As one into despare.
    To be opprest with such a page,
Lord if my heart was saire.
        Like Dido, Cupido
           I widdle and I wary,   250
      Who reft mee and left mee
          In such a feirie farie.

Then felt I Courage and Desire
Inflame mine heart with uncouth fire
To me before unknowne,   255
    But then no blood in me remaines
Vn-burnt or -boyld within my braines
By loves bellowes blowne.
    To drowne it ere I was devourde
With sighs I went about   260
    But ay the more I shoope to smoor'de
The bolder it brake out,
        Ay preasing but ceasing
          While it might break the bounds.
        Mine hew so foorth shew so   265
          The dolour of my wounds.

250 warye] wearie C5 261 smoor'de] smoored C5

With deidlie visage paill and wan,
Mair like ane Atomie nor man,
255   I widderit cleine away.
     As wax befoir the fyre I felt
My hart within my bosome melt
And pece and pece decay,
     My vaines, with brangling like to brek
260 (My punsis lap with pith),
     So feruently did me infek
That I was vext thairwith,
        My hart ay did start ay
          The fyrie flamis to flie
265   Aye houping throw louping
          To win to liberty.

     Bot ô alace byde it behuiffit
Within my cairfull corpis me incluissit
In presoun of my breist
270   With sichis sa Sowpit and ouirset
Like to an fische fast in the net
In deid-thraw vndeceist
     Quha thocht in vaine dois striue for strenth
For to pull out her head
275   Quhilk profitis na thing at the lenth
Bot haistes hir to heir deid,
        With wristing and thristing
          The faster still is scho,
        Thair I so did lye so
280   My death advancing to.

254 nor man] nor ane man La 256 As] Lyk La 261 feruently] *om.* La 262 was]
am C1 266 win to] com to La 267 O] 3it C1; och La behuiffit] behuissit C2
268] Within my cairfull corpis me incluissit incluissit] luiffit La 269 In] And
C1 270 sa sowpit] sobbit La 271 fast] fanggit La 273 Quha] Quhais C1 for] be
La 274 her] heir C2 275 Quhilk] It La 278 still is] stykis La 279 Thair] And
C1 did] dois C1

With deadly visage, pale and wan,
More like Anatomie than man,
I withered cleane away.
    As waxe before the fire I felt   270
Mine heart within my bosome melt
And piece and piece decay.
    My veines by brangling like to break,
My punses lap with pith,
    So fervency did mee infect   275
That I was vext therewith.
        Mine heart ay, it start ay
            The firie flames to flee,
        Ay howping through lowping
            To leape at libertie.   280

    But O alas it was abusde,
My carefull corps kept it inclusde
In prison of my breast,
    With sighs so sopped and ou'rset
Like to a fish fast in a net   285
In deadthraw undeceast,
    Which, though in vaine, it strives by strength
For to pul out her head,
    Which profites nothing at the length
But hastning to her dead.   290
        With thristing and wristing
            The faster still is sho.
        There I so did lye so,
            My death advancing to.

287 for] by C5

The mair I wrestlit with the wynd
The faschter still my self I fynd,
Na mirth my mynd micht mease.
　　Mair noy nor I had neuer nane,
285　I was sa alterit and ouirgane
Throw drowth of my disease.
　　Than weakly as I micht I rayis,
My sicht grewe dim and dark,
　　I stakkerit at the windil-strayis,
290　No takin I was stark,
　　　　Baith sichtles and michtles
　　　　　I grewe almaist at ainis,
　　　　In angwische I langwische
　　　　　With mony grievous grainis.

295　　With sober pace I did approche
Hard to the Riuer and the Roche
Quhairof I spak befoir
　　Quhais running sic a murmure maid
That to the Sey it softlie slaid.
300　The craig was high and schoir.
　　Than pleasur did me so prouok
Perforce thair to repaire
　　Betwix the Riuer and the Rok
Quhair hope grew with dispaire.
305　　A trie than I see than
　　　　Of CHERREIS in the braes.
　　Belaw to I saw to
　　　　Ane bus of bitter SLAES.

282 The faschter still] The faster still C1; In faster stait La 283 micht] could C1 La 284 had] tried C1 285] *om.* La 287 Than] 3it C1 La 293-94] *om.* La 295 I did] so I La 296 Hard to] Towardis La 298 running] cwmming La murmure] rumour La 299 That] As C1; And La softlie] swiftlie C1 300 The] Ore C1 was high and] ore clewch ore C1; was stay and La 301 Than] Thair C1 302 thair] for C1 306 in] on C1

The more I wrestled with the wind 295
The faster stil my selfe I finde.
No mirth my minde could mease.
 More noy than I had never none,
I was so alterd and ou'rgone
Through drouth of my disease. 300
 Yet weakly, as I might, I raise,
My sight grew dimme and dark,
 I staggered at the windling strayes,
No token I was stark.
  Both sightles and mightles 305
   I grew almost at once.
  In anguish I languish
   With many grievous groanes.

 With sober pace yet I approach
Hard to the River and the Roch 310
Whereof I spake before.
 The river such a murmure made
As to the sea it softly slade.
The Craige was stay and shore.
 Then Pleasure did me so provoke 315
There partly to repaire
 Betwixt the River and the Rocke
Where Hope grew with Despare.
  A tree then I see then
   Of Cherries on the Braes 320
  Below too I saw too
   A bush of bitter Slaes.

298 than] then C5

201

The CHERRIES hang abune my heid
310 Lyke twinkland Rubies round and reid
So hich vp in the hewch,
    Quhais schaddowis in the river schew
Als graithlie glansing as thay grewe
On trimbling twistis tewch
315   Quhilk bowed throw burding of thair birth
Inclining downe thair toppis.
    Reflexe of Phœbus of the firth
Newe colourit all thir knoppis
        With dansing and glansing
320   In tirles dornik champ
        Ay streimand and gleimand
        Throw brichtnes of that lamp.

    With earnest eye quhil I espye
The fruit betwixt me and the skye
325 Halfe gaite almaist to hevin,
    The craige sa cumbersume to clime,
The trie sa hich of growth and trim
As ony arrow evin.
    I cald to minde how Daphne did
330 Within the Laurell schrink
    Quhan from Appollo scho hir hid.
A thousand times I think
        That trie then to me then
        As he his laurell thocht.
335   Aspyring but tyring
        To get that fruit I socht.

312 schaddowes] schaddow La 316 Inclining] In hanging C1 317 of] in C1 La
318] Orecouerit all the knoppis C1; Now cullorit all þair toppis La 320 tirles]
tuik lik La 321] Quhilk streimet and gleimet C1; With streming and leming La
322 brichtnes] lichtnes C1; lycchtles La 323 quhil I] I can C1; I þair La 326-27]
The craig so heych of growth and tryme La 329 cald] call C1 La 330 Within]
Into La 333 then] þair La 334 he his] hich as C1 La 335 Aspyring] Espyring C1;
And spying La tyring] trying La 336 that] the C1 La socht] thocht La

The Cherries hang aboue mine head
Like trickling Rubies round and red
So high up in the Heugh,   325
    Whose shadowes in the rivers shew
As graithly as they grew
On trembling twists and teugh
    Whiles bow'd through burden of their birth,
Declining downe their tops.   330
    Reflexe of Phœbus off the firth
Now coloured all their knoppes
        With dancing and glancing
            In tirle as Dornick champe,
        Which streamed and leamed   335
            Through lightnes of that lampe.

    With earnest eye while I espy
That fruite betwixt me and the skye,
Halfe gate almost to Heaven,
    The Craige so cumbersome to climb,   340
The tree so tall of growth and trim
As any arrow even,
    I calde to minde how Daphne did
Within the Lawrel shrinke
    When from Apollo she her hid.   345
A thousand times I thinke
        That tree there, to mee there
            As hee his Lawrel thought,
        Aspyring but tyring
            To get that fruite I sought.   350

325 river] rivers C5 327] As graithly as they grewe C5 333 glansing as] colourd as
C4 334 tirle as] tirleis C4 trile as C5 338 The] That C5

To clime the Craige it was na buit
Lat be to presse to pull the fruit
In top of all the trie.
340   I saw na way quhairby to cum
Be ony craft to get it clum
Appeirandly to me.
    The craig was vgly, stay and dreiche,
The trie heich, lang and smal.
345   I was affrayd to mount sa hich
For feir to get ane fall.
        Affrayit to say it
            I luikit vp on loft
        Quhiles minting quhiles stinting
350   My purpose changit oft.

    Then Dreid with Danger and Dispaire
Forbad my minting anie maire
To raxe aboue my reiche.
    'Quhat, tusche', quod Curage, 'man, go to.
355   He is bot daft that hes ado
And spairis for euery speiche.
    For I haue oft hard wise men say
And we may see our sellis
    That fortune helps the hardie ay
360   And pultrones plaine repellis.
        Than feir not nor heir not
            Dreid, Danger or Dispaire.
        To faȝarts hard haȝarts
            Is deid or thay cume thaire.

337 the] þat La 343 craig] rok La 344 heich lang] bayth hie La 345 mount] mynt La 347 Affreyit] I freyit C1 349 stinting] staying La 350] I changit pvrposis oft 351 Dreid] deid La 352 my minting] me mounting C1; me mynting La 354 Quhat tusch] Tuich La 356 And spairis for every] That stayis for every C1; That spairis ony La 357 For I haue] I haif La wise] suyth La 358 And] As La sie] sie it C1 361] Then feir nocht / Nor heir nocht Ja 363] hasardis La 364] Is dreid danger and dispair La thay] C1; thy C2

    To climb that Craige it was no buite,
Let bee to prease to pul the fruite
In top of all the tree.
    I knew no way whereby to come
By any craft to get it clum,   355
Appearandly to mee.
    The Craige was ugly, stay and dreigh,
The tree, long, sound and small.
    I was affraide to climb so high
For feare to fetch a fall.   360
        Affrayed, I stayed
           And looked up aloft,
        Whiles minting, whiles stinting,
           My purpose changed oft.

    Then Dread with Danger and Despare   365
Forbade me minting any mare
To raxe above my reach.
    'What? Tush!' quoth Courage, 'man, go to.
He is but daft that hath to doe
And spare for everie speach.   370
    For I have oft heard sooth men say,
And we may see't our selves,
    That Fortune helps the hardie ay,
And pultrons ay repels.
        Then care not and feare not   375
           Dread, Danger nor Despare.
        To fazards, hard hazards
           Is death or they come there.

375] Then fear not and hear not C4; Then feare not and feare not C5

365   'Quha speidis bot sic as heich aspyris,
    Quha tryumphis not bot sic as tyris
    To win a nobill name,
        Of schrinking quhat bot schame succeidis?
    Than do as thou wald haif thy deidis
370 In register of fame.
        I put the caice thou nocht preuaild
    Sa thou with honor die.
      "Thy life bot not thy curage faild"
    Sall Poetis pen of thee.
375   Thy name than from fame than
          Sall neuir be cut aff.
       Thy graif ay sall haif ay
         That honest Epitaff.

      'Quhat can thou losse quhen honor lyuis?
380 Renowne thy vertewe ay reuyuis
    Gif valiauntlie thou end'.
       Quod Danger, 'Hulie, freind, tak heid.
    Vntymous spurring spillis the Steid.
    Tak tent quhat ȝe pretend.
385   Thocht Courage counsell thee to clim,
    Bewar thou kep na skaith.
      Haif thou na help bot Hope and him
    They may beguyle the baith.
       Thy sell now can tell now
390   The counsell of thae Clarkis
       Quhairthrow ȝit I trowe ȝit
         Thy breist dois beir the markis'.

369 thy] þai La 371 preuaild] preuaill C1; prevellis La 373 faild] faill C1; faillis La 378 That] Ane C1 La 383 steid] speid C1 La 387 hope and] hope in C1; god and La 388 They] He C1 the] ȝe C1 390 thae] these C1

Who speeds but such as high aspyres,
Who triumphs not but such as tyres   380
To win a noble name?
   Of shrinking what but shame succeeds?
Then doe as thou would have thy deeds
In register of fame.
   I put case thou not prevailde: 385
So thou with honour die,
   "Thy life but not thy courage failde"
Shal Poets pen of thee.
      Thy name then from Fame then
         Can never be cut aff.   390
      Thy grave ay shal have ay
         That honest Epitaph.

   'What canst thou losse when honour lives?
Renowne thy vertue ay revives
If valiantly thou end'.   395
   Quoth Danger, 'Huly, friend, take head.
Vntimous spurring spilles the stead.
Take tent what yee pretend.
   Thogh Courage counsel thee to climb,
Beware thou kep no skaith.   400
   Have thou no helpe but Hope and him,
They may beguile thee baith.
      Thy sell now can tell now
         The counsel of these Clarkes,
      Wherethrow yet, I trow yet,   405
         Thy breast doth beare the marks.

404 these] those C4

'Brunt bairn with fyre the danger dreidis:
Sa I beleif thy bosome bleidis
395   Sen last that fyre thou felt.
     Besydis this, seindill tymis thou seis
That euer Curage keipis the keyis
Of knawledge at his belt.
     Thocht he bid fordwart with the gunnis
400   Small powder he prouydis.
     Be not ane novice of the Nunnis
That saw not baith the sydis.
       Fuil-haist aye almaist aye
         Ouirsylis the sicht of sum
405   Quha huikis not nor lukis not
         Quhat eftirward may cum.

     '3it Wisdome wischis thee to wey
This figour of Philosophey,
A lessoun worth to leir
410   Quhilk is in time for to tak tent
And not when time is past repent
And buy repentance deir.
     Is thair na honour efter lyfe
Except thou slay thy sell
415   (Quhairfoir hes Attropus that knyfe,
I trow thou can not tell,
       That but it wald cut it
         That Clotho skairse hes spun)
       Distroying thy joying
420   Befoire it be begun.

395 last that] first the C₁ 396 this] that C₁ La thou] C₁ La; the C₂   397 euer]
every C₁ 398 at] be C₁ La 399 bid] go La 401 of] with La saw] sies C₁; red La
404 Ouirsylis] Oresettis C₁ 405 huikis] luikis La luiks] huikis La 407 3it] Bot
La wischis thee to wey] wisses thee to wie C₁; biddis the wyslie wey La 408
This figour] the sentence C₁ La 412 And] Ay La 415 that] the C₁ 417 That]
Who 418 That Clotho] Quhilk etherch La

'Burnt bairne with fire the danger dreads.
So I believe thy bosome bleeds
Since last that fire thou felt.
    Besides that, seindle times thou sees   410
That ever Courage keeps the keyes
Of knowledge at his belt.
    Though he bid fordward with the Gunnes,
Smal powder he provides.
    Be not a Novice of that Nunnes   415
Who saw not both the sides.
        Fooles haste ay, almaist ay
            Ou'rsyles the sight of some
        Who luikes not or huikes not
            What afterward may come.   420

    Yet Wisedome wisheth thee to wey
This figure in Philosophy,
A lesson worth to leare,
    Which is in time for to take tent
And not when time is past repent   425
And buy repentance deare.
    Is there no honour after life
Except thou slay thy sel?
    Wherefore hath Atropus that knife?
I trow thou canst not tell,   430
        Who but it would cut it
            Which Clotho scarce hath spun,
        Destroying the ioying
            Before it be begun.

418 or] who C5 433 the] thy C5

'All ouirs ar repuit to be vyce,
Ore hich, ore law, ore rasch, ore nyce,
Ore heit or ʒit ore cauld.
　　Thou seemes vnconstant be thy sings.
425　Thy thocht is one ane thousand things.
Thou wattis not quhat thou wald.
　　　　Let fame hir pittie on the powre
Quhan all thy banes ar brokin.
　　　　ʒone SLAE suppose thou think it soure,
430　May satisfie to slokkin
　　　　　　Thy drouth now, O youth now,
　　　　　　　　Quhilk drownis thee with desyre.
　　　　　　Aswage than thy rage, man.
　　　　　　　　Foull water quenches fyre.

435　　'Quhat fule art thou to die of thrist
And now may quench it gif thou list
So easile but paine.
　　　　Maire honor is to vanquisch ane
Nor feicht with tensum and be tane
440　And outher hurt or slaine.
　　　　The prattick is to bring to passe
And not to enterprise
　　　　And als guid drinking out of glas
As gold in ony wise.
445　　　　I leuir haue euer
　　　　　　Ane foule in hand or tway
　　　　　　Nor seand ten fleand
　　　　　　　　About me all the day.

421 repuit to be vyce] recknit to be vice C1; stet wys La　422 rasch ore nyce] rich
ore wyis C1　426 wattis] wait La　428 Quhan] Quhill C1　430 May] Will La　431-
32] Thy thrist now I traist now/Gif that thou wald it preife C1 La　432 drownis]
C1; drowins C2　433] I say to it may to C1; And may to I say to La　434] thy
painis all releife C1 La　435 of] for C1　436 now] syne C1; thow La　gif] quhen C1
440 ather] nowther La　441] Now all the practick is to passe C1　443 And als]
Now as C1　guid] giud C2　444 wise] wayis La　445 I leuir] I had lever C1　446]
In hand ane foull or twa La　447 fleand] thowsand La　448] Abone my heid all
day La　About] Aboue C1

All ou'rs are repute to be vice,   435
Ou'r high, ou'r low, ou'r rash, ou'r nice,
Ou'r hote or yet ou'r cold.
    Thou seemes unconstant by thy signes.
Thy thought is on a thousand things.
Thou wats not what thou would.   440
    Let Fame her pitty on thee powre
When all thy bones are broken.
    Yon Slae, suppose thou think it sowre,
Would satisfie to sloken
        Thy drouth now of youth now,   445
            Which dries thee with desire.
        Asswage then thy rage then.
            Foule water quencheth fire.

    'What foole art thou to die a thirst
And now may quench it if thou list   450
So easily but paine?
    More honour is to vanquish ane
Than fight with tensome and be tane
And either hurt or slay.
    The practick is to bring to passe   455
And not to enterprise,
    And as good drinking out of glasse
As gold in any wise.
        I lever have ever
            A fowle in hand or tway   460
        Then seeing ten flying
            About me all the day.

449 a] of C4 454 slay] slaine C5 461 Then] Than C4 C5

'Luik quhair to licht befoir thou loup
450 And slip na certenty for Houp
Quha gydis thee bot be gesse'.
        Quod Currage, 'Cowartis takis na cuire
To sit with schame, sa thay be suire.
I like thame all the lesse.
455   Quhat plesure purchest is but paine
Or honor wyn with ease?
        He will not lye quhair he is slaine
That douttis befoir he deis.
                For feir than I heir than
460   Bot onlie ane remeid
                That latt is and that is
                        For to cut of the heid.

        'Quhat is the way to heill thy hurt,
Quhat way is thair to stay thy sturt,
465 Quhat meinis may mak thee merrie,
        Quhat is the comfort thou cravis
Suppose thir Sophistis thee decewis?
Thou knawis it is the Cherrie
        Sen for it only thou bot thristis.
470 The slae can be na buit.
        In it also thy health consistis
And in na vther fruit.
                Thou quaikis now and schaikis now
                        And studyes at our strife.
475   Advise thee it lies thee
                        On na les nor thy life.

449 to] thow C1 La 456 wyn] woone C1 latt is] lattis C2 464 stay] slay La 467 thir] the C1; thayis La 473 now] aye C1 studies] standis La 475 thee] 3it La

'Looke where thou lights before thou loupe
And slip no certainty for Hope,
Who guides thee but be gesse'.   465
    Quoth Courage, 'Cowards take no cure
To sit with shame, so they be sure.
I like them all the lesse.
    What pleasure purchast is but paine
Or honour won with ease?   470
    He wil not lye where he is slaine
Who doubts before he dies.
        For feare then I heare then
           But onely one remead,
        Which latt is and that is   475
           For to cut off the head.

    'What is the way to heale thine hurt?
What way is there to stay thy sturt?
What meanes to make thee merrie?
    What is the comfort that thou craves?   480
Suppose these Sophists thee deceaves,
Thou knowes it is the Cherrie,
    Since for it onely thou but thirsts.
The Slae can bee no buite.
    In it also thine health consists   485
And in none other fruite.
        Why quakes thou and shakes thou
           Or studies at our strife?
        Advise thee, it lyes thee
           On no lesse than thy life.   490

465 be gesse] begesse C3 463 thou lights] thou light C4 C5 470 Or honour
won] Of honour win C4 475 latt is] lattis C3 490 no lesse] nolesse C3

'Gif ony patient wald be pancit,
Quhy suld he loup quhan he is lancit
Or schrink quhen he is schorne?
480   For I haue hard Chirurgianes say
Oft tymes deferring of ane day
Micht not be mend the morne.
       Tak tyme in tyme or tyme be tint
For tyme will not remaine.
485   Quhat forssis fyre out of the flint
Bot als hard match againe?
              Delay not and stay not
                     And thou sall sie it swae,
              So gets ay that sets ay
490   Stout stomackis to the brae.

'Thocht all beginnings be most hard
The yschew is plesand efterward,
Then schrink not for ane schoure.
       Fra anes that thou thy grening get
495 Thy paine and trauell is forȝet,
The sweet exceidis the soure.
       Go to than quicklie, fear not thir
For hope gude hap hes hecht.
       Quod Danger, 'Be not soddane, Sir,
500 The mater is of wecht.
              First spye baith, syne try baith,
                     Aduisement dois na ill.
              I say then, ȝe may then
                     Be wilfull quhen ȝe will.

481 deferring] defferand C1; posponing La ane] the C1 482 Micht] May C1 La
485 forssis] force hes La C2 487 and] nor C1 489 that] as C1 La 491 begin-
nings] beginning La 492] anes rycches haif than efterward La And yschewis]
The end is C1 493 Then] Now C1 494 grening] ganning La 497 than] now C1
La 498 hes heichte] haddis heiche La 499 soddane] dreddand La 500 weichte]
mycht La 501 syne] and C1 La 503 then] to C1

'If any patient would be pansde,
Why should he loupe when he is lansde
Or shrinke when he is shorne?
    For I have heard Chirurgians say
"Oft-times deferring of a day   495
Might not be mend the morne".
    Take time in time ere time be tint
For time will not remaine.
    What forceth fire out of the flint
But as hard match againe?   500
        Delay not nor fray not
            And thou shall see it sa:
        Such gets ay as sets ay
            Stout stomackes to the brae.

    'Though all beginning be most hard   505
The end is pleasant afterward,
Then shrinke not for no showre.
    When once that thou thy greening get
Thy paine and travel is forget.
The sweete exceeds the sowre.   510
    Goe to then quickly, feare no thir,
For Hope good hap hath height'.
    Quoth Danger, 'Be not sudden, Sir,
The matter is of weight.
        First spy both then try both,   515
            Advisement doth none ill:
        Thou may then, I say then,
            Be wilfull when thou will,

511 no] not C4

505   'Bot ʒet to mynd the proverbe call:
         Quha vsis perrellis perische sall,
         Schort quhile thair lyfe them lastis'.
             'And I haif hard', quod Hope, 'that he
         Sall nevir schaip to sayle the Se
510   That for all perrils castis.
             How many throw dispaire ar deid
         That neuer perrellis preiuit,
             How many also, gif thou reid,
         Of liues we haue releiuit
515   Quha being, euin deing,
                 But danger, bot dispaird?
             A hunder I wunder,
                 Bot thou hes hard declaird.

             'Gif we twa hald not vp thy hart,
520   Quhilk is the cheife and noblest part,
         Thy wark wald not gang weill,
             Considdering thae companions can
         Perswade a sillie simpill man
         To haʒard for his heill.
525   Suppose thay haue desauit some
         Or thay and we micht meit,
             Thay get na credit quhair we come
         In ony man of Spreit.
                 Be ressoun thair tressoun
530   Be vs is first espyit,
                 Reveiling thair deiling
                     Quhilk dowe not be denyit.

505 the proverbe] thir proverbs C1 507 lyfe them] lyffis C1 La 508 quod hope
that] that hope quod C1 509 Sall] Maid C1; Suld La schaip] schip C1; scheip
La 513 gif thou] as we C1; gif ʒe La 514 we haue] hes bene C1 La 515] Some
deing some being C1; Quha being sum deing La 516 bot dispaird] or dispaire
C1; and dispair La 517] That I haue hard declair C1 519 we twa] vertew La 521
would] will C1 522 thae] that C1; thy La 523 simpill] simpll C2 525 desauit]
disswadit C1 526 thay and we] we and thay C1 La 528 man] men La 530 is] was
C1

'But yet to mind the proverbe call:
Who uses perils perish shall: 520
Short while their life them lasts'.
    'And I have heard', quoth Hope, 'that he
Should never shape to saile the sea
That for all perils casts.
    How many through Despare are dead   525
That never perils priev'd?
    How many also, if thou read,
Of lives have we releiv'd,
        Who being, even dying,
           But Danger but desparde?   530
        A hunder, I wunder,
           But thou hast heard declarde.

    'If we two hold not up thine heart,
Which is the chiefe and noblest part,
Thy works would not goe well,   535
    Considering these companions can
Disswade a silly simple man
To hazard for his heale.
    Suppose they have deceived some
Ere we and they might meete,   540
    They got not credance where we come
In any man of sprite.
        By reason their treason
           By us is plainely spyde,
        Revealing their dealing,   545
           Which dow not be denyde.

521 Short while] Shortwhile C3 536 these]C4 the C3 541 not] no C5

'With sleikit Sophismis seiming sweit
As all thair doings war discreit
535 Thay wische thee to be wise,
Postponing tyme from hour to hour,
Bot, faith, in vnderneath the flour
The lurking serpent lyis
Suppois thou seis hir not a styme
540 Till tyme scho sting thy fute.
Persawis thou not quhat precious tyme
Thy slewthing dois ouirschute?
Allace man, thy cace than
In lingring I lament.
545 Go to now and do now
That Curage be content.

'Quhat gif Melanchollie cum in
And get an grip or thou begin?
Than is thy labour lost
550 For he will hald thee hard and fast
Till tyme and place and fruit be past,
Till thou giue vp the ghost,
Thane salbe grau'd vpon the stane
Quhilk on thy graue beis laid,
555 "Sum tyme there liued sik a ane",
Bot how suld it be said?
"Heir lyis now but prise now
Into dishonors bed
Ane cowart" as thou art,
560 "That from his fortune fled".

---

533 sleikit sophismis] sleikit sonats C1; sleikie sophismes La   535 wische] wis C1
La 540 Till tyme] Till þat La   sting] stang C1 La   542 oreschute] ourfleit La
543 than] man La 545 do now] do La 551] *om.* La   fruit] all C1 552 Till] That
C1; Quhill La 553 grau'd upon the stane] gravin on the stane C1 La 554 beis] is
C1 La 556 how suld] how sall C1; heir sall La 557 now] new La 558 dishonors]
dishonorit La   560 That] Quhilk La

With sleekie Sophismes seeming sweete,
As all their doing were discreet,
They wish thee to be wise,
 Postponing time from houre to houre,   550
But faith in underneath the flowre
The lurking serpent lyes
 Suppose thou seest her not a stime
While that she sting thy foote.
 Perceives thou not what precious time   555
Thy sleuth doth overshoote?
   Alas man, thy case man
    In lingring I lament.
   Goe to now and doe now,
    That Courage be content.   560

 'What if Melancholy come in
And get a grip ere thou begin?
Then is thy labour lost
 For he will hold thee hard and fast
Til time and place and fruite be past,   565
And thou give up the ghost.
 Then shal be graven upon that place
Which on thy tombe is laide
 "Sometime there liv'd such one", alas,
But how shal it bee said?   570
   "Heere lyes now but prise now
    Into dishonours bed
   A cowart", as thou art,
    "Who from his fortune fled".

551 in] is C5

'Imagyne, man, gif thou were laid
In graue and syne micht heir this said,
Wald thou not sweat for schame?
    Yes faith I dout not bot thou wald
565 Thairfoir gif thou hes eyis, behald
How thay wald smoir thy fame.
    Go to and mak na mair excuse,
Now life or honor lose
    And outher thame or vs refuis,
570 Thair is na vther chose:
        Considder togidder
          That we can neuer dwell.
        At length ay at strength aye
          Thae pultrons we expell,

575   Quod Danger, 'Sen I vnderstand
I That counsall can be na command,
haue na mair to say
    Except gif that he thocht it gude
Tak counsall 3it or 3e conclude
580 Of wyser men nor thay.
    Thay ar bot rakles, young and rasche
Suppois thay think vs fleid.
    Gif of our fellowschip you fasche,
Gang with thame, hardlie beid.
585   God speid you, thay leid 3ou
          That hes not meikill wit.
        Expell vs and tell vs
          "Heirefter comes not 3it"'.

561 Imagine man] Imagine than C1; Immagening La 562 this] that C1; it La
564 Yes] 3it La 568 Now] Or La   573 at] be C1; by La 574 Thae] Sic C1
578 gif that he thocht] that gif he think C1; bot gif thow think La 579 3e] we
La 580 nor] than C1 581 rakles] witlesse C1 582 thay] 3e La 584 thame hardlie
beid] thame hardlie be it C1; hardie beit La 587 and] 3e will La 588 comes not]
quhat cumis La

'Imagine, man, if thou were laid 575
In grave and syne might heare this said,
Would thou not sweat for shame?
    Yes, faith, I doubt not but thou would,
Therefore, if thou have eyes, behold
How they would smore thy fame. 580
    Goe to and make no more excuse
Ere life and honour losse
    And either them or us refuse,
There is no other chose.
        Consider togidder 585
           That we doe never dwell.
        At length ay but strength ay.
           The pultrons we expell'.

    Quoth Danger, 'Since I understand
That counsell can be no command, 590
I have no more to say
    Except if that you thinke it good,
Take counsel yet ere ye conclude
Of wiser men then they.
    They are but rackles, young and rash, 595
Suppose they thinke us fleit.
    If of our fellowship ye fash,
Goe with them, hardly be it.
        God speed you, they lead you
           Who have not meekle wit. 600
        Expell us, yeeil tell us,
           Heereafter comes not yet'.

592 you] yee C4

Quhyle Danger and Dispair retyrit,
590 Experience came in and speirit
Quhat all the matter meind.
With him came Ressoun, Wit and Skill
And thay began to speir at Will,
'Quhair mak ʒe to, my freind?'
595 'To pluk ʒone lustie CHERRIE, loe',
Quod he, 'and not the SLAE'.
Quod thay, 'Is thair na mair adoe
Or ʒe cum vp the brae
Bot to it and do it,
600 Perforce the fruit to pluck?
Weill brother, some vther
Wer meter to conduct'.

'I grant ʒe may be gude aneuch
Bot ʒit the haʒard of ʒon hewch
605 Requyris ane grauer gyde.
As wise as ʒe ar may gang wrang
Thairfore tak counsaill or ʒe gang
Of some that standis besyde.
Bot quhilk wer ʒone thrie ʒe forbad
610 ʒour company richt now?'
Quod Will, 'Thre prechours to perswad
The poysond SLAE to pow.
Thay tratlit and ratlit
A lang halfe houre and mair.
615 Foul fall thame, they call thame
Dreid, Danger and Dispaire.

591 all] *om.*La 592 came] come La 595 pluk] pull C1 597 cum] gang C1; win La 601] *om.* La 602 Wer meter] Wer better C1; Our mater La 604 of ʒon] of ane C1; vp the La 605 grauer] better C1; greittar La 609 ʒone] thai La 613] Thay trattell thay rattell C1 Thay] Thy C2 615 fall] haist La

222

While Danger and Despare retir'de
Experience came in and spear'de
What all the matter meande.   605
   With him came Reason, Wit and Skill.
Then they began to aske at Will
'Where make you to, my friend?'
   'To pluck yon lustie Cherrie, loe'
Quoth he, 'and quyte the slae'.   610
   Quoth they, 'Is there no more adoe
Ere yee win up the brae
     But doe it and to it,
       Perforce your fruite to pluck?
     Well, brother, some other   615
       Were better to conduct.

'We grant yee may be good enough,
But yet the hazard of yon heugh
Requyres a graver guide.
   As wise as yee are may goe wrang,   620
Therefore take counsell ere ye gang
Of some that stands beside.
   But who were yon three yee forbade
Your company right now?'
   Quoth Wil, 'Three preachers to perswade   625
The poysonde Slae to pull.
     They tratled and pratled
       A long halfe houre and mare.
     Foul fal them, they call them
       Dread, Danger and Despare.   630

223

'Thay ar maire faschious nor of feck.
Ʒon faiʒardis durst not for thair neck
Clim vp the Craig with vs
620   Fra we determinit to die
Or else to clime Ʒone CHERRIE trie,
Thay baid about the bus.
      Thay ar conditionate like the Cat,
They wald not weit their feit
625   Bot Ʒit gif of the fruit we gat
Thay wald be faine to eit.
        Thocht thay now, I say now
          To haʒard hes na hart
        Ʒit luck we and pluck we
630   The fruit thay wald haue part.

      Bot fra we get our voyage wun
Thay sall not than the CHERRIE con
That wald not enterpryse'.
      'Weill', quod Experience, 'Ʒe boist
635 Bot he that countis without his oist
Oft tymes he countis twyse.
      Ʒe sell the Beir skin on his back,
Bot byde quhill Ʒe it get.
      Quhen Ʒe haue done its tyme to crak.
640 Ʒe fische befoir the net.
        Quhat haist Sir, Ʒe taist Sir
          The CHERRIE or Ʒe pow it.
        Bewar Ʒit, Ʒe ar Ʒit
          Mair talkatiue nor trowit'.

617 feck] effect La 618 faiʒardis] faissard C1; hasarddis La thair] his C1 620
Fra] For C1 determinit to] determinate war to C1; determenit La 621 Ʒone]
the La 624 They] That C1 their] her C1 626 be] haif La 631 fra] gif C1 632
the] our C1 637 sell] sie La 640 Ʒe fisch] Fisch not C1 641 taist] traist La 642
that] quhat La

'They are more fashious than of feck.
Yon fazards durst not for their neck
Climb up the Craige with us.
    Fra we determined to die
Or then to climbe the Cherrie tree,   635
They bode about the bush.
    They are conditionde like the Cat,
They would not weete their feete,
    But yet if any fish we gate
They would be apt to eate.   640
        Though they now, I say now,
            To hazard have no heart,
        Yet luck we or pluck we,
            The fruite they would not parte.

'But when we get our voyage wun   645
They shal not then a Cherrie cun
Who would not enterprise'.
    'Well', quoth Experience, 'ye boast
But he that reckon'd but his hoast
Oftimes he counteth twise.   650
    Ye sell the Baires skin on his back
But bide while ye it get.
    When ye have done its time to crack.
Ye fish before the net.
        What haste, sir, ye taste, sir,   655
            The Cherrie ere yee pow it.
        Beware, sir, ye are, sir,
            More talkative nor trowit'.

639 we] they C4 650 counteth] counted C4 658 trowit] trow it C5 660 he] ye
C5

645   'Call Danger back againe', quod Skill,
    'To se quhat he can say to Will,
    We see him schod sa strait.
        We may nocht trow that ilkane tellis'.
    Quod Curage, 'We concludit ellis.
650 He seruis not for our mait
      For I can tell ʒou all perqueir
    His counsaill or he cum'.
        Quod Will, 'Quhairto suld he cume heir?
    He can not hald his tung.
655   He speikis ay, and seikis ay
            Delay of time be driftis.
        He greuis vs and deues vs
            With sophistries and schiftis'.

        Quod Ressoun, 'Quhy was he debard?
660 The tale is ill may not be hard.
    ʒit let vs heir him anis'.
        Than Danger to declair began
    How 'Hope and Curage tuik the man
    And led him all thair lanis,
665   For thay wald haif him vp the hill
    But outher stop or stay.
        And quha wes welcomer nor Will?
    He wald be formaist ay:
        He culd do and suld do,
670   Quha ever wald or nocht.
        Sic speiding proceding
           Vnlikelie was, I thocht.

646 To] And C1 647 sa] to C1 La 649 Curage] Danger La 650 mait] nait C2
652 or he cum] and ʒe will C1 654] He can not hald him still C1; For to behald
his cunning La 656] Delayis of tymes be drifts C1 658 sophistries] sophistrie
La 661 him] þame La 664 And led] To leid La 665 haif] haist C1 vp] win La

'Call Danger back againe', quoth Skil,
'To see what he can say to Wil,   660
We see him shoad so straite.
    We may not trow what each one tels'.
Quoth Courage, 'We concluded els.
He serves not for our mate
    For I can tel you all perquiere   665
His counsel ere he come'.
    Quoth Hope, 'Whereto should he come here?
He cannot hold him dum.
        He speaks ay and seeks ay
           Delayes oft times and drifts   670
        To grieve us and dieve us
           With Sophistrie and shifts.

    Quoth Reason, 'Why was he debarde?
The tale is ill cannot be heard,
Yet let us heare him anes'.   675
    Then Danger to declare began
How Hope and Courage tooke the man
To leade them all their lanes,
    How 'They would have him up the hill
But either stoppe or stay,   680
    And who was welcomer than Will?
He would be foremost ay.
        He could doe and should doe
           Who ever would or nought.
        Such speeding proceeding   685
           Vnlikely was, I thought.

670 Delayes] delay C5 684 nought] dought C5

'Thairfoir I wischt them to be war
And raschlie not to run ouir far
675 Without sik gydis as ȝe'.
Quod Curage, 'Friend, I heir ȝou faill.
Remember better on your taill.
ȝe sayd it culd not be,
Besydis that ȝe wald not consent
680 That evir we suld clim'.
Quod Will, 'For my part I repent
We saw them mair nor him
For thay ar the stayer
Of vs alsweill as he.
685 I think now they schrink now.
Go fordwart, let thame be.

'Go, go, we do not heir bot guckis.
Thay say that voyage never luckis
Quhair ilk ane hes ane vote'.
690 Quod Wisdome grauelie, 'Sir, I grant,
We were na war your vote to want.
Some sentence heir I note.
Suppois ȝe speak it bot be gesse
Some fruit thairin I fynd.
695 ȝe wald be fordward, I confesse,
And cummis oft tymis behynd.
It may be that thay be
Dissauit that never doutit.
Indeid, Sir, that heid, Sir,
700 Hes meikill wit about it'.

---

673 wischt them] wisse him C1 674 raschlie] ryche La 675 Without sik gydis] With sic ane gyde C1 676 ȝou] ȝe C1 678 culd] micht C1 679 Beside] Besyddis La ȝe] he La consent] be content La 682] That we saw you or him C1 687 go we do not heir] to quhat do we heir C1 689 ilk ane] ilk man C1 690 grauelie] grathlie C1 691 na] the C1 692 heir] now C1 La 694 I] we La 697 thay] may C1

'Therefore I wisht him to beware
And rashly not to run ou'r far
Without such guides as wee'.
    Quoth Courage, 'Friend, I heare you faile.   690
Take better tent unto your tale:
Ye said, "It could not be".
    Besides that, ye would not consent
That ever we should clim'.
    Quoth Wil, 'For my part, I repent   695
We saw them more than him
        For they are the stayare
            Of us as wel as hee.
        I thinke now they shrinke now,
            Goe forward, let them bee.   700

    'Goe, goe, we doe nothing but guckes.
They say the voyage never luckes
Where each one hath a vote'.
    Quoth Wisedome gravely, 'Sir, I grant,
We were no worse your vote to want.   705
Some sentence now I note.
    Suppose you speake it but be gesse,
Some fruite therein I finde.
    Ye would be foremost, I confesse,
But comes oft-times behind.   710
        It may be that they bee
            Deceivd that never doubted.
        Indeed, sir, that head, sir,
            Hath meekle wit about it'.

707 be gesse] begesse C3

Than wilful Will began to rage
And sware he fand na thing in age
Bot anger, yre and grudge,
   'And for my selfe', quod he, 'I sweir
705 To quyte all my companions heir
And thay admit the Iudge.
   Experience is growne sa auld
That he begins to raue.
   The laif but Curage are sa cauld,
710 Na haʒarting they haif.
      For Danger far stranger
         Hes maid them nor they war.
      Go fra thame, we pra thame
         That nouther dow nor dar.

715   'Quhy may not these thre leid this ane?
I led ane hunder all my lane
But counsall of them all'.
   'I grant', quod Wisdom, 'ʒe haue led
Bot I wald speir how many sped
720 Or furderit but ane fall?
   But vther few or nane I trow.
Experience can tell.
   He sayis, that man may wyte bot ʒow
The first tyme that he fell.
725   He kennis now quhais pennis now
         Thou borrowit him to flee.
      His wounds ʒit quhilk sounds ʒit
         He gat them than throw thee'.

702 sware] sweir La fand] saw La the] you C1 La 707 is] hes La 711 far] for C1 La 712] Hes ever maid thame ware C1; He maid þame go fra þame La nor] than 713] We pray þame La 715 these three] we three C1; we twa La 716 all my lane] myne allane C1 720 furderit] fordward C1 721] For thair is nane or few I trow C1 723 He] Men C1 man may] he may C1; man La 725 kennis] kenins C2 726 him to flee] fra the clarkis C1 727 sounds] stoundis La 728] I trowe dois beir the markis C1; He gat þame euir of þe La

Then wilful Will began to rage,   715
And swore he saw nothing in age
But anger, yre and grudge.
 'And for my selfe', quoth he, 'I sweare
To quyte all my companions heere
If they admit you iudge.   720
 Experience is growne so old
That he begins to rave.
 The rest but Courage are so cold
No hazarding they have,
  For Danger farre stranger   725
   Hath made them than they were.
  Goe fra them, we pray them,
   Who neither dow nor dare.

 'Why may not wee three leade this one?
I led an hundreth mine alone,   730
But counsel of them all'.
 'I grant', quoth Wisedome, 'ye have led,
But I would speere how many sped
Or furthered but a fall?
 But either few or none, I trow,   735
Experience can tell.
 He sayes that man may wite but you
The first time that hee fell.
  He kens then whose pens then
   Thou borrowed him to flee.   740
  His wounds yet, which stounds yet,
   He got them then through thee'.

'That', quod Experience, 'is trew.
730 Will flatterit him quhan first he flew
And set him in an Low.
    Will was his Counsell and conuoy
To borrow fra the blindit boy
Baith quiver, wingis and bow,
735   Quhairwith befoir he seyit to schuit
He neither ʒeild to youth
    Nor ʒit had need of any fruit
To quench his deadly drouth,
        Quhilk pynis him and dwynis him
740   To deid, he wattis not how.
        Gif Will than did ill than
            Himselfe remembers now.

    'For I Experience was thair
Like as I vse to be all quhair
745 Quhat tyme he wytit Will
        To be maist cause of his mischeif.
For I my self can be ane preif
And witnes thairintill.
        Thair is na boundis bot I haif bene
750 Nor hidlingis fra me hid
        Nor secret thingis bot I haif sene
That he or onie did.
        Thairfoir now no moir now
            Let him think to conceild
755   For quhy now, euin I now
            Am detbond to reveild.

729] Than quod Experience is it trew C1 730 first] that C1 734 wingis and] and his C1 735 seyit to] sayit La 736 neither] never C1 La 740 he wattis] I wat C1 La 742 remembers] considder C1; remember La 743 For] First La 745 wytit] wytis C1 La 746 maist cause] the cause C1; maist La 747 For I] I La ane] na La 750 hidlingis] heich things C1; secreittis La 754 conceild] conceill C1; recyll La 756 reveild] reveill C1 La

'That', quoth Experience, 'is true.
Will flattered him when first he flew.
Will set him in a low.   745
    Will was his counsell and convoy.
Will borrowed from the blinded Boy
Both Quaver, wings and bow
    Wherewith before he say'd to shoote
He neither yeeld to youth   750
    Nor yet had need of any fruite
To quench his deadly drouth
        Which pines him and dwines him
            To death, I wot not how.
        If Will then did ill then,   755
            Himselfe remembers now.

'For I Experience was there,
Like as I use to bee all where,
What time hee wited Will
    To be the ground of all his griefe,   760
As I my selfe can bee a priefe
And witnes thereuntill.
    There are no bounds but I have beene
Nor hidlings from mee hid,
    Nor secret things but I have seene   765
That he or any did.
        Therefore now, no more now
            Let him thinke to concealde.
        For why now, even I now
            Am debtbound to reveald.   770

'My custome is for to declair
The treuth and nevir eik nor pair
For onie man ane jot.
760   Gif wil-full Will delytis in leis,
Exampill in thy self thou seis
How he can turne his cote
    And with his langage wald alluir
Thee ʒit to brek thy bainis.
765   Some tyme thou knawis gif he was suir,
Thow vsd his counsell ainis
        Quha wald ʒit be bald ʒit
           To wrak thee, wer not we.
      Think on now, of ʒon now',
770   Quod Wisdome than to me.

    'Weill', quod Experience, 'gif that he
Submittis himself to ʒow and me
I wait quhat I suld say,
    Our gude advyse he sall nocht want
775 Provyding alway gif he grant
To put ʒon Will away
    And banische baith him and Dispair
That all gude purpose spillis.
      Sa he will melle with them na mair,
780 Lat them twa flyte thair fillis.
        Sic coissing but loissing
          All honest men may vse.
      'That change now wer strange now',
        Quod Ressoun, 'to refuse'.

758 treuth] treuh C2 nevir] nather C1 La 763 wald] till C1 764 ʒit] for C1 765 thou knawis] ʒe sawe C1; thow saw La he was] ʒe war C1 767 be bald] behauld C1 La 768 wer not] war than C1; war nor La 771 Weill] Than C1; I will La 772 Submittis] Will come C1 774 Our gude advyse] Gif he be wise C1 775 gif] that C1 La 779 will] wald C1 them] vs C1; him La

'My custome is for to declare
The truth and neither eke nor paire
For any man a ioate.
    If wilful Will delytes in lyes,
Example in thy selfe thou sees   775
How he can turne his coate
    And with his language would allure
Thee yet to breake thy bones.
    Thou knowes thyself if he be sure,
Thou usde his counsell ones   780
        Who would yet, behold yet,
            To wreak thee, were not wee.
        Thinke on, you, on yon now',
            Quoth Wisedome then to mee.

    'Wel', quoth Experience, 'if hee   785
Submits himselfe to you and mee
I wote what I should say.
    Our good advise he shall not want
Providing alwayes that hee grant
To put yon Will away   790
    And banish both him and Despare
That all good purpose spils,
    So he will mell with them no mare
Let them two flyte their fils.
        Such cossing but lossing   795
            All honest men may use'.
        'That change now were strange now',
            Quoth Reason, 'To refuse'.

783 you] yon C5

1597 Cherrie

Quoth Will, 'Fy on him when he flew
That powde not Cherries then anew   800
For to have staide his hurt'.
    Quoth Reason, 'Though he beare the blame
He never saw nor needed them
While he himselfe had hurt.
    First when he mistred not, he might.   805
He needs and may not now.
    Thy folly when he had his flight
Empashed him to pow.
      Both hee now and we now
        Perceives thy purpose plaine   810
      To turne him and burne him
        And blow on him againe'.

    Quoth Skil, 'What would wee longer strive?
Far better late than never thrive.
Come, let us helpe him yet.   815
    Tint time we may not get againe.
We waste but present time in vaine'.
'Beware', with that quoth Wit,
    'Speak on, Experience, let see.
We think you hold you dumb'.   820
    'Of bygones I have heard', quoth he,
'I know not things to come'.
      Quoth Reason, 'The season
        With slouthing slydes away.
      First take him and make him   825
        A man if that you may'.

800 anew] a new C3 813 would wee] should wee C4

1597 Cherrie

Quoth Will, 'If he be not a man
I pray you sirs, what is he than?
He lookes like one at least'.
    Quoth Reason, 'If he follow thee 830
And minde not to remaine with mee,
Nought but a bruital beast.
    A man in shape doth nought consist
For all your tanting tales
    Therefore, sir Will, I would yee wist 835
Your Metaphysick failes.
        Goe leare yet a yeare yet
            Your Logick at the schooles.
        Some day then yee may then
            Passe Master with the Mules'. 840

Quoth Will, 'I marvel what you meane.
Should I not trow mine own two eyne
For all your Logick schooles?
    If I did not, I were not wise'.
Quoth Reason, 'I have told you thrise 845
None ferlies more than fooles.
    There be more senses than the sight
Which ye ov'rhaile for haste,
    To wit, if ye remember right,
Smel, hearing, touch and taste. 850
        All quick things have sic things,
            I meane both man and beast.
        By kinde ay we finde ay
            Few lackes them at the least.

843 your] you C5 847 more] mo C4 851 sic] such C3

1597 Cherrie

'So by that consequence of thine   855
Or Syllogisme said like a swine,
A Kow may learne thee laire.
 Thou uses onely but the eyes,
She touches, tastes, smels, heares and sees,
Which matches thee and maire.   860
 But since to triumph yee intend
As presently appeares,
 Sir, for your Clergie to be kend,
Take yee two asses eares.
  No Miter perfyter   865
   Got Midas for his meed.
  That hood, sir, is good, sir,
   To hap your braine-sick head.

 'Ye have no feele for to defyne
Though yee have cunning to declyne   870
A man to be a moole.
 With little work yet yee may vowde
To grow a gallant horse and good
To ride theron at Yoole.
 But to our ground where wee began   875
For all your gustlesse iests.
 I must be master of the man
But thou to bruital beasts,
  So wee two must bee two
   To cause both kinds be knowne.   880
  Keep mine then from thine then
   And each one use their owne'.

1597 Cherrie

Then Will as angry as an ape
Ran ramping, swearing, rude and rape.
Saw he none other shift. 885
    He would not want an inch his wil
Even whether't did him good or ill
For thirty of his thrift.
    He would be formest in the field
And master if he might. 890
    Yea hee should rather die than yeeld
Though Reason had the right.
        'Shal he now make mee now
            His subiect or his slave?
        No, rather my father 895
            Shall quick goe to the grave.

    'I height him while mine heart is haile
To perish first ere he prevaile,
Come after what so may'.
    Quoth Reason, 'Doubt yee not indeed? 900
Ye hitte the naile vpon the head,
It shall bee as yee say.
    Suppose yee spur for to aspire
Your bridle wants a bit.
    That mare may leave you in the myre 905
As sicker as yee sit.
        Your sentence repentance
            Shall learn you I believe
        And anger you langer
            When yee that practick prieve. 910

886 his] of C4 901 Ye] Yet C3 905 mare] C4 C5; marke C3 908 learn] C4 C5;
leave C3

785　Than altogidder they began
　　　To say 'Cum on, thou martyrit man
　　　And do as we deuyse'.
　　　　　Abasd ane bonie quhyle I baid
　　　And musd or I my answere maid.
790　I turnd me ainis or twyse
　　　　　Behalding euerie ane about.
　　　I feird to speik in haist.
　　　　　Some seimd assurd, some dred for dout,
　　　Will ran Reid-wood almaist:
795　　　　With wringing and thringing
　　　　　　　His hands on vther dang.
　　　　　Dispair to, for cair to,
　　　　　　　Wald needs himselfe go hang.

789 And musd or I my] And muissit or I C1; I maysit or I my La　790 I] And C1
794 Will] Some C1

'As yee have dyted your decreet,
Your prophecy to bee compleat
Perhaps and to your paines.
   It hath beene said and may be so,
A wilful man wants never woe   915
Though he get little gaines.
   But since ye thinkt an easie thing
To mount above the Moone
   Of your owne fiddle take a spring
And dance when yee have done.   920
      If than, sir, the man, sir,
         Like of your mirth, hee may.
      But speare first and heare first
         What he himselfe will say'.

   Then altogether they began   925
And said, 'Come on, thou martyrde man,
What is thy will? Advise'.
   Abasde a bony while I stood
And musde ere I mine answere made.
I turnd me once or twise   930
   Beholding every one about
Whose motions movd me maist.
   Some seemd assured. Some dread for doubt.
Will ran red wood for haist
      With wringing and flinging   935
         For madnes like to mang.
      Despare too for care too
         Would needs himselfe goe hang.

923 But] C4; And C3 928 stood] bade C5

Quhilk quhen Experience persauit,
800 Quod he, 'Remember gif we rauit
As Will alledgit of laite
Quhen as he sware na thing he saw
In age bot anger slack and slaw
And cankerit of consait.
805 3e culd not luck as he alledgit
That all opinions sperit.
He was sa frak and fyerie edgit
He thocht vs four bot feirit.
"Quha pansis on chancis",
810 Quod he, "na worschip winnis.
Ay some best sall come best
That hap weill rak well rinnis",

'3it', quod Experience, 'behauld
For all the tales that he hes tauld
815 How he himselfe behaues.
Because Dispaire culd come na speid,
Lo quhaire he hangs all bot the heid
And in ane withie waues.
Gif 3on be suir, ains thou may se,
820 To men that with thame mellis:
Gif thay had hurt or helpit thee
Considder be thameselfis.
Than chuse the to vse the
Be vs or sic as 3one.
825 Say sone now, haue done now,
Mak outher aff or one.

---

799 Quhilk quhen] Fra time C1; Quhill than La 800 gif we rauit] 3e ressauit
C1; gif he raiffit La 802 na thing] nocht else C1 La 805 3e] He C1 La 808 vs
four bot] not to be C1; ws sone bot La 809 on chancis] quhat chanchis La
817 Lo] Luik C1 819 3on be suir ains] thou be sory C1; þou besuir now La 820
To] Two C1 821 had] haue C1 823 the] 3e C1 the] 3e C1 824 Be] With C1

Which when Experience perceivd,
Quoth he, 'Remember if I ravde   940
As Will allegde of late
   When as he swore nothing he saw
In age but anger slack and slaw
And cankred in conceite.
   Ye could not lucke as he alledgde   945
Who all opinions spearde.
   He was so frack and firie edgd
He thought us foure but feard.
      "Who panses what chanses",
         Quoth hee, "no worship wins.   950
     To some best shal come best
        Who hap wel rack well rins",

   'Yet', quoth Experience, 'behold,
For all the tales that ye have told,
How hee himselfe behaves.   955
   Because Despare could come no speed,
Loe heere he hings all but the head,
And in a widdy waves.
   If you be sure once thou may see
To men that with them mels.   960
   If they had hurt or helped thee
Consider by themsels.
      Then chuse thee to use thee
        By us or such as yon,
      Syne soone now, have done now,   965
        Make either off or on'.

954 ye have] he hes C4   957 heere] where C4

'Persaues thou not quhairfra proceids
The frantik fantasies that feids
Thy furious flaming fyre
830   Quhilk dois thy bailfull breist combuir
That nane bot we', quod thay, 'can cuir
Nor knawis quhat dois requyre.
    The persing passion of thy Spreit
That waists thy vitall breath
835   Hes holit thy heavie hart with heit.
Desyre drawes on thy death.
        Thy punsis Renuncis
          All kynd of quiet rest.
        That fever hes ever
840   Thy person sa opprest'.

    Quod thay, 'Were thou acquaint with Skill,
He knawis quhat humors dois thee ill
Quhair thou thy cares contrakis.
    He knawis the ground of all thy griefe
845 And Recept to for thy releife.
All medicines he makis'.
    'Cum on', quod Skil, 'content am I
To put my helping hand
Provyding alwayis he apply
850 To counsall and command.
        Quhill we than', quod he than,
          'Ar myndit to remaine,
        Gif place now in cace now
          Thou get vs not againe.

829 flaming] flamyis of La 831 That nane bot we] Bot nane bot we C1 knawis] kennis C1 833] The passions of thy pensiue spreits C1; The passiones of þi persing spreit La 834 vitall] fatall C1; wettal La 835 Hes holit] Hes healit C1; Hes held La heit] heits C1 836 death] drewth La 837 renuncis] denuncis C1 840 sa] ay C1 843 Quhair thou] Quhair throw La 845 recept to for] recepts to for C1; recepie for La 848 put my] put to my La 852 remane] returne La 854 Thou] 3e La

'Perceivst thou not wherefra proceeds
The frantick fantasie that feeds
Thy furious flamming fire
   Which doth thy bailfull brest combur,   970
That none indeed', quoth they, 'can cure
Nor helpe thine hearts desire.
   The piercing passions of the spirit,
Which wastes thy vitall breath,
   Doth hold thine heavy heart with heate.   975
Desire drawes on thy death.
      Thy punces pronounces
         All kinde of quyet rest.
      That fever hath ever
         Thy person so opprest.   980

'Couldst thou come once acquaint with Skil,
Hee knowes what humours doth thee ill,
And how thy cares contracts.
   Hee knowes the ground of all thy griefe
And recipies of thy reliefe.   985
All medicines hee makes.'
   Quoth Skil, 'Come on, content am I
To put mine helping hand,
   Providing alwayes hee apply
To counsel and command.   990
      While wee, then', quoth he then,
         'Are minded to remaine,
      Give place now, incace now,
         Thou get us not againe.

971 none indeed] none C4 977 pronounces] renounces C4 985 recipies of]
recipies for C4

855 'Assuire thy selfe gif that we sched
  Thou sall not get thy purpose sped.
  Tak tent. We haif thee tald.
   Haif done and dryue nocht aff the day.
  The man that will not quhen he may
860 He sall not quhen he wald.
   Quhat wald thou do, I wald we wist,
  Except or gif vs oure.
   Quod he, 'I think me mair than blist
  To fynde sick famous foure
865   Besyde me to guyde me
    Now quhen I haue to doe
   Considering the swidering
   3e fand me first into.

  'Quhen Currage crau'd ane stomack stout
870 And Danger draue me into dout
  With his companione Dreid,
   Quhylis Will wald vp aboue the aire,
  Quhyllis I was dround into dispaire,
  Quhylis Hope held vp my heid.
875   Sic pithie resounis and Replyis
  On euery side thay schewe
   That I, quha wes not verie wyis,
  Thocht all thair tales was trewe.
   So mony and bony
880   All problemis thay propond
   Baith quicklie and liklie.
    I marveld meikill ond.

857 we] I C1 861 wald thou] will you C1; will thow La 862 Except] Accept La 863 than] nor C1 La 866 to doe] ado C1 868 3e] I La 869 Quhen Currage crau'd] Than Currage with C1 870 draue] drewe C1 873 dround into] arplonit in La 878 was] wer C1 880 All] Auld C1 La propond] expound C1 882 marveld] marvell C1

250

'Assure thy selfe if that we shed   995
Thou shalt not get thy purpose sped.
Take heede. Wee have thee told.
        Have done and drive not off the day.
The man that will not when he may,
He shal not when hee would.   1000
        What wilt thou doe? I would we wist.
Accept or give us our'.
        Quoth I, 'I think me more than blest
To finde such famous foure
                Beside mee to guide mee   1005
                        Now when I have to doe,
                Considering what swidering
                        Ye found me first into.

        'When Courage cravd a stomack stout
And Danger drave mee into doubt   1010
With his companion Dread,
        Whiles Wil would up above the aire,
Whiles I am drownde in deepe Despare,
Whiles Hope held up mine head.
        Such pithie reasons and replies   1015
On every side they shew,
        That I, who was not very wise,
Thought all their tales were true.
                So mony and bony
                        Old problemes they proponit,   1020
                But quickly and likely,
                        I marvell meekle on it.

1013 am] was C4   1021 But] Both C4

'3it Hope and Currage wan the feild
Thocht Dreid and Danger nevir 3eild
885 Bot fled to fynde refuge.
   Swa fra 3e four met thay were fayne
Because 3e cauld thame back againe
And glad that 3e war Iudge
   For thay were fugitiue befoir,
890 Now ar thay frank and fre
   To speak and stand in awe na moir'.
Quod Ressoun, 'Swa suld be
   Oft tymes now but crimes now,
      Bot evin be force it falls
895   The strang ay with wrang ay
         Puttis waiker to the walls

   'Quhilk is a fault, thou man confesse.
Strenth is not ordaynd till oppresse
With rigour by the richt
900   Bot be the contrair to sustein
The waik anes that oreburdenit bein
Als meikill as thay micht.
   'So Hope and Currage did', quod I,
Experimented like,
905   'Schaw skild and pithie resouns quhy
That Danger lap the dyke'.
      Quod Dreid, 'Sir, tak heid, Sir,
         Lang speiking part man spill.
      Insist not 3e wist not
910   We went aganis our will'.

884 nevir] wald not C1 886 Swa fra 3e four met] Fra we conveind sa C1; Swa fra the foure come La 887 3e] he C1 La 888] Thay glaid to get him iudge C1 889 For] Quhair C1 La 891 in] na C2 893 now] *om*. La 894] Men being forced falls C1 falls] faillis La 896] Pusis waikar to wallis La 897 thou] 3e C1 898 till] to C1 La 901 anes] *om*. La 904 Experimented] Weill exprementit C1; Experience sic La 905] Schaw Skills and Wills occasion quhy C1; Schew Skill and Wit reassonis quhy La 908 man] will C1 909, 911 3e] we C1 La

'Yet Hope and Courage wan the field
Though Dread and Danger never yeeld,
But fled to finde refuge.   1025
  Yet when ye foure came, they were faine
Because ye gart us come againe.
The griende to get you iudge
  Where they were fugitive before.
Yee made them frank and free   1030
  To speak and stand in aw no more'.
Quoth Reason, 'So should bee.
    Oft-times now, but crymes now,
      But even perforce it fals:
    The strong ay with wrong ay   1035
      Puts weaker to the wals,

'Which is a fault, ye must confesse.
Strength was not ordained to oppresse
With rigour by the right,
  But by the contrare, to sustaine   1040
The loaden which ovrburthend beene,
As meekle as they might'.
  'So Hope and Courage did', quoth I,
Experimented like,
  'Show skilde and pithy reasons why   1045
That Dangcr lap thc dykc'.
    Quoth Danger, 'Sir, take heed, sir,
      Long spoken part must spill.
    Insist not we wist not
      We went against our will.   1050

1038 to] for to C5

'With Curage 3e were sa content
3e never socht our small consent.
Of vs 3e stand na aw.
    Thair logique ressouns 3e allowit.
915 3e wer determined to trow it
Alledgence past for law:
    For all the proverbs they pervsit,
3e thocht them skantly skild.
    Our ressouns had bene als weill rusit
920 Had 3e bene als weill wil'd
        Till our side as 3our side
           Sa trewlie is it termd.
        We see now in thee now
           Affection dois affermd'.

925   Experience then smyrkling smyld.
'We are na barnis to be begyld',
Quod he and schuik his heid.
    'For authours quha alledgis vs,
Thay may not ga about the bus
930 For all thair deadly feid:

915 determined] determinate C1 trow it] trowit La 917 they] 3e C1; we La 918 them] vs C1 919 rusit] vsit C1; refusit La 920 willit] will it La 922 is it] as wes C1; I may La C3 termit] term it La C3 C4 923 We] I C1C3 924 affermd] affermit C1; afferm it La 925 then smyrkling smyld] thairat blinkt and smylit C1 927 schuik] schuit La 929 ga] win C1 930, *infra*: Printed by R.W. Cum Privilegio Regali C1; A sonet made be the same author [a version of **59**, 'Supreme Essence,' follows]; Finis quod mongomerie La

'With Courage ye were so content
Ye never sought our smal consent.
Of us ye stood not aw.
    Then Logick lessons ye allowit
And was determined to trow it.   1055
Alleageance past for Law.
    For all the proverbs wee perusde,
Yee thought them skantly skild.
    Our reasons had beene as well rusde
Had ye beene as well wilde   1060
        To our side as your side,
           So truely I may tearme it.
        I see now in thee now,
           Affection doth affirm't'.

    Experience then smirking smilde.   1065
'We are no bairnes to be beguild',
Quoth he and shooke his head.
    'For Authors who alledges us
They stil would win about the bus
To foster deadly feede.   1070
    For wee are equal for you all.
No persons wee respect.
    We have been so are yet and shall
Be found so in effect.
        If we were as ye were,   1075
           We had comde unrequyrde
        But wee now, ye see now,
           Doe nothing undesirde.

1055 trow it] trowit C3 1062 terme it] tearm't C5

'There is a sentence said by some,
1080 "Let none uncald to counsell come
That welcome weines to bee",
Yea I have heard another yet,
"Who came uncald unservd shuld sit",
Perhaps, sir, so may yee'.
1085 'Good man, grande mercie for your gecke'
Quoth Hope, and lowly lowts.
'If yee were sent for, we suspect,
Because the Doctours doubts.
Your yeares now appeares now
1090 With wisedome to be vext,
Reioycing in gloysing
Till you have tint your text.

'Where yee were sent for let us see.
Who would be welcomer than wee?
1095 Prove that and we are payde'.
'Wel', quoth Experience, 'beware,
You know not in what case you are.
Your tongue hath you betrayde.
The man may able tine a stot
1100 Who cannot count his kinch.
In your owne bow you are ov'rshot
By more then halfe an inch.
Who wats sir if that sir
Is sowre which seemeth sweet.
1105 I feare now ye heare now
A dangerous decreete.

'Sir, by that sentence yee have said
I pledge ere all the play bee plaid
That some shall lose a laike.
    Since yee but put me for to prove   1110
Such heads as help for my behove,
Your warrand is but waike.
    Speare at the man your selfe and see,
Suppose you strive for state,
    If hee regrated not how hee   1115
Had learnd my lesson late
        And granted hee wanted
            Both Reason, Wit and Skill,
        Compleaning and meaning
            Our absence did him ill.   1120

'Confront him further face for face
If yet hee rewes his rackles race.
Perhaps and ye shall heare.
    For ay since Adam and since Eve
Who first thy leasings did believe,   1125
I sold thy doctrine deare.
    What hath beene done even to this day
I keep in minde almaist.
    Ye promise further than ye pay,
Sir Hope, for all your haste.   1130
        Promitting unwitting,
            Your heghts yee never hooked.
        I show you I know you,
            Your bygones I have booked.

1135 'I would incace a count were cravd
Shew thousand thousands thou deceivde
Where thou was true to one
        And by the contrare I may vant
Which thou must, though it grieve thee, grant
1140 I trumped never a man
        But truely told the naked trueth
To men that meld with mee
        For neither rigour nor for rueth
Bot onely loath to lie.
1145   To some yet to come yet
                Thy succour shall be slight
        Which I then must try then
                And register it right'.

        'Ha ha', quoth Hope and lowdly leugh,
1150 'Ye'r but a prentise at the pleugh.
Experience, yee prieve,
        Suppose all bygones as yee spacke,
Ye are no Prophet worth a plack
Nor I bound to believe.
1155 Yee should not say, sir, till yee see
But when yee see it, say'.
        'Yet', quoth Experience, 'at thee
Make many mints I may
                By signes now and things now
1160   Which ay before mee beares
                Expressing by gessing
                        The perill that appeares'.

1135 would] could C4

Then Hope replyde and that with pith
And wisely weighd his words therewith
Sententiously and short.   1165
    Quoth hee, 'I am the Anchor grip
That saves the Sailers and their ship
From perill to their port'.
    Quoth hee, 'Oft times that Anchor drives
As wee have found before   1170
    And loses many thousand lives
By shipwrack on the shore.
        Your grips oft but slips oft
           When men have most to doe
        Syne leaves them and reaves them   1175
           Of my companion too.

'Thou leaves them not thy selfe alone
But to their griefe when thou art gone
Gars Courage quite them als'.
    Quoth Hope, 'I would ye understood.   1180
I grip fast if the ground be good
And fleets where it is false.
    There should no fault with mee be found
Nor I accusde at all.
    Wyte such as should have sound the ground   1185
Before the Anchor fall.
        Their leede ay at neede ay
           Might warne them if they would
        If they there would stay there
           Or have good anchor-hold.   1190

1176 my companion] thy conpanion C4

'If yee read right it was not I
But onely Ignorance whereby
Their Carvels all were cloven.
    I am not for a trumper tane'.
1195 'All', quoth Experience, 'is ane.
I have my processe proven,
    To wit that we were cald each one
To come before wee came.
    That now obiection ye have none
1200 Your selfe may say the same.
        Ye are now too farre now
            Come forward for to flee.
        Perceive then ye have then
            The worst end of the tree'.

1205   When Hope was gald into the quick
Quoth Courage, kicking at the prick,
'Wee let you well to wit
    Make hee you welcomer than wee,
Then bygones bygones, farewell he.
1210 Except hee seeke us yet
    Hee understands his owne estate.
Let him his chiftanes chuse
    But yet his battel will bee blate
If hee our force refuse.
1215   Refuse us or chuse us
        Our counsel is hee clim
    But stay hee or stray hee
        We have none help for him

1194 trumper] trumpet C4

'Except the Cherrie be his chose.
Bee ye his friends, wee are his foes,   1220
His doings we despite.
    If we perceive him satled sa
To satisfie him with the Slae
His company we quite'.
    Then Dread and Danger grew so glad   1225
And wont that they had wun.
    They thought all seald that they had said
Sen they had first begun.
        They thought then they mought then
            Without a partie plead   1230
        But yet there with Wit there
            They were dung downe indeed.

    'Sirs Dread and Danger', then quoth Wit,
'Ye did yourselves to mee submit.
Experience can prove'.   1235
    'That', quoth Experience, 'I past.
Their own confession made them fast.
They may no more remove,
    For if I right remember mee
This maxime then they made,   1240
    To wit, "The man with Wit should wey
What Philosophs had said'
        Which sentence repentance
            Forbade him deare to buy'.
        They knew then how true then   1245
            And preasde not to reply.

Though he dang Dread and Danger down
Yet Courage could not overcome,
Hope heght him such an hyre.
1250　　He thought himselfe so soone he saw
His enemies were laid so law
It was no time to tyre.
　　　　Hee hit the yron while it was hait
Incace it might grow cold
1255　　For he esteemde his foes defaite
When once he found them folde.
　　　　　'Though we now', quoth hee now,
　　　　　　'Have been so free and franke,
　　　　　　Vnsought yet ye mought yet
1260　　　　　For kindnesse cund us thanke.

　　　　'Suppose it so as thou hast said
That unrequyrde wee offered aide
At least it came of love.
　　　　Experience, yee start too soone,
1265　Yee dow nothing while all be done
And then perhaps yee prove
　　　　More plaine than pleasant, too, perchance,
(Some tell that have you tryit)
　　　　As fast as you your selfe advance
1270　(Ye dow not wel deny it)
　　　　　Abide then your tide then
　　　　　　And waite upon the wind.
　　　　　Ye know sir ye ow sir
　　　　　　To hold you ay behinde.

'When yee have done some doughty deeds   1275
Syne ye should see how all succeeds
To write them as they were'.
    'Friend, huly, haste not halfe so fast
Lest', quoth Experience at last,
'Ye buy my doctrine deare.   1280
    Hope puts that hast into your head
Which boyles your barmie braine.
    Howbeit Fooleshaste comes hulie speede,
Faire heights make fooles be faine.
        Such smyling beguiling   1285
           Bids feare not for no freets
        Yet I now deny now
           That al is gold that gleets.

'Suppose not silver all that shines.
Oft times a tentlesse Merchant tines   1290
For buying geare be gesse'.
    'For all the vantage and the winning
Good buyers gets at the beginning',
Quoth Courage, 'not the lesse.
    Whiles as good Merchant tines as wins   1295
If old mens tales bee true.
    Suppose the pack come to pins
Who can his chance eshew?
        Then, good sir, conclude, sir,
           Good buyers have done baith.   1300
        Advance then, take chance then
           As sundry good ships hath.

1284 make] makes C4

'Who wist what would bee cheape or deare
Should neede to traffique but a yeare
1305 If things to come were kend.
   Suppose all bygone things be plaine
Your Prophecy is but prophane.
Ye're best behold the end.
   Yee would accuse mee of a crime
1310 Almost before wee met.
   Torment you not before the time
Since dolour payes no debt.
     What by past that I past
      Ye wot if it was well.
1315   To come yet by doome yet
      Confesse ye have no feele'.

   'Yet', quoth Experience, 'what than?
Who may be meetest for the man?
Let us his answere have.
1320   When they submitted them to mee
To Reason I was faine to flee,
His counsell for to crave'.
   Quoth he, 'Since you yourselves submit
To doe as I decreet
1325   I shal advise with Skil and Wit
What they thinke may bee meete'.
     They cryde then, 'We byde, then,
      At Reason for refuge.
    Allow him and trow him
1330   As governour and iudge'.

1308 Ye're] Yee are C4; Ye had C5

So said they all with one consent,
'What he concluds, we are content
His bidding to obey.
    Hee hath authority to use,
Then take his chose whom he would chuse   1335
And longer not delay'.
    Then Reason rose and was reioysde.
Quoth he, 'Mine hearts, come hither.
    I hope this play may bee composde
That we may goe together.   1340
        To all now I shall now
            His proper place assigne
        That they heere shal say heere
            They thinke none other thing.

    'Come on', quoth he, 'companion Skill,   1345
Ye understand both good and ill.
In Physick yee are fine.
    Be medciner unto this man
And shaw such cunning as yee can
To put him out of paine.   1350
    First gard the ground of all his griefe,
 What sicknes ye suspect,
    Syne looke what hee lackes for reliefe
Ere further he infect.
        Comfort him, exhort him,   1355
            Give him your good advice
        And panse not nor skanse not
            The perill nor the price.

1335 would] will C4

'Though it be cumbersome, what recke,
1360 Finde out the cause by the effect
And working of his veines.
    Yet while we grip it to the ground
See first what fashion may bee found
To pacifie his paines.
1365   Doe what ye dow to have him haile
And for that purpose prease.
    Cut off the cause, the effect must faile
So all his sorrowes cease.
        His fever shall never
1370   From thencefoorth have no force
        Then urge him to purge him
        He will not waxe the worse'.

    Quoth Skil, 'His senses are so sicke
I know no liquor worth a leeke
1375 To quench his deadly drouth
    Except the Cherrie help his heat,
Whose sappy sloking sharp and sweet
Might melt into his mouth
    And his melancholy remove
1380 To mitigate his minde,
    None wholesomer for your behove
Nor more cooling of kinde,
        No Nectar directar
        Could all the gods him give
1385   Nor send him to mend him,
        None like it, I believe,

1368 sorrowes] sorrow C5 1373 are] is C5 1381 your] his C4 C5

'For drowth decayes as it digests'.
'Why then', quoth Reason, 'nothing rests
But how it may bee had'.
    'Most true' quoth Skil 'that is the scope   1390
Yet we must have some helpe of Hope'.
Quoth Danger, 'I am rad
    His hastines breeds us mishap
When he is highly horst.
    I would wee looked ere wee lap'.   1395
Quoth Wit, 'That were not worst.
        I meane now, conveene now
            The counsell one and all,
      Begin then, cal in then'.
          Quoth Reason, 'So I shall'.   1400

    Then Reason rose with gesture grave
Belyve conveening all the lave
To see what they would say,
    With silver scepter in his hand
As chiftane chosen to command   1405
And they bent to obey.
    He pansed long before he spake
And in a study stood
    Syne hee began and silence brake,
'Come on', quoth hc, 'conclude   1410
        What way now we may now
            Yon Cherrie come to catch.
      Speak out, sirs, about sirs,
          Have done, let us dispatch'.

1393 breeds] breed C4; bred C5 1399 in] C4 C5; on C3

1415 Quoth Courage, 'Scourge him first that skars.
Much musing memory but marres.
I tell you mine intent'.
  Quoth Wit, 'Who will not partly panse
In perils, perishes perchance.
1420 Ov'r rackles may repent'.
  Then quoth Experience and spake,
'Sir, I have seene them baith,
  In bairnlines and lye aback,
Escape and come to skaith.
1425 But what now of that now.
    Sturt followes all extreames.
  Retaine then the meane then,
   The surest way it seemes.

  'Where some hes further'd, some hes faild.
1430 Where part hes perisht, part prevaild.
Alike all cannot lucke
  Then either venture with the one
Or with the other let alone
The Cherrie for to plucke'.
1435 Quoth Hope, 'For feare folke must not fash'.
Quoth Danger, 'Let not light'.
  Quoth Wit, 'Bee neither rude nor rash'.
Quoth Reason, 'Yee have right'.
   The rest then thought best then
1440   When Reason said it so
   That roundly and soundly
    They should together goe

To get the Cherrie in all haste
As for my safety serving maist
Though Dread and Danger feard   1445
   The peril of that irksome way
Lest that thereby I should decay
Who then so weake appearde
   Yet Hope and Courage hard beside
Who with them wont contend   1450
   Did take in hand us for to guide
Vnto our iourneyes end
     Impleadging and waidging
       Both two their lives for mine,
     Providing the guiding   1455
       To them were granted syne.

   Then Dread and Danger did appeale,
Alledging it could not be well
Nor yet would they agree
   But said they should sound their retreate   1460
Because they thought them no wise meete
Conductores unto mee
   Nor to no man in mine estate
With sicknes sore opprest
   For they tooke ay the nearest gate   1465
Omitting oft the best.
     Their nearest, perquearest
      Is always to them both
     'Where they, sir, may say, sir,
       What recks them of your skaith?   1470

1470 your] their C5

'But as for us two now we sweare
By him before whom we appeare
Our ful intent is now
   To have you whole and alway was
1475 That purpose for to bring to passe
So is not theirs, I trow'.
   Then Hope and Courage did attest
The gods of both these parts
   If they wrought not all for the best
1480 Of mee with upright hearts.
     Our Chiftane than liftane
      His scepter did enioyne
   'No more there, uproare there'
     And so their strife was done,

1485   Rebuiking Dread and Danger sore,
Suppose they meant well evermore
To me as they had sworne,
   Because their neighbours they abusde
In so farre as they had accusde
1490 Them as ye heard beforne
   'Did ye not else', quoth he, 'consent
The Cherry for to pow?'
   Quoth Danger, 'We are well content
But yet the maner how?
1495   We shal now, even all now,
     Get this man with us there.
   It rest is and best is
     Your counsel shall declare'.

1491 ye] he C5

'Wel said', quoth Hope and Courage, 'now
We thereto will accord with you   1500
And shall abide by them.
  Like as before we did submit
So wee repeate the samine yet.
We minde not to reclaime.
  Whom they shal chuse to guide the way   1505
Wee shal him follow straight
  And further this man what we may
Because wee have so height,
    Promitting but flitting
      To doe the thing we can   1510
    To please both and ease both
      This silly sickly man'.

  When Reason heard this, then quoth hee,
'I see your chiefest stay to bee
That we have nam'd no guide.   1515
  The worthy counsel hath therefore
Thought good that Wit should goe before
For perils to provide'.
  Quoth Wit, 'There is but one of three
Which I shall to you show   1520
  Whereof the first two cannot bee
For any thing I know.
    The way heere so stay heere
      Is, that wee cannot clim
    Even ov'r now, we foure now.   1525
      That will bee hard for him.

'The next, if we goe downe about
While that this bend of Craiges run out
The streame is there so starke
1530   And also passeth wading deepe
And broader farre than we dow leape,
It should be idle work.
    It growes ay broader nere the sea
Sen over the lin it came.
1535   The running dead doth signifie
The deepnes of the same.
        I leave now to deave now
          How that it swiftly slides
        As sleeping and creeping
1540   But nature so provides.

'Our way then lyes about the Lin
Whereby a' warrand we shal win,
It is so straight and plaine.
    The water also is so shald
1545 We shal it passe even as we wald
With pleasure and but paine,
    For as we see the mischief grow
Oft of a feckles thing
    So likewise doth this river flow
1550 Foorth of a pretty spring
        Whose throat, sir, I wot, sir,
          You may stop with your neive
        As you, sir, I trow, sir
          Experience, can prieve'.

1533 nere] than C4 C5

'That', quoth Experience, 'I can.   1555
All that yee said sen yee began
I know to be of truth'.
    Quoth Skill, 'The samine I approve'.
Quoth Reason, 'Then let us remove
And sleepe no more in sleuth.   1560
    Wit and Experience', quoth he,
'Shall come before apace.
    The man shall come with Skill and mee
Into the second place.
        Attour now you foure now   1565
            Shall come into a band
        Proceeding and leading
            Each other by the hand'.

    As Reason ordeinde, all obeyde.
None was ov'r rash nor none affraide   1570
Our counsel was so wise.
    As of our iourney Wit did note,
We found it true in every iote.
God bles'd our interprise.
    For even as wee came to the tree   1575
Which, as yee heard mee tell,
    Could not be clum, there suddenly
The fruite for ripnes fell
        Which hasting and tasting
            I found myselfe relievde   1580
        Of cares all and sares all
            Which minde and body grievde.

1574 bles'd] bless C4 1579 hasting . . . tasting] tasting . . . hasting C4

Praise be to God my Lord therefore
Who did mine health to mee restore
1585 Being so long time pinde.
Yea blessed bee his holy Name
Who did from death to life recleame,
Mee who was so unkinde.
All Nations also magnifie
1590 This everliving Lord,
Let me with you and you with mee
To laude him ay accord
Whose love ay wee prove ay
To us above all things,
1595 And kisse him and blesse him
Whose Glore eternall rings.

OTHER POEMS

Ȝe hevinis abone with heavinlie ornamentis
Extend ȝour courtingis of þe cristall air,
To asuir colour turne ȝour elementis
And soft þis seasoun quhilk hes bene schairp and sair.
Command the cluddis that thay dissolue na mair   5
Nor ws molest with mistie Vapouris weit
For now scho cummis, the fairest of all fair,
The mundane mirrour of maikles margareit.

The myildest may, the mekest and modest,
The fairest flour, þe freschest flourisching,   10
The lamp of licht, of ȝouth the lustiest,
The blythest bird of bewtie maist bening,
Groundit with grace and godlie governing
As A per C, aboue all elevat
To quhome comparit is na erthlie thing   15   97
Nor with the goddis so heichlie estimat.

The goddes diana in hir hevinlie throne
Evin at the full of all hir maiestie
Quhen scho belevit that dainger wes þair none
Bot in hir sphere ascending vp maist hie   20
Vpon this nymph fra that scho caist hir ei
Blusching for schame out of hir schyire scho slippis,
Thinking scho had bene phoebus verelie,
At quhose depart scho fell into the eclips.

The Asteres cleir and torchis of the nicht   25
Quhilk in the sterrie firmament wer fixit,
Fra thay persavit dame phoebes lost hir licht
Lyik diamontis with cristall perlis mixit
They did discend to schyne this nymph annixit,
Vpon hir schoulderis twinkling euerie on   30
Quhilk to depaint it wald be ouer prolixt
How thay in ordour glisteris in hir goun.

Gif scho had bene into the dayis auld
Quhen Iupiter the schap of bull did tak
35 Befoir europe quhen he his feit did fauld
Quhill scho throw courage clam vpon his bak,
Sum greater magik I wait he had gart mak
Hir to haue stollin be his slichtis quent
For to haue past aboue the зodiak
40 As quein and goddes of the firmament.

97ᵛ   With goldin schouris as he did clemene
He wald this virgine furteouslie desave
Bot I houp in the goddes hemene
Quhilk to hir brother so happie fortoun gave
45 That scho salbe exaltit by the laif
Baith for hir bewtie and hir nobill bluid
And of my self ane seruand scho sall have
Vnto I die, and so I doe conclud.

103

Luiffaris leif of to loif so hie
зour ladyes and thame styill no mair
But peir the erthlie E per sie
And flour of feminine maist fair.
5 Sen thair is ane without compare
Sic tytillis in зour sanges deleit
And prays the pereles preclair
Montgomrie maikles margareit,

Quhose port and pereles pulchritud,
10 Fair forme and face angelicall
Sua meik and full of mansuetud
With vertew supernaturall,
Makdome and proper memberis all
Sa perfyte and with Ioy repleit
15 Pruiffis hir but peir or peregall
Of maidis the maikles margareit.

102.48, *infra*: finis quod A. Montgomrie Mq

Sa wyse in ȝouth and verteous,   98
Sic ressounis for to reull the rest
As in greit age wer marvelous,
Sua manerlie, myld and modest,   20
Sa grave, sa gratious and digest
And in all doings sa discreit,
The maist bening and boniest
Mirrour of maidinis margareit.

Pigmalion that ane portratour   25
Be painting craft did so decoir
Him self þairwith in paramour
Fell suddanlie and smert þairfoir.
Wer he alyve he wald deploir
His folie and his love forleit   30
This fairer patrone to adoir
Of maidis the maikles margareit.

Or had this nymphe bene in these dayis
Quhen Paris Iudgit in Helicon,
Venus had not obtenit sic prayis.   35
Scho and the goddessis ilkone
Wald have preferrit this paragon
As marrowit but matche most meit
The golden ball to bruik alone,
Merveling in this Margareit   40

Quhose nobill birth and royall bluid
Hir better nature dois exceid.
Hir native giftes and graces guid   98ᵛ
Sua bonteouslie declairis Indeid
As waill and wit of womanheid   45
That sua with vertew dois ouerfleit,
Happie is hie that sall posseid
In mariage this margareit.

Helpe and graunt hap, gud hemene,
50   Lat not thy pairt in hir Inlaik
Nor lat not doulful destanie,
Mishap or fortoun worke hir wraik.
Graunt lyik vnto hir self ane maik
That will hir honour luif and treit
55   And I sall serve him for hir saik.
Fairweill my Maistres Margareit.

163   **104**   **Ane anser to ane heland manis Invectiue maid be**
         alexander montgomry

Fyndlay m^{c}connoquhy, fuf m^{c}fadȝan,
Cativilie geilȝie with þe poik braik,
Smoir ennary cakin trewis, breikles m^{c}bradȝan,
Ȝeill fart fast in baquhidder or þe corne schaik,
5   In steid of grene gynger ȝe eit gray gradȝan.
For lyce in ȝour lunschoch ȝe haif na Inlaik.
Mony muntir moir in mvggis of mvre madȝan
Sawis seindill saffroun in sawse for þer sarkis saik.
Ocknewling occonnoquhy ocgreigry m^{c}grane
10   With fallisty muntir moy
         Soy in scho sorle boy,
         Callin feane aggus endoy,
            Firry braldach ilkane.

253   **105**

Irkit I am with langsum luvis lair
Oursett with Inwart siching sair,
For in the presone of dispair
         I ly
5   Seing Ilk wicht gettis sum weilfair
         bot I.

103.56, *infra*: A.M. Mq
104.5, 6 *rev.* (*6 / 5, LH* margin) 7 sawse] saw(ts; *del.*)se Ba
105.1 with langsum] with (inwart siching sair; *del.*) langum Ba

My hairt is pynd and persit so with panis 253[v]
Quhill teiris over my visage ranis
And makis the blud within my vanis
   To dry. 10
Quha ma sic greif resist aganis
   Bot I?

My mad misfortoun dois me so commve
That I may newyr rest nor ruve
Bot wary all the goddis abve 15
   The sky
That every leid obtenis thair luve
   bot I.

All nobill hairtis of natour Ar inclynd
Quhair thay find constance to be kynd. 20
Thairfoir to me scho sowld hir mynd
   apply,
Sen non Is for hir persone pynd
   bot I.

The facultie of famenene Is so 25
Vnto thair friend To be his fo
Syne meuis him Lufe, he is ago
   forthy.
Vncourtesly thus keill thay mo
   than I. 30

Thay covet not the man that thay may get,
For him thay hald as propper det.
On strangeris ay thair myndis ar set
   to spy.
Thus Mo bene sett outwith thair net 35
   nor I.

14 That] Thy Ba 21 Thairfoir to me scho] Thairfoir (to me; *superscript*) scho
Ba 35 sett outwith] settoutwith Ba

Grit fule I am to follow the delyte
Of thame that hes no faith perfyte.
Thairfoir sic cumpany I quyt
40   denny.
Off all my wo hes non the wyt
             bot I.

Quhat wounder Is thocht I do weip and pleid
This fellon crewall lyfe I leid,
45 The quhilk but dowt wilbe my deid
             In hy,
For every man obtenis remeid
             bot I.

My lady hes ane hairt of stone so hard
50 On me to rew scho hes no regard
Bot bustously I am debard
             ay by,
And every man gettis sum reward
             bot I.

p. 51   **106   The xxiij sphalme translait be him**

The Lord most hie
I knaw wilbe
Ane hird to me,
I can not lang haif stress nor stand in neid.
5 He makis my lair
In feildis most fair
Quhair I but cair
Reposing at my plesour saifly feid.
He sweitly me convois
10 To plesand springis

105.50 On] (for; *del.*) on Ba 54, *infra:* ffinis quod Montgomery
106.5 lair] leare Me 6 most fair] sa feare Me 7] That I but ceare Me; That with-
out care Mi1 8] Repose and at my pleasure safely feede Me; I doe repose, and at
my pleasure feede Mi

Quhair nothing me annoyis
Bot plesour bringis,
He makis my mynd
Fit to sic kynd
That fors or feir of foe can not me greif,   15
He dois me leid
In perfyt tred
And for his name he will me nevir leif.

Thocht I sould stray
Ilk day by day
In deidly way   20
3it will I not dispair nor feir non ill
For quhy, thy grace
In every place   52
Dois me Imbrace,   25
Thy rod and schiphirdis cruk confortis me still,
        In dispyt of my foo
        My tabill growis,
        Thow balmis my heid with Ioo,
        My cup overflowis,   30
    Kyndnes and grace
    Marcy and pace
Sall fallow me for all my wretchit dayis
        And me convoy
        To endles Ioy   35
In hevin quhair I salbe with the alwayis

13 makis] bringis Ba; giues Me Mi1 14 Fit to] peace in Me Mi1 15] That feare of foes, nor force, cannot me reaue Me Mi1 foe] (feir; *del.*) foe Ba 16] By him I am lead Me Mi1 19 stray] stay Mi1 20 Ilk] even Me Mi1 22] Yet wald I be assurd, and feare none ill Me Mi1 25 Dois] Doth Mi1 29 Ioo] joye Me Mi1 34-5] Then endles joy, sall me convoy Me Mi1 36 salbe with the] with thee sall be Me Mi1 36, *infra*: ffinis translait be montgomry

Appendix

Selected Songs

a About a bank

Andrew Blackhall

Lyric: Wq 1 III: *om.* Sc 3 I 4: q q Wc 5 I 3: cF Wc 6 III 4: cG Sc Ta 8 III 3: *rest om.* Sc 9 IV 2: qB Wb

to a busse to heer the birds ———— beer Ther
lo - di - ous through na - tour of the

year Some sing - ing, some spring - ing so
nim - ble so trym - blie, the

high in - to the skye So by.
birds they flew me

11 I 3: cD Wc II 1: cD Ta 12 III 1–3: c m Sc 13 cc Sc 14 II 1–2 cF D Ta 16 III 4
mG Sc

b Befor the Greeks

Be - for   the   Greeks   did   en - ter -
They set   a   Coun - sel   sag   and

prise   The Tro - jan   town   in   arms   to
wise   A - pol - lo's   an - swer   for   to

go   how they should   speed and
know

Lyric: Ta 3 I 1–2: c c Ed Ta 6 I 1–2: c. q Ed IV 3: cD Ta 7 1–2 I: cG cA Ed Fo
I 3: nat. Ed IV I: *om.* Ta

have   suc - cess   In   that   so

great   a   bus – si – nes

12–16 IV: c cF cB–flat c.F qF cC cD mC m.F Ta 15 I: *repeated* Ed 15–16 III:
mF cE cF mG Ta

c Come my children dere

Lyric: Ta 4 I 2: m K 5 *and passim* I: *rest om.* K 12 I 2: m K

For it   is   no   earth - ly   thing

Bot a   love   far a -   bove

oth - er   loves -   all   I   say,

24 I: c c Ta

d Even death behold I breath

Even
else

death   be -
dol - lour

hold   I
af - ter

breath,
death

my breath pro -
sould slack when

cures   my
I   wer

paine.
slaine

Bot   des - ti -

nies   dis -
daine   who

span   my

fat - all

Lyric: Sc 1: *om.* Rc 5 I: c q q Fo 9 I: c c Rc Ta 12 I: c. q Sc

14–22 I: c.C qB cG cF cF cE mF cE qE cD cB m.A Rc 14 I 1–2: c c Fc Fo Ta
18 I 3–4: cFcE Fc Fo Ta 20 I: c q q Fc Sc Fo Ta 22 I: m. Sc 23 I: m Sc

28 I: c. B sq AD Fo 29 q FEFG Ta

e In throw the windowis

Lyric: Fc

11 I 3–4: mFc Ed Ta III 3–4: mTa 13 III: cA B A G Ta 14 III: mG cF–sharp
G Ta 15 III: cG G c.B qC Ta 16 I 4: G Fc Ed Ta III: cD G c.B qC Ta 17 III:
m.D qCB cA Ta 18 III: cG A C D Ta

19 I 4: C–nat. Ed 19–20 III: cF qE D cE mD B cC Ta 21 III: cE E E A Ta 22
III: cC mD c.F qE Ta 23–24 III: mD qC D E D cB B qA G cA Ta 24 I 4:
F–sharp Fc Ta 25 III: c.G qG Ta 26 sB Ta

f Lyk as the dumb Solsequium

Lyric: Fo 2 IV 3–4: m Wt 3 I 1–3: mA cA Wq Rc Mi2 Ed III 1–4 m cA Ed2 4
I: cF F G G E E Rc; c. q F c.G qF cE E Mi2 Ed I 1–2: c. q F–sharp Wq Ta I
2: F Ed2 II 1–2: m Ta 4 I 5–6: cE E Fo 5 I: m c m.D Rc Ed Ta 1–3: m cD
Wq I 3: qF E Mi2 III: m. Ta III 1–4: m m Wa IV: m m Wt 6 I 4–6: c.E qD
E F Wq; c. qF Ed2

7 I: cG A G F mE E Ed2 I 3–6 m Ed1 III 3–6 c m Wa 8 I: cE m cF m cG Rc I
6: cG Mi2 III 4–6: c c c Wa 9 I 1–3: m cA Wq Mi2; mA c c cG Ed1 III: m. m
c Wa IV: m m mF cC Wt 10 I: cF qA c.G qR cE E Fo; cF F G G E E Rc I
1–2: cF qE F Mi2 II 1–2: m Ta III 3–4: m Wa IV 1–2: c.D qC Wt 11 I: c m
m.D Rc; m c mD Mi2 Ed IV: c c sD Wt 11 (*second ending*) c c.D qC sD Mi2

g Quhat Mightie Motione

Quhat might- tie mo -tione so my mynd mis - chievis?
Quhat rest - less rage my Re - son so be - reives?

Quhat vn - couth cairs all throu my corps do creep?
Quhat rest - less loth of meit, of drink, of sleep?

I knou not nou vhat Coun- ten -ance to

Lyric: Ed 5–6 III: cA C qB A G F cG G mA Wt Ta 9 IV 3: qF A Ta

keep   For   to   ex - pell   a

poy-sone that I   prove   A - lace   a -

lace   that   evir I leirnd to   Love

15 II: m A A Ed   16 III 1: A Ed